Hollywood Beauty

Hollywood Beauty

Linda Darnell and the American Dream

by Ronald L. Davis

University of Oklahoma : Norman and London

By Ronald L. Davis

A History of Opera in the American West
(New York, 1965)
Opera in Chicago (New York, 1966)
The Social and Cultural Life of the 1920s (ed.) (New
York, 1972)
A History of Music in American Life (Melbourne,
Fla., 1980–82)
Hollywood Anecdotes (with Paul Boller)
(New York, 1987)
*Hollywood Beauty: Linda Darnell and the American
Dream* (Norman, 1991)

Library of Congress Cataloging-in-Publication Data

Davis, Ronald L.
    Hollywood beauty : Linda Darnell and the
American dream / by Ronald L. Davis. — 1st ed.
        p.   cm.
    Includes index.
    ISBN 0-8061-2327-3
        1. Darnell, Linda, 1921–1965.   2. Darnell,
Linda, 1921–1965— Family.   3. Darnell
family.   4. Motion picture actors and
actresses—United States—Biography.   I. Title.
PN2287.D285D38   1991
791.43'028'092—dc20
[B]   90-50685
                                                      CIP

The paper in this book meets the guidelines for
permanence and durability of the Committee on
Production Guidelines for Book Longevity of the
Council on Library Resources, Inc.

With affection and gratitude to
Undeen,
Monte,
Calvin,
Lola,
and especially Monetta.

This story is yours.

Contents

Illustrations

Illustrations

Preface

Linda Darnell's life was a tragedy—an American tragedy—like Judy Garland's and Marilyn Monroe's and James Dean's, all of whom became cult figures. For each of them fame meant failure and victory spelled defeat. It is the story of hundreds of Hollywood and Broadway stars, yet in Linda's case the pursuit of the great American dream discloses pitfalls for an entire family. Hers is a story that could be repeated in the music business, sports, the corporate world, politics, higher education—any realm of contemporary life where the quest for success erodes human relationships and humane values. But Linda Darnell's life was also unique. Despite a veneer of worldliness and sophistication, she never stopped being what she was at the outset—a shy, sensitive girl from a working-class family who realized that to survive in the Hollywood jungle one had to be tough and calculating and dedicated to a projection of self in ways she never was. That was her principal tragedy, with everything else a radius from the central drama. Having been admired since childhood for her beauty, Linda Darnell at fifteen was thrust into a glamorous, self-serving world she had no capacity to understand. She struggled heroically to become her own person, with no solid family foundation to build on and the weight of sudden fame pressing down on her. Her legend tarnished early, in part because her story was commonplace, all too typical of the tinseled milieu that created her, yet reflecting the realities of Hollywood more graphically than the public cared to contemplate.

Like Linda, I grew up in the Oak Cliff section of Dallas. Mine was the neighborhood adjacent to where the Darnells had lived only a brief time before. Linda Darnell had been a favorite movie star of mine, although all the great stars of Hollywood's golden era were my favorites. The top choice depended on what films I had seen the previous week, but they were all beautiful people casting spells that fed an only child's fantasy world. Certainly, Linda Darnell held no exclusive fascination for me, except that she came from Dallas and had attended a rival high school. I never met her, made no pilgrimage to her old neighborhood, but saw all of her pictures. In the late 1940s and early 1950s I saw practically everybody's pictures and still recollect images, dialogue, and musical passages from movies I haven't seen since.

After graduating from college and teaching several years at state universities in Kansas and Michigan, I came back to Dallas as a history professor at Southern Methodist University the year Linda Darnell died. Some time later I became director of the SMU Oral History Program on the Performing Arts, which houses hundreds of interviews dealing with the big studio system. By then the city I had grown up in was no more, transformed into the sprawling Dallas–Fort Worth metroplex, and the great movie palaces along Elm Street I had frequented as a child soon vanished, except for the Majestic, which historic preservationists managed to salvage. Their place had been taken by multiscreened cinemas in shopping malls throughout the outer city and suburbs, clones of those springing up all across the country.

One afternoon I walked into a faculty club reception to discover a staff psychologist I had known casually for years standing in front of me. Without being pushy, she suggested I should interview her for the university's oral history collection. I agreed that might be pleasant, but jokingly asked what we'd talk about. She gave me a warm smile and said, "I went to school with Linda Darnell. She was Monetta then. We were Texanitas together during the Texas Centennial. Believe it or not, there are still several of us around." I returned to my office thinking that a series of oral histories on Linda Darnell might be a sound suggestion for a performing arts project, and shared the idea with my secretary, who at the time was transcribing six lengthy interviews with actor Gregory Peck and had become absorbed in her own fantasies. She mumbled something unintelligible after I'd relayed the notion, but she clearly resented the interruption and seemed thoroughly unimpressed. "I went to school with Linda Darnell, too," she muttered, turning off her transcriber. "My brother had some dates with her."

So I decided to begin collecting data on Linda by interviewing my own secretary, strictly for the university's oral history archives. Next came the psychologist, who sat in my office and dissected with keen insight a unique personality. I became fascinated with the story after just two accounts—partly because I found anything dealing with the movies interesting, but also because they brought back images from my own boyhood. Neighbors and, eventually, Darnell family members deepened my involvement until I became haunted by characters in a plot I identified with intimately. Then on one of my interviewing trips to California, still for the SMU archives, I decided to contact Linda's older sister Undeen. "Let's see how this goes," I told my secretary. "If it turns out well, I may have a book to write." Certainly the story behind the scenes was far more gripping than anything I had viewed on the silver screen.

The interview with Undeen Darnell Hunter went beautifully, and I recognized why I internalized the story to the extent I did. These were *my* people, the kind of people I had grown up with. Linda had merely realized the dream many of us shared in the decades before and after World War II. The trick would be to write about the Darnells without allowing too much of my own family to creep in. I began talking with everyone I could locate who had worked on a Darnell picture, begging for additional leads. I asked Otto Lang, who had been close to Darryl Zanuck—first as Zanuck's ski instructor in Sun Valley, later as a producer at Twentieth Century–Fox—what he remembered about Linda. "I knew her only slightly," he said. "But Dorris, the friend who just served us coffee, knew her well. They came to Hollywood together." Lang's friend turned out to be Dorris Bowdon Johnson, widow of screenwriter Nunnally Johnson, who had indeed been on the train with Linda when, as a fourteen-year-old girl, she first went to California for a screen test.

By this time there was no turning back. I eventually found my way to Monte Darnell's secluded valley in Oregon, with Mount Shasta just over the horizon, and spent two days feeding dogs, pigs, chickens, and finally a couple of exhausted Texans, and talking about her sister's career and the impact it had on her family. Thanks to a spring vacation I was able to spend a week in London, where Calvin Darnell, Linda's brother, added a dimension I had merely glimpsed before. Jeanne Curtis not only shared with me her recollections of Linda, but much of her friend's personal memorabilia. Finally in Charleston I met Lola Marley Leaming, Linda's adopted daughter, whose sensitivity and insight were beyond expectation. I also acquired a sister in the process—at least that's the way I feel about Lola.

We arranged to get acquainted over breakfast at the motel she had suggested on the telephone. "This is going to be tough for me," Lola said on our way out. "If you had written me four years earlier, I wouldn't have talked to you. I think I can handle it now. But I'd like to walk around and show you old Charleston and get to know you before we plunge in." I immediately warmed to her openness and quickly knew her contribution would be special. She volunteered some of the more sensitive information as we strolled around the Battery, pointing out Fort Sumter off in the distance. "You know my family better than I do," Lola claimed and started asking me questions. I shared with her news I had learned only days before—that her Uncle Cal was dying of cancer in London. "I'm still very angry at him," she confessed and told me why. "You know, Lola," I found myself saying, "Cal was in an extremely flaky period of his life then. He was in no condition to be an uncle to you." I proceeded to explain. We spent the afternoon at her home interviewing, asking each other questions. By evening I felt like a member of the family and promised to return for the Spoleto Festival the following May (which I did, with pleasure).

After some discussion we decided to have dinner at her home rather than go out. Putting the meal together turned into a team effort, with an occasional cat or dog covetously looking on. "I hope Mother would be proud of me," Lola confided as she worked in the kitchen, "and of her grandchildren. Somehow I think she would be." I thoroughly agreed. After dinner Lola's husband Ab and I stayed at the table finishing our beer, while Lola cleared the dishes and attended to her two children. When Valerie, Lola's daughter by a previous marriage, discovered I knew her mother's Uncle Cal, I became a celebrity. Ab started to explain how Lola still had bad feelings over Cal's disappearance at the time of Linda's death. "Now, Ab," Lola admonished, "Ron and I talked about that this afternoon, and I think I finally understand. Eighteen years is long enough to be mad at someone." I found tears filling my eyes.

The debts I owe are clearly personal. I deeply thank Virginia Crawford Chancey, my favorite psychologist and a grand lady, without whose suggestion Linda Darnell would have remained just another figure in a mythic gallery for me. To Eleanor Kline Solon, my secretary and friend for many years, I offer eternal gratitude. Eleanor's encouragement and support were essential in my coming to see her former classmate's success as a tragic slice of the American experience. The final product is rightly dedicated to Undeen, Monte, and Calvin Darnell and Charlotte Marley Leaming as well as to their sister and mother. Without their cooperation this biography would have been little more than a sketch. Each became a friend and urged me to write honestly, insisting Linda would have demanded that.

To other members of Linda's family I extend sincere appreciation, especially to Cleo Brown Johnson, a marvel in her nineties, with a spirit to reckon with. Linda's friends were legion, but my special thanks go to Jeanne and Richard Curtis, Trudi Dieterle, Maria Flores, Thomas Hayward, Mary Healy, Henriette Wyeth Hurd, Dorris Bowdon Johnson, Carol Bruce, Gladys Witten, and Yvonne Wood. In every instance their contribution was generous and valuable.

Personal gratitude must be extended to the administration of Southern Methodist University, most notably Dean R. Hal Williams and Provost Hans Hillerbrand, who approved a semester's leave from teaching to begin writing the manuscript. Constructive criticism of the initial draft was offered by my colleagues Luis Martin, Judy J. Mohraz, Paul Varg, and David J. Weber, as well as friends and relatives, especially Chris Anderson, Lee Breeden, Ruth Anne Breeding, Marilyn B. Davis, Ruth L. Davis, Jack and Lee Long, Trudy McMurrin, Joan Rosendahl, Ghada Saffar, Marilee Skwirz, Teryna Snyder, and Carol Weber. The entire manuscript was typed and put on a word processor by Shirley Atkins, Kathleen Triplett, Susan Meyn, and Tom Culpepper. They know the evolution of the finished product better than anyone. Finally, I recognize the encouragement and emotional support given by my son in spirit, Manuel Antonio Colom, who shared a number of interview situations with me and vicariously became part of Linda Darnell's family. For Tony, Cleo Johnson—Linda's maternal aunt—became "Aunt Cleo," and he her "Dallas grandson" from Guatemala. His role was vital throughout.

RONALD L. DAVIS

Dallas, Texas

Hollywood Beauty

Before Dawn

It was pouring rain, just as it had for days in Atlanta. Linda Darnell, only a few years earlier Hollywood's "girl with the perfect face," sank into gloom. Linda wasn't a girl anymore, not that that particularly bothered her. She was forty-one, a little puffy, with a thick waist she had fought most of her life. Yet her arms and legs were pencil thin, so that she wore ankle-length dresses and long sleeves whenever possible. Sitting alone in her Atlanta hotel room in March 1965, she was painfully aware that she no longer resembled the young beauty who had adorned the Technicolor screen in *Blood and Sand*, *Centennial Summer*, and *Forever Amber*. Those pictures were from another life, made by an unsophisticated girl from Texas who hadn't learned how to survive in the Hollywood jungle, who hadn't yet become bitter. Since then she had grown angry, disillusioned, bewildered, disappointed, yet somehow managed to keep her sense of humor and most of her integrity. Individuals may have let her down, but she hadn't lost her childlike faith in people. Even after everything else was gone, no one could rob her of her ability to love, although the pain of loving unwisely burned without remedy.

Linda Darnell, once considered Hollywood's Glory Girl, pulled herself off the bed and poured half an inch of vodka into a tumbler. Within an hour it would be time to leave for the theater. Exhausted, she began fixing her face, mechanically bringing to life the beauty that had once lifted a shy school girl to international fame. Hers was the fantasy come true for a Depression generation that needed to believe in magic and fairy godmothers. Brushing her cheek with rouge, she tried to remember when her appearance hadn't been more important than anything else. Even when she was tired and wanted out, there was always someone to push her toward success, promising her a life of tinsel and riches if she would do their bidding. But the tinsel soon tarnished, and what was left was hard work and eventually heartbreak. Despite her despondency that afternoon in Atlanta, she found her mirror image smiling back, as she thought of the folly of her own success. She finished the vodka and began tying a scarf around her hair.

Long before necessary she was in her dressing room at the Atlanta Community Playhouse, ready for the evening's performance. As she stood waiting to make her entrance, a young actor appeared at her side. "You haven't forgotten the prop change tonight have you, Miss Darnell?" he asked, ruining her concentration. "Don't you dare upset an actor or actress before they step out on a goddamn stage," she snapped at him later. "And don't treat me as if I were an amateur. I may not be the greatest actress in the world, but by damn I'm a professional!"

For the rest of their run the young actor fawned over her, and she hated that still more. She had been told since she was fifteen how special she was, but she'd learned better, the hard way. Invariably the Hollywood leeches were the ones who flattered most, told her what she wanted to hear, even when she knew it wasn't so. But she'd never allowed herself to become hard. Probably she'd even encouraged the lies, wanting to believe what she knew she shouldn't, at least for the moment. When the whole world is picking you apart, and you're projected larger than life on the screen—your emotions, face, voice, everything—magnified until a single wrinkle looks like a canyon, life can get pretty frightening.

Linda remained depressed throughout her Atlanta run, nauseated and run-down, despite the vitamin shots and Miltown (an anti-anxiety drug). She liked acting on the stage, liked the feel of a live audience, and left Atlanta confident she had played her part well, never suspecting she had given her last performance. After two grueling months on the road she needed a rest, and decided to spend Easter relaxing with her dearest friends, Jeanne and Richard Curtis, at their new home in Glenview, Illinois, a Chicago suburb. She had met the Curtises eighteen years earlier, on the set of *Unfaithfully Yours*, and the couple had grown closer to her than her own family. Although the Darnells loved each other in their crazy way, somehow they had become alienated; Mama Pearl had seen to that, just as she had seen to everything else.

Linda often thought of Pearl, although she hadn't visited her mother in recent years. "They always said you'd never die, Mama, as long as I lived, because we're so much alike," Linda frequently remarked, and certainly the similarities had grown sharper. Pearl had become bedridden and lived in a convalescent home, her eyesight too poor to read, but the family still suffered from the impact of her influence, as though she were still active. Monte, Linda's younger sister, worked as a nurse nearby and looked in on her mother, while Cal, her brother, had moved to England, escaping as best he could the hurts of the past. Only Undeen, the eldest, had sustained a marriage, had children, and found contentment in the simple pleasures of homemaking. In many ways Linda envied her sister, who, even when they were children, had been referred to as the white sheep of the family. She was the one the rest depended on. Undeen had largely raised her younger sisters and brother, and they all adored her for her sincerity. Linda dabbed her eyes with a handkerchief on the plane bound for Chicago, as she thought how different life might have been for them all had Pearl not forced the Hollywood dream on them. "I never wanted this," Linda often said after achieving stardom. But she knew she wouldn't have had it any other way.

Within a few days after joining the Curtises, Linda felt better than she had in months. Emotionally she came alive again, spending hours with Jeanne cooking and shopping, shocking Richard with her ribald humor, then covering her face with her hands like a naughty child. "Linda," Dick told her, "in all my years in the Marine Corps I never met a sergeant who could outswear you. You're the only woman I know who can be dressed like a queen and blow someone right out of the air with her language." She gave a raucous laugh and said in her husky voice, "Well, I've got more balls than most men do! If there's anything I hate, it's a weak man."

But Linda wasn't as tough as she liked to appear. When she and Jeanne discovered a family of raccoons in the backyard, Linda insisted on putting food out for them, sitting for hours in the dark waiting for them to appear. She had always loved animals; all four of the Darnell children delighted in taking care of helpless creatures, perhaps to give themselves some semblance of power, when they themselves were victims of the domineering Pearl. "Do you know what I would really like to have done?" Linda asked Jeanne one day. "I would like to have been a doctor. Medicine fascinates me." Suddenly she turned remorseful, haunted again by what life might have been, had the Hollywood dream remained merely a fantasy.

The Curtises' next-door neighbor saw Linda emptying garbage one morning, but didn't recognize her without makeup. Later, when Dick had to fly to Los Angeles on business, the actress drove with Jeanne to the airport. "Dick's one of a kind," Linda said on their way back. "He's the only real man left." Patricia,

Jeanne and Dick's sixteen-year-old daughter, was in Glenview, eagerly awaiting the arrival of Linda's adopted daughter Lola, who was scheduled to join her mother the following week. Lola and Patty were the same age and had grown up almost like sisters. Although their personalities were very different, Lola felt far closer to Patty than she did to any of her cousins.

On Thursday, April 8, Jeanne, Patty, and Linda spent a quiet evening at the Curtises' town house. The women worked into the night sorting through the receipts necessary for filing Linda's income tax return, and after bundling everything up for her accountant, Linda happened to notice that *Star Dust*, one of her early movies, was showing on television. Smiling, she snapped on the set in the living room shortly after midnight and said to Jeanne and Patty, "Let's stay up and watch this. We need some laughs."

The credits had no sooner come on than Linda was transported back to her first months in Hollywood. Lola's father, J. Peverell Marley, had been the cinematographer on *Star Dust*. "I used to wait for him after we'd finished shooting and spill my guts to him," Linda commented to Patty and Jeanne. "I sure never thought I'd end up marrying the guy." She smiled at Jeanne. "Pev may not have been the most polished man in the world, but he was dependable and honest. And he understood Hollywood. He taught me a lot." She lit a cigarette and began watching her scenes. "Linda giggled all the way through the picture," Jeanne remembered later. Since the film parodied some of Linda's own adventures breaking into movies, she became nostalgic. "We ought to order a print of this to show Lola when she comes," she suggested. "I'll call Darryl Zanuck tomorrow. The son of a bitch owes me *something* for those thirteen years!"

Linda laughed when the movie was over. Jeanne switched off the television set around 2:30 in the morning, carrying the two ashtrays they had filled to the kitchen sink. "I sure hope that coffee doesn't keep us awake," Linda commented. She found a book on wild animals to read before going to sleep, and they went upstairs and got into their pajamas. Linda kept coming over to Jeanne's bed in the room where they both were sleeping, to show her pictures of snakes she found fascinating, but Jeanne thought they were repulsive. Finally around 3:30 they fell asleep. The next thing Jeanne remembered was hearing Patty come in and say, "Mother, wake up. I have cold cream on my face, and it's running into my eyes. There's something wrong. There seems to be a lot of heat."

Jeanne bolted out of bed and threw on a light. The three of them went into the hall and walked to the top of the stairs, looking down into the living room. "We could see a glow, not flames, but a glow, like from an electric heater," Jeanne said later. Calmly they decided to investigate. They went into the bathroom, and each grabbed a wet towel." We came back to the head of the steps and there was a *whoosh* sound," Jeanne recalled. "It seemed like a jet engine. Then flames shot up the stairs to within one step of where we were standing. Apparently the heat was there in the living room, and then it exploded. Whether opening the bedroom doors had created a draft, I don't know. But instantly the heat became very intense, and the flames came up the stairs and then receded. It was like a whirlwind of flames." By now the smoke had started, curling out from the woodwork and creeping over the floor. The two women ran to call the fire department, each picking up a different phone and keeping the other from getting through. "You hang up, Linda," Jeanne shouted, "and I'll dial." They were a little more excited, but basically still calm. Jeanne reached the Glenview Fire Department, then rejoined Linda.

By this time smoke was engulfing the whole upstairs, and they decided to wait by a window. Jeanne looked around, but couldn't find Patty. Linda said, "I think she's at the foot of your bed." They found the girl—frightened, crouched by her mother's bed. Jeanne grabbed her daughter and dragged her to the window. The smoke and heat were growing more intense by the second. Suddenly even the carpet felt so hot they could barely stand on it. The aluminum blinds on the window were hot, and Jeanne couldn't touch the crank to open the glass. "Nobody has any idea of the heat," she explained later. "It's excruciating, and you're literally blowing to expel the heat from your body. It's like sitting in the hottest oven imaginable, only there was smoke mixed in with this."

Finally Jeanne grabbed the blinds and broke the window, because they had to have air. She managed to get the window open, but the smoke was stifling. "Get Pat out," Linda said, still with no hint of panic. Jeanne got Patty up on a chair and out the window, ordering her to jump. It was a two-and-a-half story drop, but Patty jumped onto the concrete patio, breaking her leg, heel, and ankle, and fracturing a vertebra. Jeanne assumed Linda was right behind her. She worked herself out onto the ledge and turned to help her friend. When Linda failed to take her hand, Jeanne realized she wasn't there. Jeanne went back in, but the heat and smoke drove her out again. By now firefighters were arriving. Jeanne was back on the ledge, hanging onto the roof. She kept calling to Linda, but there was no answer. "There's a lady inside," Jeanne yelled to the firefighters. "Get her out." They thought she said "baby" and tried to break through the large plate glass window in the living room. Meanwhile, people were running all over the lawn.

It was a rainy morning, and now about 5:10. David Mundhenk, a young neighbor, had made his way to the sliding glass door in back after spotting a figure in the living room silhouetted against the flames and smoke. He smashed the window with a shovel and tried to enter, cutting his wrist badly, only to be driven back by the smoke. The figure inside suddenly disappeared into the roaring inferno, and David heard a muffled cry through the crackle of flames that enveloped the living room. Jeanne was still screaming, "There's a lady in there!" Firefighters found Patty and soon got her mother off the ledge with a ladder. Somebody handed Jeanne a coat and a pair of galoshes, and she hurried around to the front yard. Meanwhile firefighters were inside, crawling around wearing oxygen masks, looking for a baby.

On the stairs they found a bedspread, a blanket, and a sheet Linda had pulled off the bed to wrap herself in. Apparently terrified of jumping, she had descended the stairs into a blinding wall of smoke, feeling her way along the banister, and attempted to go out the front door. "Linda had very weak wrists and ankles," Jeanne explained, "and I'm sure she was afraid to get out on the ledge and jump." She may have made it to the door, but couldn't turn the deadbolt, which would have been hot. Confused and disoriented by the heat and smoke, she evidently panicked and fell.

Firefighters found her on the living room floor, conscious but with second-and third-degree burns over ninety percent of her body, including her face. Jeanne arrived at the front door just as they were carrying Linda out. They took her to an ambulance, only to discover the vehicle's back door was jammed. Workers tried to pry it open, but couldn't. They put Linda in a police car and drove her to Skokie Valley Community Hospital. Almost immediately another ambulance arrived, and Patty and David Mundhenk, whose wrist was gushing blood, were put inside. Since Jeanne was still on her feet, a friend drove her to the hospital, arriving shortly before Patty was taken into surgery. Already reporters were swarming the corridors, hungry for a story about a

Hollywood celebrity. One put his foot in front of the cart wheeling Patty Curtis into the operating room, trying to stop it long enough to ask questions, but a police officer ran over and drew his pistol. Doctors soon had Jeanne's burns and cuts bandaged, while they kept Linda in an emergency room, working over her frantically, calling in additional staff. A tube had been inserted into her throat to ease her breathing, and she was given fluid and plasma intravenously for shock. "Mother," Patty said just before she was taken into surgery, "Linda is alive. I know, because she was in the booth next to me in emergency and she was swearing. You should have heard the language. I didn't see her, but I know she's alive."

Pearl and Monetta

Although she couldn't swim a stroke, Maggie Pearl grew up playing along the Tennessee River, on the outskirts of the village of Clifton, Tennessee, where in 1886 she had been born. Fir trees blanketed the hills east of the valley, while watermills and tanneries stood on the banks of the merging streams. Forty years later Maggie Pearl would be Mrs. Roy Darnell, the harridan behind the adolescent girl Hollywood made a star at fifteen. But at the turn of the century Maggie Pearl was just the beautiful, strong-willed daughter of Mary York and Thomas Gaugh Brown.

When she was ten, Maggie Pearl found an abandoned skiff and crawled inside. Soon she was lost in fantasies of resplendent actresses and all the nice things she had seen in mail order catalogues at her father's store. From afar she gradually heard voices. She sat up to find the skiff had been swept out into the river. Along the bank townspeople were yelling, pointing as the tiny craft made its way into turbulent water. A neighbor ran down the boardwalk to Tom Brown's store, finding Tom in the adjoining saloon. Immediately Tom and some friends dashed toward the river, located a boat, and began rowing toward the runaway skiff. Mary Brown waited on the sidelines, wringing her hands and murmuring prayers, as baby Cleo screamed and cried into her mother's skirts. Tom and the men finally reached Maggie Pearl, but not until she had added plenty of excitement to the town's sleepy afternoon. "She was always a colorful person," Pearl's sister Cleo said later. "She was always looking for something more than just the ordinary."

In many ways Maggie Pearl took after her father. She even looked more like him than did the other three children. Tom Brown was half Cherokee, and as a young man had traveled with a circus. Later he became a musician, mastering several instruments, but particularly the fiddle. He formed his own band, and every spring his musicians played on the river boats up and down the Tennessee and Mississippi rivers. Maggie Pearl ached to go with him, but had to content herself with imitating distant thespians she dreamed of joining. Dressed in Mary's high heels and long dresses, Pearl performed for sister Priscilla and baby Cleo—singing, dancing, reciting rhymes, telling jokes. "She had such dreams," said Cleo. "She was never content to sit down like most children."

If the religious, somewhat introverted Mary had reservations about Maggie Pearl's flamboyance, her protests were offset by Tom's encouragement. Maggie Pearl was the apple of his eye. She grew up without spankings, extroverted, spoiled, often driving her mother to distraction. More than once Maggie Pearl waded out into the river, yelling to the helpless Mary that she was going to drown herself unless she got her way.

But Maggie Pearl's pampered childhood came to an end in February 1901, when Tom Brown died. Mary carried on as best she could, but the modest affluence Tom had provided dwindled into poverty. Maggie Pearl continued her dreams, but was devastated by her father's premature death. She became a problem child, more disposed than ever to command attention, even talking back to elders. Uncle Jim, her mother's half brother, came to be something of a father figure, but Jim was scarcely more than a boy himself and no match for Maggie Pearl.

So when Lawrence Ketroe came to town and began paying the girl notice, most family members were relieved. Ketroe, a handsome, smooth-talking Italian in his late thirties, happened onto Maggie Pearl enroute to the local hotel and commented on what a pretty girl she was. He found out where she lived and shortly paid a call. Maggie Pearl was intrigued with Ketroe's kindness and debonair appearance, which reminded her of her father. When Uncle Jim learned that a traveling man was courting his niece, he threatened to go for his shotgun. But Maggie Pearl would tolerate no interference; she knew there was a world beyond the river's bend and was determined to see it. On May 27, 1905, Maggie Pearl and Ketroe appeared before a justice of the peace and were married. The bride turned fifteen two months later.

The newlyweds immediately left town, traveling to Cajun country. Maggie Pearl experienced her first taste of ethnic foods and learned to cook. Her husband took her to dances, where she outdid herself, always the center of attention. But again the laughter was cut short. Money ran out about the time Maggie Pearl learned she was pregnant. Ketroe brought her back to Tennessee—not to Clifton, but to nearby Hohenwald, where Maggie

Pearl's cousin George took them in. There Richard was born.

Ketroe continued his travels while Maggie Pearl remained in Hohenwald. Evelyn, their second child, was born during one of his absences. George proved generous, but Maggie Pearl grew restless. Eventually there were rumors that Ketroe had killed a man. Then he failed to return from a trip. Maggie Pearl felt the insecurity she had experienced when her father died, only now she was away from home, with two babies to support. Ketroe showed up later at Mary's place in Clifton looking for his wife, but Pearl was still with Cousin George. "We never saw him again," Cleo recalled.

Mary's finances had meantime grown desperate, and she decided to take Priscilla and Cleo to live with her half brother and sister in Oklahoma Territory. After selling what they could, the family left Maggie Pearl behind to arrange her divorce. They went by boat down below Shiloh, then boarded a train for Indian Territory. Mary's folks, George and Florence, had adjoining farms near Ardmore, the territory's largest town. Maggie Pearl followed about a year later with her babies.

Pearl's attitude had changed. With her children she was strict and unbending. She seemed cynical, already nostalgic for her youth. She was still high-strung, wanting things to move faster than they normally do. Yet life on an Oklahoma farm in 1907 was drudgery. Every hand was needed, and all but the smallest children had to help hoe and pick cotton. Since there were few schools, Mary worried about her younger children's education, and shortly after Oklahoma became a state she moved them to Anadarko. Maggie Pearl went to work in a boarding house, leaving her mother to look after Richard and Evelyn, but the old fantasies of a more glamorous life never left her.

When Maggie Pearl discovered that Geronimo, the Apache chief, was a prisoner at Fort Sill, she made a trip to see him. She visited the nearby Caddo Reservation, made friends with some of the Indians there, and brought home a beaded deerskin purse that became one of her treasures. "She was always very proud of her Indian blood," a family member recalled, "and goodness knows she loved to go on the warpath."

In 1913 Maggie Pearl decided to move to Texas. Mary offered to keep Richard and Evelyn, but Pearl wanted them near her. She took a train to Dallas, then a city of just under 100,000, with its heart still in the soil. To Pearl, Dallas represented bright lights, freedom, and the restoration of lost dreams. Yet with no education to speak of, her opportunities were limited. Pearl found a job as domestic help with the Lewis family in Oak Cliff, a suburb that preserved the ambience of a small town.

To take the job with the Lewises, Pearl had to find a place to leave Richard and Evelyn, and decided on a Christian orphanage a few blocks away. She signed the necessary papers and faithfully went to visit them every Sunday. One week she found Richard and Evelyn gone. They had been legally adopted, and officials at the orphanage refused to tell her by whom. "She almost lost her mind," Pearl's sister Cleo said. "We all did. It was such a blow."

Pearl searched for her children frantically. She felt betrayed, mistrusted people all the more, became filled with anger and hate. At the same time the loss reawakened a religious impulse she had acquired from her mother, causing her to grow overly puritanical. She joined the Oak Cliff Christian Church, learned to fear God, and became schooled in repression. But through it all ran the guilt of having abandoned her babies and the rage at having them stolen from her.

At twenty-three Pearl had lost some of her robust beauty, yet was still an attractive woman. Her face, weathered by wind and sun, had grown angular. Her straight black hair fell below her knees. She was dark and thin, teeming with energy. She was quick in her movements, quick tempered, quick to form opinions. "Everything had to be done right now," a neighbor remembered, "and she wanted it all her way." Yet Pearl could be terribly funny, even if her lack of education was readily apparent.

At the Lewises' Pearl customarily walked out front to bring in the mail. Soon she struck up an acquaintance with the postman, a shy fellow given to few words. Pearl began waiting for him, as their exchanges grew longer. Calvin Roy Darnell had been born in a log cabin on the Brazos River. His father was an itinerant school teacher, although Roy had grown up a farm boy. His family later moved to Denton, just north of Dallas, where his mother supplemented the family income by taking in boarders. Shortly after Roy and his brother Earl were employed by the Dallas post office in 1910, the rest of the Darnells moved to Dallas, buying a cottage in Oak Cliff.

Roy proved to be three years older than Pearl, and she thought of him as a fine southern gentleman. He was easygoing and spoke in quiet, gentle tones. Eventually Roy asked Pearl out. He was dazzled by her energy, wit, and endless monologues. Pearl loved the movies, and the couple had one of their first dates at a downtown theater. On March 19, 1915, Pearl Ketroe and Roy Darnell were married in the Adolphus Hotel, Dallas's newest and grandest.

Roy's family soon found Pearl difficult. For a brief time the couple lived with Earl and his wife, Annie, but that lasted only a short while, causing an estrangement between Roy and his brothers and sisters. Since Roy was the kind of husband who could sit in a room for hours and not say a word, Pearl quickly found him a bore. When her constant talking got the best of him, Roy would simply announce, "Pearl, I'm going fishing," and off he went. Once they were married, Pearl no longer worked, devoting herself to lodge and charity functions. Occasionally she managed to coerce Roy into taking her to a dance, where she embarrassed her husband by flouncing around in full skirts, as she danced by herself to the fast numbers. Maggie Pearl never liked anything slow.

On Sundays the couple went to church, and Pearl continued her search for Evelyn and Richard. She kept a photograph of her children on the mantle and talked about them incessantly. While Roy by no means earned big money, he provided his wife with a security she had not known since childhood. She loved knick-knacks and costume jewelry and, of course, the movies. After Roy was promoted to the position of clerk in the central post office, Pearl frequently took a streetcar downtown to meet him for an early show, basking in Hollywood dreams. The couple's first baby, Undeen Therese, was born in March 1918, and Pearl immediately began concocting plans for her future. Undeen was a pretty girl, soft in disposition. Pearl grew determined the child would become the actress she herself had wanted to be. Undeen would have dancing and elocution lessons and all the things a pretty girl needed to prepare herself for the movies.

With World War I over, Pearl coaxed Roy into taking a family vacation. They had laid aside a few dollars, and Pearl longed to see Hollywood. In October 1919, the couple packed up baby Undeen and left for California, spending several days in Los Angeles. Pearl was overjoyed. Leaving Undeen with Roy, she went to watch movies being made and even managed to get hired as an extra for a crowd scene. "She was thrilled to death!" Undeen said later. "She used to tell us about it. She so wanted to be a movie actress."

Pearl returned home more determined than ever that Undeen should be a star. The child was enrolled in all sorts of classes, even before she was old enough. "I was much too shy," said Undeen. "I couldn't sing or act. I just didn't have the talent." But Pearl held firm and the lessons continued, even though Roy complained about the cost. There were baby contests, then pageants and lodge shows, never with any success. The child's reluctance simply made Pearl more adamant. "I always thought of myself as the ugly duckling," Undeen said. "I just felt doomed. Finally Mother decided that dumb Undeen wasn't going to make it."

Pearl took out her frustrations bickering with Roy. Everything was his fault. He refused even to talk to her, much less take her exciting places like men in the movies did. "I grew up with Mother just raising Holy Ned all the time," Undeen recalled. Soon the Darnells moved into a simple frame cottage on Alabama Street in a middle-class neighborhood in south Oak Cliff. They were living there when Pearl accidentally discovered Richard playing in a yard not far from where she had worked. Richard and Evelyn had been adopted by the Bennetts, a religious family of modest means, who had done the best they could for the children. Pearl immediately introduced herself as their rightful mother and demanded the children be returned to her, eventually haranguing and threatening trouble. Richard periodically found a way to visit his mother, and Evelyn later ran away to live with the Darnells for a time. "I remember Richard carrying me on his shoulders across a vacant field," said Undeen. "I was so proud, because he was so handsome. I always wanted an older brother."

She also hoped for a baby sister and got her wish on the evening of October 16, 1923. The new baby, born at home, had dark eyes and coal black hair already an inch long. "I remember standing by her bed the night she was born," Undeen said. "Dad reached over and tweaked her hair, and he said, 'Well, hello Tweedles.'" They named her Monetta Eloyse, although the world would know her as Linda. To her family she always remained Tweedles.

Beautiful even as a child, Monetta was a quiet girl, unusually obedient, trying to avoid domestic turmoil that only got worse. At times she seemed withdrawn, happily cutting out paper dolls in a world of her own. "Being five years older, I thought she was a pest," Undeen said, although the girls grew up sharing a room and most of their childhood secrets. While Undeen considered Monetta more outgoing than herself, playmates remember her as timid, anything but a show-off. Yet Pearl had ambitions from the start. There was something in the way Monetta handled herself that made Pearl know she had her star this time. She would see to it. So Monetta grew up hearing how one day she would be a movie actress. "Tweedles always said she was going to be out in Hollywood," Undeen recalled, "from the time she was a tiny kid. She just seemed to be Mother all over again."

When Monetta was two, the Darnells bought a home around the corner from where Richard and Evelyn lived. Pearl talked less openly about her estranged children, so they existed only as rumor among neighborhood gossips. Prophetically the new house was on Hollywood Street, which dead-ended into the recently completed Sunset High School. The modest five-room bungalow had essentially the same floor plan as all the other houses on its street. Inside, floral wallpaper surrounded overstuffed furniture, with family pictures all around. Out front big sycamore trees shaded the yard, while cedar bushes screened the porch swing from the street. Texas was crawling with scorpions and insects, so it was always a good idea to shake shoes and check the swing before sitting down.

Within a few years there were two more Darnell children: Monte Maloya, born in 1929, and Calvin Roy, Jr., born fourteen months later. Monte, named for one of Pearl's old boyfriends, was expected to be the boy. She infuriated her mother by not talking until she was five years old, preferring to point at whatever she wanted. "They thought I was retarded," said Monte. "I did grow up the ugly duckling. I was really an embarrassment to Mother." Cal for years was called Sonny. Like Monetta, he had beautiful black hair and thick, long eyelashes. Pearl kept him in shoulder-length curls and dresses until he was almost six. "She actually raised me like a girl," he admitted later.

Eleven years older than Monte, Undeen seemed almost like a second mother, and she did spend much of her time babysitting and looking after her brother and sisters. "She was so normal and quiet," Monte recalled. "Mother took a deep breath about an hour before she got up in the morning and never quit talking until about two hours after she went to bed." Monetta also felt protective toward Monte and Cal, showing them the attention and patience she herself craved. "That girl was my idol," said Monte. Neither of the younger children communicated much with Roy, although they loved and respected him. "Dad was strict," Undeen remembered, "but we could get around him. He would correct you, but he was the one you could wrap around your little finger. It was Mother who ruled the roost."

Monte and Cal, the closest in age, fought the typical childhood battles, but the two of them spent hours together catching lizards and horned toads and tormenting bugs on the front walk. In the morning they sat on the curb waiting for the milk wagon to make its rounds, so Monte could pet her favorite draft horse. Pearl was a fierce disciplinarian, and none of the children dared cross her. Undeen once got a thrashing when Monetta rammed a leg through the wire on top of a rabbit pen out by the garage. Another time Monetta climbed a plum tree Roy had planted, then suddenly started screaming. "Pretty soon my mother came out, just a-cussing," Undeen remembered. Pearl shook Monetta, to make the child tell her what was wrong. Crying, the girl pointed to her back. An asp had dropped down the back of her dress and was stinging her. After Monetta stopped screaming, Pearl grabbed an ax and chopped down the plum tree!

Around the neighborhood it was whispered that Mrs. Darnell was a screwball. She usually just pulled her hair back into a knot behind her head, and already her skin showed the wrinkled look of older farm women. But it was her aggressive, meddlesome personality that put people off. The Crawfords, who lived a block away, avoided her as much as possible. "I passed by their house going to school every morning," said Virginia Crawford. "Mrs. Darnell was an intense woman. In my romantic memory I picture her as having a kind of gypsy intensity. I have the impression she was a rather dramatic person in a very undramatic setting." Virginia's sister Rita remembered Pearl as "always in motion. My mother claimed she went from door to door like a child with a sand pail, dipping out a certain amount at each door in exchange for a little gossip. She stirred up trouble up and down the street. After the first visit, Mother was never home to Mrs. Darnell." Louise Lamm, who grew up three houses down the street, felt Pearl was downright mean. "All the kids in the neighborhood were afraid of her," Louise claimed. "She really didn't want us near her house, and chased us away." Mrs. Cannon lived next door to the Darnells and would warn the neighborhood children:

"You be careful. Mrs. Darnell's mean. She chased Mr. Darnell all over the backyard yesterday with a butcher knife in her hand!"

Roy, on the other hand, was consistently praised as hardworking and meek. "I never heard Mr. Darnell say over one or two words," Louise Lamm said. "He was completely henpecked. I'm sure he was very fond of his children; he just didn't have any real say in what happened." Roy was always "a shadowy figure," according to Virginia Crawford. "I think it was the typical situation of a nice man who was just dominated by this space-filling woman."

The neighbors were even less fond of the family's penchant for pets, all kinds of pets—chickens, rabbits, white mice, an Irish setter, and a huge turtle out in the backyard. "Those children kept snakes and all kinds of bugs around," their Aunt Cleo said. "I was afraid to lie down in that house for fear of what I'd wake up and find in bed with me." Cal was an avid collector of asps and scorpions, which he kept in jars. "I didn't cross the street, but I always took a wide swath around the sidewalk when I passed their house," Virginia Crawford declared.

Monetta loved animals, too, and would carry around a pet rabbit. She had a canary once, but the cat from next door ate it and she cried and cried. She was growing into a gorgeous child—thin, but with her mother's olive coloring and limpid dark eyes. "She was always so sweet and kind and had a smile on her face all the time," said Dolly Elder, Monetta's closest school friend. "I just thought she was the prettiest thing I'd ever seen." Monetta was studious and smart, consistently making high marks and never giving her teachers any trouble. "Everybody thought she was a beautiful girl," Louise Lamm agreed, "but they really didn't pay much attention to her. She was so shy and reserved."

Monetta's shyness increased when she became ill during the third grade and lost an alarming amount of weight. Pearl was afraid she might have tuberculosis, and the neighborhood chatter was that she did. Monetta was ordered to have complete bed rest and missed several weeks of school. Pearl tried to keep her entertained, but became more possessive than ever. Since Monetta was put on a diet of liver three times a week, Pearl insisted the whole family eat it. Within a few months the patient revived, but seemed more docile than ever.

"Monetta was the one that Mrs. Darnell had singled out for success," Virginia Crawford said, "and nothing was going to stop her." So when Monetta started back to school, she also resumed her music and elocution lessons, which she had taken faithfully since she was four. She played the piano, recited poems, and was always dancing and showing off around the house. During the summer the Darnell kids and the Harrison children from next door would put on skits out in the backyard. "Tweedles was always out there being the shining light," Undeen remembered. "I would always slink into the background. We charged our parents a penny to watch the show, so I was usually in charge of the money."

Monte and Cal also took music and elocution lessons and were entered in every pageant Pearl's lodge women held. Cal even won a cup in a beauty contest. When he was four, he appeared in a lodge show wearing white satin pants, looking like Little Lord Fauntleroy. "Mother was determined to make somebody a star," Undeen said. But Cal phrased it more harshly: "She had this grand determination to push her children toward show business one way or another. Mother was a dragon, a fire-eating dragon." Still, Monetta was enough like her mother to find the dream of stardom captivating. "When Tweedles came along, with all the natural talent and beauty that she had, they were just two peas in a pod," observed Monte. "One complemented the other."

Classmates recalled Monetta's being "pretty well kept at home." While other girls walked from school in clusters, Monetta usually walked by herself. When classmates asked her to join them, she was friendly, even though she had little in common with them. Much of Monetta's time was spent doing her school work in the room she shared with Undeen. She was exceptionally talented in art, and as a youngster drew paper dolls and sold them for a penny each. When her class listened to Walter Damrosch's music appreciation series on the radio at school, Monetta drew pictures illustrating the selections they heard for most of the other pupils.

The Depression hit Dallas less severely than it did the country's more heavily industrialized cities, since the discovery of oil in East Texas stimulated the local economy, but hard times touched the city's working classes, both financially and psychologically. Pearl's lodges prepared food for the Salvation Army, and she herself worked at several local missions. "I remember going down to the breadlines and sitting there with the other kids," recalled Monte. "And I remember men standing in line as we rode into town." Roy still loved to fish and hunt, frequently staying away for days at a time. Once he brought home a giant catfish, which he put in a washtub for the kids to see. Eventually it wound up as food for the needy. "Dad fed an awful lot of people during the Depression," Monte said. "I've seen him bring home three hundred squirrels at a time, and I remember staying up watching him skin them."

Hard times also brought a wave of lawlessness to the Southwest, and the unpaved streets of west Dallas spawned the notorious Clyde Barrow and Bonnie Parker, who for two years robbed and terrorized the Texas-Oklahoma-Louisiana area, making headlines and thrilling a humdrum public. In May 1934, after the elusive desperadoes had been shot through with bullets in the piney woods of Louisiana, their bodies were returned to Dallas and taken to separate funeral homes. Bonnie Parker's was brought to McKamy-Campbell, just across the river from Oak Cliff. That night large crowds gathered outside both funeral homes, waiting to view the bodies. Mrs. Campbell was one of Pearl's lodge women, so Pearl called and made arrangements for a private showing. The whole family went, although Undeen and Roy stayed in the car. "I remember seeing Bonnie Parker lying on a table," Monte said, "the first dead person I'd ever seen. She had very blonde hair and looked beautiful." On the drive home all four children were piled in the back seat of Roy's 1929 Chevrolet, not saying a word. Monte sat on Monetta's lap, while Undeen held Cal. Finally Monte whispered to Monetta, "What were all of those black things all over her?" Monetta leaned down and said, "Honey, those were bullet holes." Monte was terrified.

Unhappy and bored, Pearl craved sensationalism and sniffed it out at every opportunity. If there was none, she created it, pushing her way to the front. She made waves in the PTA, became chairman of the Good Cheer Committee of the Oak Cliff Society of Fine Arts, and was an active member in the Woman's Benefit Association, an insurance group that sponsored clubs and activities for members. On Saturdays the WBA provided elocution and dance lessons for members' children, and Pearl saw to it that Monetta had both. "Monetta's mother was very ambitious for her daughter," remembered Frances Brown, who taught the elocution classes. "Monetta didn't stand out particularly, except that she was so sweet and considerate. In her theater work she wasn't outstanding. But her mother was right behind her everywhere she went."

When Monetta was in the sixth grade, Pearl learned there was to be a talent contest at Lida Hooe School, where all her younger children attended. She made sure Monetta entered, sold tickets for the event, and trotted out the whole family to attend. Monetta wore a pale blue satin dress with tiny pink rosettes and won first place for singing "Alice Blue Gown" in a clear soprano voice. "I thought she looked so pretty that night," her classmate Charloise Hufstedler said. "She wasn't really beautiful, because she was just a kid. She was skinny and had no figure at all. But I think that's when it all started, when she won that prize in sixth grade. From then on Monetta just didn't have much time for anything else. She and her mother were determined she'd go to Hollywood."

Discovery

Like hundreds before and after her, Pearl Darnell envisioned Hollywood as an escape from working-class tedium, and for her Monetta was the ticket. She mustered every resource available, meager as they were. Over the next two years Monetta sang "Alice Blue Gown" in talent shows all over Dallas, performing practically every week. In more cases than not she won the prize. She appeared three times on the "Kiddie Show" originating from the downtown Melba Theater, broadcast locally over radio station WRR, each time winning first or second prize. Inez Teddlie, who played piano for the "Kiddie Club" contestants, remembered Monetta's doing a simple dance wearing a flashy costume and singing "Only a Gypsy." "With her dark coloring she looked very pretty. She didn't seem to have a great deal of talent, either for singing or dancing. She had poise and appeared older than her years. But it seemed to be her mother's idea that she be on."

In 1936 the big show in Dallas was the Texas Centennial. The state fair grounds were refurbished, and President Franklin Roosevelt himself came to inaugurate the occasion. Sally Rand brandished her fans, while big names from all segments of the entertainment industry were on hand. From early June through late November the Texas Centennial relieved for some ten million visitors the bleakness of the Depression. Monetta was hired by Centennial officials to perform a Mexican hat dance. Pearl took Monte and Cal out to the fair grounds to see their sister perform, and just as they walked past the Sinclair Oil dinosaurs, Pearl spotted a group of Indians in full ceremonial garb. "To my utter terror and disgrace," Cal said, "my mother pulled up her skirts and crawled through a fence and started hugging all of those Indians, which sent me into tears. It was the most frightening moment of my childhood. But she actually knew those Indians from Anadarko."

When school started in the fall, Monetta continued to make high marks despite having to devote practically every afternoon to dance lessons, music practice, or play rehearsals. She appeared twice in nearby Fort Worth, was on a number of WPA theatre programs, and was featured in every lodge, church, and school program Pearl could manage. The Dallas Little Theater accepted her into its teenage class and through that she auditioned for a local screen test. When the Cathedral Players of St. Matthews Episcopal Church produced the southwestern premiere of T. S. Eliot's *Murder in the Cathedral*, Pearl made certain Monetta tried out. She got a part, becoming the group's youngest member. While Undeen babysat Monte and Cal, Roy drove Monetta and Pearl across town for evening rehearsals, even though he thought the whole business was nonsense and refused to budge from the car.

In addition to everything else Monetta spent afternoons modeling, eventually for Southwestern Style Shows, a Dallas fashion show. Actress Dale Evans, then a local band vocalist, worked luncheon shows with Hyman Charninsky's orchestra at the Baker and Adolphus hotels when Monetta was modeling junior miss dresses. "She was a very sweet, unassuming child," said the future queen of the cowgirls. "She was exceptionally beautiful, but very unspoiled."

Occasionally Monetta would invite her friend Dolly Elder along with her to rehearsals or photography sessions. The two girls often spent Saturday afternoons downtown window shopping, going to movies, or looking at cosmetics and nail polish in the dime stores. Whereas most girls wore sweaters and skirts to school, Monetta always looked more sophisticated. "That's one of the things that made her different from the rest of us," schoolmate Eleanor Kline remembered. "Monetta always looked gorgeous, with full makeup and her hair absolutely beautiful." But classmates found her beauty intimidating. "I think she must have had a hard time dealing with the fact that her peers were in awe of her," Virginia Crawford said. "You had the impression of isolation, not by her choosing at all, but by the fact of her singular beauty." Yet Monetta bit her fingernails badly. "We used to laugh about it," Dolly Elder recalled. "She would always complain about my nails being long and hers looking so ratty. She had all colors of nail polish, and we'd have fun trying to make our nails polka dot or plaid. But her life was hard. It seemed that somebody else was always in command, telling her what to do, when to do it, which way to look. It's a good thing she had an easy disposition or she couldn't have handled it."

Monetta herself later said, "I've been working since I was eleven. I never got to do the things most girls do. I never attended a school dance, never took a spin in a cut-down jalopy. I worked. I was a lonely child and grateful to anyone who liked me. I guess my craving for affection goes back to my childhood, when I didn't have much of it." She was a responsible girl, trying to make people happy. "Stand straight, smile, tell them you're sixteen," Pearl would instruct when they went for modeling interviews. Monetta learned early the premium on dressing well and acting grown up. It seemed the route to acceptance.

Virginia Crawford happened to board a streetcar one Saturday morning a block before Monetta did. Virginia was sitting toward the back so Monetta didn't notice her. "Her head was down," Virginia recalled, and she was "so shy she almost didn't look at anybody." She was carrying a small makeup kit, across the side of which were three-inch letters spelling out her name. "I'm sure her mother put those letters on there, and I think she was a little embarrassed. She sat very demurely on that front seat, ducking her head, almost covering up the lettering with her arm. My impression is that her mother invariably found ways to attract attention, which only emphasized Monetta's self-effacement. I think she was embarrassed, but was powerless to resist. Things were happening to her in spite of herself."

Nor was Roy strong enough to stop the force pushing his family toward something beyond their control. As Pearl became increasingly absorbed with Monetta's reputation, Roy took over some of the domestic duties. Pearl was never much of a housekeeper, so what was done either Roy or Undeen did. "Poor Roy, regardless of how tired he was, he didn't complain," Pearl's sister Cleo said. "I never heard him say anything that would indicate his inner feelings. He did whatever Pearl told him to do, and he accepted it without any controversy whatsoever."

When Cleo or her sister Priscilla came to visit, Pearl would stay up all night chattering. "We didn't know what a show was," Cleo maintained, "and we certainly didn't know what spotlights were, but she would tell us all about show business and the spotlights and all the shows she'd seen." Occasionally Pearl and Priscilla and a few neighbor ladies gathered for gossip and a glass of blackberry wine, which they insisted wasn't really drinking. "They only drank those ghastly sweet things," Cal said later, "but those old cats used to knock back the blackberry wine. Pearl had this intense moral thing, yet I think she had very strong sex drives and didn't know how to deal with them."

Once Pearl caught the smell of success, Monte and Cal grew up largely on their own. Roy frequently worked nights and didn't always come home immediately afterwards, and Undeen was ready to graduate from high school and find a job. Neighbors recall the younger Darnell children coming into the grocery store to buy something for lunch and stocking up on junk food. Monte was developing a personality as headstrong as her mother's, while Cal was growing into a handsome boy whom the neighborhood women fawned over. He detested his long curls, and Monte hated them too, especially since Pearl had cut her hair short. One day the children located some scissors, and Monte tore into Cal's curls, much to his delight and hers. "Mother came in and about killed both of us," recalled Monte. "She cried like a baby and kept those curls in a box in the cedar chest."

It was simply assumed that someday Monetta would be a movie star. "I used to go by and look at the marquee of the Bison Theater up on the corner," Monte said. "This was before I even started school. We'd go up there to the candy store, and I'd look at that marquee and I'd think, 'Someday it's going to read MONETTA DARNELL.' I knew it as well as she did."

In the bedroom Monetta and Undeen shared each had her own wall for tacking up movie star pictures. Monetta's favorite was Tyrone Power, although she also liked Loretta Young. "We both dreamed of Hollywood," said Undeen. "She dreamed of acting out there. I just wanted to go out and see the stars." Monetta would sit for hours in front of their dresser, posing and primping before its three big mirrors. "I guess that should have told us she was going to be an actress," Undeen declared.

Monetta hated housework. Undeen was the homebody, but Pearl decided that since Undeen washed the dishes, Monetta should dry them. No sooner would the family finish supper than Monetta would decide it was time to practice the piano, leaving Undeen with a table full of dirty dishes. "Mother, I wish you'd make Tweedles come in here and help me with these dishes!" Undeen protested one evening after a hard day. Pearl yelled for Monetta to go help in the kitchen, but had to repeat the order a second time. Monetta swished past Monte and took a stance in the doorway, glaring at Undeen. "Someday I'm going to Hollywood," she shouted, hands on hips, "and I'll have a maid to do my dishes."

Family members knew all about Monetta's tantrums, even if friends didn't. At her worst they were a match for Pearl's. "Mother and Tweedles were just alike," said Undeen. "They both thought the same way and had terrible tempers. They had quite a few arguments, and I can remember Tweedles looking at me so angry she could spit." She once broke a pair of lamps she knew Pearl liked. It was a tense moment when Undeen had to tell her mother what happened. "But that was Tweedles's way of getting back at Mother."

Whether Monetta herself really wanted to be a movie star is a difficult question to answer. Monte claimed, "She had ambition as much as Mother ever did, not only the ability but the desire to do it." Cal said, "Tweedles wanted to become a film star because Mother wanted her to be. She didn't know what else to do. She certainly had the gift. It just came naturally for her." Monetta herself admitted, "Mother really shoved me along, spotting me in one contest after another. I had no great talent, and I didn't want to be a movie star particularly. But Mother had always wanted it for herself, and I guess she attained it through me." For both Monetta and Pearl, becoming a movie star was pure fantasy; neither understood the work involved nor the measures necessary to sustain success once it was attained. Both were therefore doomed to disappointment after their euphoria cooled.

So successful had the Texas Centennial been in 1936 that the state fair officials decided to repeat the celebration the next year, calling it the Pan American Exposition. This time a group of attractive teenage girls called Texanitas welcomed special guests, decorated floats, and appeared in the local press day after day. Virginia Crawford became a Texanita; so did Louise Lamm's older sister. Bill Langley, who headed photographic publicity for the fair, had the job of selecting the lucky girls.

One day, after interviewing scores of pretty girls, Langley was ready to go home. His secretary stopped him: "Mr. Langley, there's one more girl here I think you should see." Langley refused, insisting he had more than enough candidates already. "Please," his secretary said. "If I were you, I'd take a look at this one." Langley gave in, determined not to be impressed. In walked "the most gorgeous creature," with black hair and skinny legs, yet the most beautiful eyes he had ever seen. In her hand was a makeup kit labeled "Monetta Darnell." She stood five feet three inches and was as flat chested as a child. "What do you want?" Langley snorted. "To become a model," the girl answered. She was shy, but poised. "What makes you think you can model?"

asked Langley gruffly. "I know I can," she returned politely. "And someday I'm going to be a movie star."

Langley handed her an application and hired her despite the fact that she was underage. At fourteen Monetta was the youngest of the Texanitas, and Bill Langley was to become her "Uncle Willy" for life. When Pearl found out Virginia Crawford was also a Texanita, she called up and asked Virginia to keep an eye on Monetta. "It really was an age of innocence," Virginia said. "There was no problem with school girls being models at that time, because there were clucking mother-hen types taking care of us. It was fun, but I know Monetta got all the plum notices."

In September 1937 Monetta entered Sunset High School, making the honor roll every semester she was there, but showing particular interest in Spanish and art. Outside commitments, plus a combination of allergies, forced her to be absent from school frequently, although her grades rarely suffered. "She seemed to do it with such ease," Dolly Elder said. Monetta dated very little, since Pearl kept her busy and closely chaperoned. Her love of animals continued, however, as did Cal's and Monte's.

The younger children habitually lost pets around the house, and it was not unusual for Roy to stand in his shorts before the bedroom bureau yelling, "Pearl! Come in here and get this garter snake out of my sock drawer." One Easter, he bought the family two dyed Easter chicks at Sears Roebuck. One was pink, the other blue. The pink one died in less than a week, but the blue one, a rooster the children named Weedy, grew up in a box under the kitchen stove and later had the run of the house. "He was just one of the family," Monte and Undeen agreed. When Weedy got big, the children dressed him up. Monetta painted his toenails and spurs, and Pearl made him a pair of trousers, with a place for his tail feathers to stick through, and a cape that tied under his neck. "He was really a handsome fellow," said Monte. "Whenever we couldn't find Weedy, we'd go into the front bedroom and there he'd be up on the vanity seat in front of a long mirror preening himself."

Eventually Weedy took to roosting on the backs of the beds, so Pearl made another trip to Sears and bought him a baby crib of his own. Unfortunately for neighbors, as Weedy got older he learned to crow. "I'd have to put him under the covers with me about four o'clock in the morning and try to keep him there," Monte remembered. Sometimes the children would infuriate him until he chased them. Monte and Cal would joyously leap on their bed to get away from him, while the rooster paced below, sharpening his claws on the rug.

Weedy sat at the table and ate off a plate whatever the family ate—fried chicken, pinto beans, potatoes, hot peppers, everything. Finally he became so paralyzed he no longer could walk. Pearl took him to a veterinarian. "What do you feed this chicken?" the unsuspecting vet asked. "Oh, he eats table scraps," Pearl told him. "He eats what we do." Poor Weedy was immediately placed on a stringent diet of chicken feed. Pearl had to moisten his food and force it down his throat. "They had to carry him around on a pillow for a month or two," said Undeen, "because he still couldn't walk. But with all the chicken food and vitamins they poked down him, he raised up again."

Once Monetta entered Sunset High, her work schedule became even more hectic. Roy frequently picked her up at school, dutifully driving her to rehearsals. Whenever the girl's future was mentioned, Roy urged her to become a schoolteacher like his father or a secretary, something secure, and give up this nonsense of becoming an actress.

But as the Depression persisted, Americans seemed obsessed with escapism, and schoolgirls everywhere dreamed of movie stars. Hollywood appeared a modern gold rush, Tinseltown, and for a democracy without an established nobility, it produced an American royalty. Far more than its politicians, movie stars since Mary Pickford and Douglas Fairbanks had become America's gods and goddesses. Their only rivals were a handful of sports heroes who still lacked the controlled publicity to lift themselves to the height of celebrity. Movie stars, on the other hand, represented the American dream in materialistic terms an emotionally undernourished public could accept and emulate.

Newspapers across the country doted on announcements of new starlets who had been discovered by the Hollywood studios. This or that lucky girl was "being groomed for stardom." It was the crowning of the homecoming queen turned into a national craze, and Dallas was not exempt. Oliver Hinsdell, formerly with a local theater group, returned to town as a Paramount scout, and Metro-Goldwyn-Mayer filmed "actual screen tests" on the stage of the Majestic Theater, using the Dallas winners of MGM's "official search for talent." The advertisement assured, "You'll See Movies Made Before Your Very Eyes!" Fans, captured by the mystique, flocked to the downtown movie palace. The next month the *Dallas Times Herald* suggested, "Talent sleuthing is a funny and unpredictable business," but failed to mention that the publicity involved made for lively movie attendance.

In November 1937 Twentieth Century–Fox talent scout Ivan Kahn arrived in town looking for new faces. Kahn, who had traveled all over the South, visited Dallas and Fort Worth, placing announcements in the newspapers of both cities. Pearl Darnell read the notice and insisted Monetta see him. Here was their chance. "It certainly won't hurt to try," Pearl insisted. She called up and made an appointment. "I was going to be a movie star or Mom was going to bust in the attempt," Monetta said later.

Whatever mixed feelings Monetta may have had, she showed up at Ivan Kahn's hotel suite at the appointed hour, Pearl at her side, looking her best and instructed not to mention she was only fourteen years old. Kahn assumed she was around eighteen. He looked her over, had her read for him, selected some photographs from those Bill Langley had taken, and left town saying, "Maybe you'll hear from us." He had done the same with dozens of others.

The report Kahn turned in later to Lew Schreiber, Twentieth Century–Fox's casting director, indicated his enthusiasm: "Will photograph more beautifully as she progresses—reads well—has a particular cuteness, at the same time strength along with it." Monetta waited through the Christmas holidays, racing Pearl to the mailbox, hoping for Kahn's response. Finally, on January 3, the scout sent a New Year's greeting and word that the studio was interested. Monetta replied that same evening, with Pearl hanging over her shoulder: "I only hope a little prayer will be answered. You see the theatrical world is my life. I live it every day. It is my only ambition and with my will and determination for success, I cannot fail. But of course, someone who can and will must give me a chance to prove myself. Please tell them how hard I will work." She included additional references and the hope that they would soon meet again.

Another month went by. Then on February 8, a telegram arrived from Ivan Kahn's office: "Considering bringing you here for screen test. Studio to pay expenses. Could you arrange to leave Friday evening the eleventh? Anticipate you will be in Los Angeles two or three weeks. If program satisfactory wire collect your approval and we will forward letters of agreement and detailed letter of instructions." Monetta and Pearl wired that they both could be ready. Kahn mailed four copies of the test and option agreement for them to sign, stating that a check for Monetta's transportation and incidental expenses would follow. Pearl would have to pay her own way. Monetta telegraphed that the signed agreements were in the mail, as not only Pearl but Monte and Cal prepared to leave on the train with her. "I just always assumed one day we'd go to Hollywood," said Monte. "It was almost like, 'Well, now it's time to go to California because Tweedles is going to be a movie star.'"

While Sunset High School buzzed with excitement, Monetta was photographed by local reporters, who wished her well. Dolly Elder stopped by with some gifts, and Roy drove them to the station. "I'd never been out of Texas," Monetta said later, "never ridden on a train, had never stayed in a hotel." Neither had she ridden in a taxi, or seen an orange tree or the ocean. "Before I came to Hollywood I dreamed that movie people led lives of ease and luxury, that their wants were filled before they could mention them, and that life was a smooth succession of pleasure. I was very young and naive." Yet in February 1938 the American dream seemed within her grasp.

Along with Monetta Darnell, Ivan Kahn had discovered two other girls during his southern travels, both in Louisiana. One was Dorris Bowdon, who would play Rosasharn in John Ford's *The Grapes of Wrath* and marry screenwriter Nunnally Johnson. The other was Mary Healy, who with her husband, Peter Lind Hayes, would enjoy a successful career in radio and television. Mary and Dorris were in their early twenties when Twentieth Century-Fox signed them in 1938. Neither made more than a few pictures, although Dorris came to know the industry well through her husband.

Dorris Bowdon, from Memphis, Tennessee, was an English and speech student at Louisiana State University when a New Orleans critic saw her in a school play and recommended that Ivan Kahn take a look at her. Kahn visited LSU and found Dorris a unique personality. His assessment to Twentieth Century–Fox was: "New type on screen—reads well and could be developed—for type of roles somewhat similar to Bette Davis." Dorris received a letter from the studio asking her to report for a screen test in February. "In absolute rapture I went home for the holidays and told my mother I was going to make the trip to Los Angeles," she recalled. "Mother thought it was outrageous for me to quit school before I had my degree. She had also been persuaded by the press that Hollywood was a den of iniquity and that I shouldn't go near it. But I knew it was a kind of Cinderella break for me."

Dorris caught the train in New Orleans for California. At the station there was a band and great fanfare as Mary Healy boarded the same car. Mary had been a singer since she was a child and had built a local reputation performing over radio station WWL in New Orleans. At the time she met Ivan Kahn she was working as a secretary at the Twentieth Century–Fox Film Exchange and singing evenings at the Roosevelt Hotel. Kahn saw her both places and felt she might develop the qualities that spell box office success. He reported to Twentieth Century-Fox: "This girl has a fine natural singing voice and a swell delivery of her songs—pretty—vivacious—intelligent." Mary, too, received a wire that she had been selected by Twentieth Century–Fox for a screen test.

"I was a very introverted girl," Dorris Bowdon confessed later, "rather shy and insecure. And Mary was just the opposite. Mary was a marvelous extrovert. She would break into song at anything. My first impression was that she was a terrible show off." Since Mary was something of a local celebrity, New Orleans made sure she had a grand send-off, and she boarded the train with the band playing and "orchids from here to there." As Mary remembered it, "I got on the train and saw this very pretty young girl with big blue eyes and a little black hat, turned up all around. Her heart was broken because she'd been going with a boy back home. We were so different—like two people from outer space." Once they arrived in California the girls would room together and become best friends.

The next evening the train pulled into Dallas, where there was more fanfare, a lot of press and picture-taking—all arranged by the studio. Both Dorris and Mary were surprised. Amid the flurry Monetta Darnell and her mother, brother, and sister got on board, carrying a large picnic basket with a top that lifted at either end. Pearl had reserved a compartment, and the children were whisked in and the door shut. Once the train started, the basket was carefully opened. Inside, with towels stuffed all around, was Weedy, their pet rooster! "There was never any thought of not taking him," Monte said. "We knew Dad would probably wring his neck and have him for dinner." The children had fed Weedy well in hopes that he would be sleepy and quiet.

It was a long trip, especially for Weedy and the children. "Things are very dull on this old train," Monetta wrote Dolly Elder. "You can't write, read, draw, or even sleep." Eventually she met Mary and Dorris and discovered they were bound for Hollywood too, and the three soon fed each other's excitement. "I learned that Monetta was very young," Dorris recalled. "She was a darling, sweet, extraordinarily beautiful girl, but almost a totally provincial girl. She had never been out of Dallas before. Her mother was her cross, not that Monetta seemed particularly aware of it. Apparently her mother was living out a dream of wealth and fame based on her daughter. She wanted so much to make this giant step and was truly hell-bent. She was a woman of obvious limitations, and she was a pusher." Mary said, "I'll always remember that little girl, such a beautiful child. I looked at her and thought, 'So pretty!' Her eyes were very unusual, very arresting. But I felt she was rather sad. I thought she was warm and sweet, but a little lost somehow. Her mother seemed like a farm lady with a hatchet face and a harsh voice, and Monetta was this beautiful child who didn't seem to belong to this woman at all."

Their train was met in Los Angeles by Ivan Kahn and representatives from the Twentieth Century–Fox publicity department. The young hopefuls were taken directly to a radio station where Tyrone Power was doing a broadcast. "You cannot imagine how breathtaking that was for us!" recalled Dorris. Monetta was dressed in her mother's coat and a little flat-topped porkpie hat with a veil that Pearl had worn on the train earlier. Almost apologetically Monetta whispered, "This is my mother's hat." Her instincts were those of a child, and thrown into a strange environment, what poise she had vanished. "You couldn't do anything to destroy that exceptionally beautiful face," Dorris said, "but instead of letting that face be the thing everyone saw, her mother was trying to make her look older."

Dorris was the most mature of the three and appeared somewhat removed from the others. "I think she looked down on all of us a little," Mary claimed later, "but at the time I was completely gaga." Studio publicists photographed the girls, arranging them on baggage carts and in unusual poses that seemed glamorous. Pearl had pulled the veil down over the porkpie hat, giving Monetta an almost ludicrous look. "It was really an old lady's hat," Dorris remembered. "Even for the fashions of the time, it was absurd." Ivan Kahn fully recognized that Monetta needed polishing, but was struck again by her superb complexion and coloring. The entourage was chauffeured to the radio station, where the three girls were photographed with Tyrone Power, Monetta's favorite star. It was a moment of excitement and terror. The Darnells were then driven to the Hollywood Plaza Hotel, where Pearl, Monetta, Monte, Cal, and a contraband Weedy checked in. "It was a beautiful day," said Monte, "and California looked like a picture postcard, with orange groves we could see as we rode in. It was just gorgeous."

Twentieth Century–Fox was not only the newest, but also the most beautiful of the motion picture lots. Its landscaping was meticulous, with hundreds of gardeners to care for its parks and flower beds. The back lot, which later became Century City, consisted of a couple hundred acres, with a natural lake and all varieties of standing sets. "It was like an adventure story for a young kid to come here," said Joe Silver, who grew up on the lot. The Cafe de Paris, with its imported French chef, served scrumptious food at modest prices, and the old Writers Building was designed like a French chateau. "It was a real showplace," said Silver.

Monetta Darnell came through the studio gates for her screen test thrilled but inwardly frightened. It was everything she had dreamed about, and her excitement was that of a child. "The thing I remember most about Monetta when we first arrived at the studio," Dorris Bowdon said later, "was her yelling and waving to all of the players we saw. I remember the astonishment on some people's faces, being greeted so warmly by somebody they had never seen before. It was kind of a sweet, childish thing to do. At the time it was horribly embarrassing to me. I was such a stuffy young girl."

A publicist was assigned to the girls, and they were taken to each of the various departments. Wardrobe women swarmed over them, and makeup experts buzzed about, discussing their blemishes as though all three were deaf. One of Monetta's eyes was found to droop slightly; something would have to be done about that. And she bit her fingernails! Her smile was too broad, showing far too much gum. It would have been a devastating experience, even for a secure person, and Monetta was scarcely that. She would have to try harder, she decided, be friendlier—do whatever they told her.

For the next two weeks she worked with the respected drama coach Florence Enright in an effort to learn the acting fundamentals and rid herself of her Texas accent. She met her share of stars and a week after arriving wrote Dolly Elder a postcard: "Gee, I'm having a marvelous time. Met and made photos with Tyrone Power and Don Ameche. Met Alice Faye, Jimmy Ritz, etc." But she indicated none of the bewilderment bottled inside.

"You can imagine the stresses on this girl," Dorris Bowdon said. "Unschooled, and a painfully unschooled mother with ambitions beyond Monetta's attainment. I'm sure Monetta was aware of her unpreparedness. I imagine her lack of self-confidence grew. It's a frequent story with girls coming into this business, who go through the trials and often very insensitive treatment. A pretty girl was chattel in Hollywood. There were more gorgeous girls in this town than anywhere else in the world."

Finally it was time for her screen test. Monetta admitted later how frightened she was on that huge soundstage with all the cameras and technicians peering down on her. She did a short sketch entitled "Two Nuts on a Sidewalk" with a young contract player named Robert Allen. By that time the studio had discovered her age and expressed concern. She clearly was too old to be cast as a child star, yet was too immature for adult roles. Then there was Pearl, who had by no means endeared herself to Ivan Kahn or studio executives. Pearl obviously represented trouble—meddlesome, petty, exasperating trouble that Hollywood moguls knew well. The last thing anybody on the Fox lot wanted was another stage mother.

For what seemed an endless week the Darnells awaited an answer. When it came, the response was that Monetta was too young. She should go back home, get all the experience she could, send updated pictures of herself from time to time, and keep in touch. Maybe in a year she would grow up enough to be reconsidered. Monetta didn't know how to interpret this message. She cried, then grew determined to show them. "That's all right, Tweedles," Monte reassured, "you'll be out here next year." The hurt intensified when Mary and Dorris both received stock contracts.

"It was hell," Monetta later said, "to go home to Dallas and have everybody ask you, 'How are you making out in Hollywood?' I hadn't a film to point out. I didn't even have an answer. I was miserable." But at Sunset High the girls were agog with excitement, thrilled even to talk to someone who had been to Hollywood. "I can remember her coming back that first time," said a friend from Spanish class. "Monetta told us they had put her in kissing classes, where she got to kiss all the leading men. We were all so envious!" Some claimed she had gone high hat, and although Ivan Kahn had cautioned her to not try to look older, she began wearing more makeup than usual.

Pearl, meanwhile, became more difficult than ever, provoking shopkeepers and dime store clerks with her demanding ways. She was quick to let the neighborhood know all about Monetta's Hollywood success, and her garrulous attitude infuriated practically everyone. Twentieth Century–Fox representatives had said Monetta needed more experience, so Pearl made sure she got as much exposure as possible. She resumed her modeling and appeared in ads for TAD Film Company, becoming a familiar face to suburban moviegoers. Shortly after entering her sophomore year of high school, she got a part in Lynn Riggs's play *Russet Mantle* with the Civic Theater, a nonprofessional group that presented plays on the fairgrounds. Critic John Rosenfield found the play "murky, morbid and frequently incoherent," but had a good word for Monetta: "Pretty Monetta Darnell and Taylor Byars were effective as a pair of Mexican menials."

She promptly wrote Ivan Kahn, informing him of her activities. TAD Film Company had agreed to shoot thirteen playlets, with Monetta featured in all of them. "I'd give *anything* if you and Mr. Schreiber could see one of them," she said. "I had a chance to play the lead in a production that ran two weeks during our state fair, but, *of all things*, Mother wouldn't let me do it on account of school. That almost killed me." She planned to study diction at the Dallas Little Theater, until Pearl found that an apprenticeship cost $1,500 a year, making it impossible.

"You'd *really* be *surprised* at how much I've *changed*," Monetta told Kahn, "since the night you saw us off, bound for home! I've really applied myself in everything you all told me to do. I certainly hope you were sincere." She had seen in a local newspaper that Dorris Bowdon had been cast in one of the studio's *Jones Family* pictures. "Wish her and Mary, too, all the luck in the world for me," Monetta wrote Kahn, "and tell them I haven't forgotten them. If you see the Ritzes and Tyrone, do me a huge favor and just ask them if they remember me. Oh, I hope *you* haven't forgot-

35

ten me!" Kahn replied, "I think it is fine that you are doing all these things to improve yourself. Keep up the good work and you will be prepared when the big chance comes."

Monetta continued to make honor-roll grades at Sunset High and was cocaptain of the pep squad. Her friend Charloise Hufstedler, the other cocaptain, insisted, "Monetta wasn't a sophisticated girl, just very down-to-earth." She spoke Spanish fluently, occasionally attending functions where she met students from Latin America. "It's the only time I ever saw her walk over and start a conversation with somebody," Virginia Crawford said.

Jaime Jorba, a teenage boy whose family had left Spain for Mexico City during the Spanish Civil War, enrolled in Sunset during Monetta's sophomore year. He came to the United States primarily to learn English. Because of her fluent Spanish, Monetta was assigned to help Jaime with his lessons. Polite, wealthy, and good looking, Jaime was invited to the Darnell home many times, where the whole family, Pearl included, grew fond of him. He and Monetta often sat on the sofa with their grammar books, teaching each other verb tenses. "They looked so cute together," Undeen remembered. Soon they developed a crush on one another, which became obvious to everyone around. It was Monetta's first romance, and in some ways her most gratifying. Their relationship was serious enough that she and Jaime wrote and visited even after she went to Hollywood.

Early in 1939, Pearl learned of another talent search from local newspapers. Impatient with not hearing anything definite from Ivan Kahn, she decided to force his hand. Monetta was now fifteen. If Twentieth Century–Fox wasn't interested in her, another studio might well be. RKO Radio Pictures was sponsoring Jesse L. Lasky's "Gateway to Hollywood" contest. Auditions were being held in cities across the nation, and local winners—a boy-girl team—were brought to Hollywood for a "screen test" on network radio. Monetta filled out an application and, during exam week, went downtown after school for an audition. Everyone read a scene from Odets's *Golden Boy*. Monetta teamed with a boy named Wayne Babb, and after several readings they were chosen the Dallas winners.

Photographs were taken, and Monetta immediately left for the opening of the Southwestern Style Show, arriving an hour late. "Gee, what a hectic night!" she wrote Ivan Kahn. "I'm really a wreck. However, I'm taking some 'vitamin pills' thrice daily and so I suppose this won't kill me. We're still a heck of a long way from Hollywood yet, but don't worry, I'll bet it won't be so very long before I'll be seeing you all again."

Lasky's "Gateway to Hollywood," sponsored by the Wrigley Company, was aired on Sunday afternoons. Young discoveries from around the country were brought to Hollywood and teamed with established stars such as Claudette Colbert, Cary Grant, and Joan Crawford. The show was divided into three ten-minute segments, featuring three boy-girl combinations each week, with the winners awarded RKO contracts. RKO would also have options on any of the runners-up they chose.

Monetta and Wayne Babb competed against winners from Salt Lake City and San Francisco, then were scheduled to appear on the national broadcast from Hollywood. Since Monetta was under age, expenses for a chaperon to California would be paid, as well as her own. When Ivan Kahn learned about her participation in "Gateway to Hollywood," he sent Lew Schreiber the clippings Monetta had mailed him with her note. "Paramount, too, seems to have their eye on this girl," Kahn warned Schreiber. "I know we were to keep tabs on her, and if we want her, I think we have to act now."

Pearl was determined that this time Monetta would be ready. On February 12, they were off again to Los Angeles. The broadcast featured Monetta in a scene from Booth Tarkington's *Clarence*, with Edward Everett Horton as guest star, but she lost in the final vote. "I think the judges must have chalked up her sublime self-assurance as unbecoming in such a youngster," Jesse Lasky wrote in his autobiography. "But in spite of the judges' decision I thought [Monetta] Darnell was the loveliest, most exciting sixteen-year-old [sic] I'd ever seen, and her talent utterly refreshing."

While they were in California, Pearl and Monetta visited Ivan Kahn, who pointed out that Twentieth Century–Fox could do nothing while RKO held an option on Monetta as a "Gateway to Hollywood" contestant. He advised her to say as little as possible about her earlier contact with Fox, go home, wait quietly, and let RKO's option expire at the end of the month. Meanwhile Kahn and Lew Schreiber outlined the terms of a contract, ready to act when the time came.

Monetta and Pearl returned to Dallas, again not sure what the situation was. Then RKO extended its option for another five weeks, leaving Twentieth Century-Fox in limbo. By this time

Darryl F. Zanuck, Fox's production head, had become aware of Monetta. He liked her photographs, ran her test footage, and thought she might have enough star quality to play the lead in *Hotel for Women*, one of his upcoming productions.

Meanwhile Monetta waited. She resumed classes at Sunset High, not knowing whether she would finish the semester. She was afraid to tell her classmates anything. A representative from Twentieth Century–Fox contacted her about the part in *Hotel for Women*, but so did RKO, asking her to sign an endorsement giving "Gateway to Hollywood" the right to use her name and picture in its search for talent. Fox wired her to do no such thing. "Please wait there until the option expires Wednesday," she was instructed, "then we will wire you about having the studio bring you here." Monetta was drying dishes and had a stack in her hand when the telegram arrived. "We always laughed," said Dolly Elder, "because her mother claimed she broke a dozen plates when they got that telegram. She threw the plates right up in the air." Again Pearl jumped the gun by notifying the local press prematurely. Ten days before RKO's option expired, Monetta's picture appeared in the *Dallas Morning News*, surrounded by photographers and reporters, with the story that she was about to be signed by a major studio. Ivan Kahn was furious.

Monetta flew to Los Angeles alone on April 5, 1939, and went on salary at Twentieth Century–Fox the next day, beginning at $75 a week. Kahn cautioned Pearl not to give out any more information, since the publicity department planned to release the story nationally. "If anything should break locally in your papers," he told her, "it would spoil the write-ups all over the country and would spoil a very good break for Monetta in a publicity way. I know I can depend on you to do this, so don't be impatient, as I think you will be able to do all the talking you want in the next couple of days." He instructed Pearl not to sign anything in Monetta's behalf. He suggested she send Monetta's best pictures to him, clearly eager to get them out of her hands. He was evasive on the issue of Pearl's coming to California, saying only that she would be hearing from Monetta soon.

Kahn wrote Pearl again two days later, repeating much of what he had told her earlier. Pearl airmailed back, "We are the happiest little family in the world over Monetta being signed with Twentieth Century–Fox. That is the one she, and us too, wanted her to be with since you had her out last year. Words cannot express how you have looked after our little girl." Pearl assured Kahn they would do whatever he and the studio said. She would sign nothing "outside of what I am supposed to sign with the studio. In other words, Monetta has sold herself to Twentieth Century–Fox. That is why I told Monetta to find out about me giving any information about her going out. So you see I know not to do anything until I get permission from you."

Pearl told neighbors her daughter was visiting her sister Priscilla in Ft. Worth. She asked Kahn to warn Monetta not to go out evenings with people she met. "You see she puts a lot of confidence in those (or some) she meets. I have told her also, but your telling her too would impress it more on her mind." Monetta was staying at the Studio Club in Hollywood, where she was closely chaperoned. But still Pearl attempted to exercise control, insisting Monetta have a room by herself and asking Ivan Kahn to caution her not to say anything about her affairs to the other girls. "I want her to be nice to them, but not mix with them."

By mid-April Kahn wired Pearl that she could at last tell her friends, neighbors, and the Dallas newspapers that Monetta had been signed by Twentieth Century–Fox. "We think it is so wonderful," she said, "for our little girl to be doing such wonderful things for such a great and grand motion picture studio as dear old Twentieth Century–Fox is. She is too happy for words knowing she is with the studio whom she learned to love from the first." Pearl quickly realized the studio had replaced her, taking control of Monetta's life. Against Zanuck and the corporate structure, even the aggressive Pearl was powerless, silenced before she began. As she herself acknowledged, Monetta had "sold herself to Twentieth Century–Fox." But Pearl knew it was she who had signed the bill of sale—and lost her power in the process.

Hollywood

Twentieth Century–Fox was a studio born during the hard times of the Great Depression. Shortly after the Wall Street crash William Fox, one of the pioneers in sound, lost his fortune, and was sent to prison for fraud. In 1935 the Fox Film Corporation, once a giant, stood on the edge of bankruptcy. Twentieth Century Pictures, on the other hand, formed two years earlier by Joseph Schenck, Darryl F. Zanuck, and William Goetz, was an aggressive production company with no studio of its own. Fox had the studio, the facilities, and an elaborate distribution network, but he was not making pictures of any great quality or mass appeal. In Darryl Zanuck, a production genius, Twentieth Century possessed the essential leadership. When the two corporations merged, Zanuck became vice president in charge of production, and the company settled into the old Fox lot, on land once known as the Tom Mix Ranch.

Although Spyros Skouras became president of Twentieth Century–Fox, Zanuck was the force that shaped the studio's destiny. Zanuck recently had been production head at Warner Brothers, where he became something of a boy wonder, guiding the Warners' transition from silent to sound pictures. Zanuck's major inheritance from Fox had been Will Rogers and Shirley Temple. Rogers would be killed in a plane crash in 1935, whereas Temple was on the threshold of growing up. Tom Mix, once the big Fox star, was gone, Janet Gaynor and Warner Baxter were coming to the end of their careers, and Loretta Young was leaving for better opportunities elsewhere. In terms of star power, Zanuck found himself in dire straits, having to create his own galaxy. He shortly brought in Tony Martin from radio, the Ritz Brothers as Twentieth Century–Fox's answer to MGM's Marx Brothers, and society columnist Elsa Maxwell, mainly for her publicity value. To these he added his real stars: Tyrone Power, Alice Faye, Don Ameche, and Sonja Henie, around whom he built most of his A pictures. When the studio contracted Monetta Darnell, Zanuck was still bolstering his star roster and enhancing his players' prestige, thereby increasing Twentieth Century–Fox's lending power so that the studio could borrow other stars it wanted in return.

Although dozens of young women poured into Hollywood daily hoping to become overnight successes, it took someone of Gene Tierney's unique beauty or Anne Baxter's dramatic skills to make a lasting impression and develop into a studio asset. Zanuck signed both Tierney and Baxter, but was convinced that Ivan Kahn's little fawn-eyed brunette from Texas also possessed the looks to grow into a saleable commodity. His major concern was her tepid personality. Zanuck felt Monetta lacked presence, a special quality that would leap off the screen and captivate audiences in film after film. Still, he had to take a chance and decided to build Monetta into an American Cinderella, an innocent from humble circumstances who happened to fit Hollywood's glass slipper.

Monetta immediately began studying with drama coach Florence Enright, whose job it was to teach newcomers how to walk, and to instill them with confidence. Enright would coach Monetta for the role of Marcia in Zanuck's *Hotel for Women*, which would be easy for her since she was to play a young model. She reported to Olive Hughes in the wardrobe department, but found her intimidating, as many did. Because Monetta was under age, California law required that she have at least three hours of schooling a day, although the time could be broken up into half-hour periods. Frances Klampt, who was in charge of the studio school, would arrange her studies around the *Hotel for Women* shooting schedule. The studio had also decided to change her name. Zanuck suggested Linda because he felt that the name would advertise her beauty and suggest a Latin quality that matched her coloring.

Twentieth Century–Fox took out an entire page in the *Motion Picture Herald* to announce its latest find. Harry Brand, the studio's publicity director, worked overtime cranking out stories about her. Linda Darnell was seventeen, according to Brand's reports, and one of six children. No mention was made of the fact that Richard and Evelyn were from her mother's first marriage. Linda was the daughter of a postal clerk from pioneering southern stock, who had worked at the same job for thirty years. Linda's mother, Margret Brown, was of French descent; the studio chose to overlook Pearl's Indian heritage. Like Scarlett O'Hara, Linda's favorite cussword was "fiddledeedee," and she had interviewed for a screen test because her mother urged it. After all, "Mother knows best," Brand quoted Linda. Later he went to great lengths to insist, "Mrs. Darnell has made it a rule never to intervene in her talented daughter's affairs unless she is asked. The result is that producers and directors welcome Mrs. Darnell on the set." He must have meant it as a warning.

Old hands around the Twentieth Century–Fox lot remembered Linda Darnell's arrival as a shy, gawky kid. "She took your breath away," said film executive Howard W. Koch. "She just sort of knocked you out. Being a young lad myself then, I thought, 'Boy, if I could just talk to her.' Of course I didn't have much luck." Joe Silver, about the same age as Linda, said, "She was a very nice, very shy girl. A beautiful girl, but very, very shy and frightened of the things she was experiencing. She was like any other kid that age. She was scared to death."

Within a few days Linda was called before the great man himself, Darryl F. Zanuck. Zanuck's secretary ushered her into his office, which stretched like a golf course. Zanuck was polite, aware of Linda's lack of sophistication. If he was not the kindly uncle that Ivan Kahn seemed to be, neither was he the satyr she discovered later. "She was so young," Joe Silver insisted. "Zanuck liked girls, but I would doubt that he had anything to do with her sexually." Film composer David Raksin said, "Darryl Zanuck had a side not many people know about. He could be a very decent man. He did a lot of things which were brutal; he did a lot of things which were inconsiderate and insensitive, but he was no punk. He was an amazing bird."

Back in Texas the Darnells awaited word from Linda. Pearl had decided to remain in Dallas until Monte and Cal's school was out before moving to California. She assured neighbors that once summer came, however, the family would be off to Hollywood. Her attitude became more insufferable than ever. Whereas earlier she would take her grocery basket through the aisles, picking out what she wanted, now she stood at the front of the store, list in hand, imperiously calling out items for an attendant to fetch. Roy still thought the whole notion of Hollywood was a mistake. He didn't approve and made that clear.

Linda began *Hotel for Women* with a mountain of expectation on her shoulders, and she felt the weight. "Here she was, fifteen and suddenly given the lead in a film," Dorris Bowdon observed. "If everything had happened to Linda five years later, I think she might have been able to handle it. But as it was, I don't believe she had a chance." The picture actually was called "Elsa Maxwell's *Hotel for Women*," which was Zanuck's way of putting Maxwell, a social force in the late 1930s, on the payroll and assuring his studio of publicity. The film's director, Gregory Ratoff, was a Zanuck henchman and a great character, whom Monetta liked. Ann Sothern received top billing on the picture, although Linda Darnell's was definitely the pivotal role.

Exciting though it was, Linda soon learned that moviemaking was not the fun she'd expected. There were interminable periods of just sitting around waiting while sets were lighted. Generally that was when she did her school work. For the most part moviemaking was dull, boring, nerve-racking work. "I'm learning what really hard work is," she told an interviewer. "At home in Dallas I used to sprawl on the lawn and dream about the nice, easy time the screen stars must be having in Hollywood, but the last two months have taught me quite another story."

Hotel for Women's cameraman was J. Peverell Marley, a veteran dating back to silent days. The son of British immigrants, Marley had been raised in California and knew Hollywood, professionally and socially. He had photographed Monetta's screen test and immediately recognized how insecure she was. Marley became her protector, calling her aside to explain the pitfalls and what to watch out for. When she was on the verge of tears, Marley encouraged her. After work she sometimes sat in his car and waited for him, then poured out her troubles. "I don't think I would have been able to stick it out if Pev hadn't been around to buoy me up," she later said. "I had grown to depend upon him so much that at the end of a scene, I'd look at him instead of the director to see how I'd done." By the end of the picture it was clear Marley had fallen in love with her.

From time to time Linda ran into her friends Dorris Bowdon and Mary Healy on the lot. Dorris had scored with *The Jones Family Down on the Farm*, Twentieth Century–Fox's equivalent to MGM's *Andy Hardy* series, and was currently finishing John Ford's *Young Mr. Lincoln*. Mary had not yet received her chance, but was being coached by Jule Styne, later composer of *Gypsy* and *Funny Girl*, in the hope that some day she would hit the screen with one of her songs. Ivan Kahn remained close to all three of them, and Linda always insisted that without him "none of my success or my dreams or happiness could have been realized."

Hollywood

But the strangeness of Hollywood soon made her feel more like Alice in Wonderland than Cinderella, and although she occasionally went out with friends from the Studio Club, she grew desperately homesick. One Monday the studio called Dallas, suggesting that some family member come out and stay with Linda. That same day Undeen had been told by the insurance company she worked for that she was going to be assigned her own office with two girls under her. "I was about four feet off the ground," Undeen remembered. "I was going to be a big executive—that was my career. I'd been planning this for years and years." She rode home on the streetcar that evening dying to tell her family the good news. The Darnells lived about four doors from the stop, and she went flying home and bounded up on the porch. Pearl was waiting at the door. "Guess what, Mother!" Undeen shouted. "Never mind what," answered Pearl. "You guess what! You're going to California Friday."

"So there went my career down the drain," Undeen said wistfully. "I didn't get to tell her what my exciting news was until later that night." But Linda needed her, and Undeen was the only one free to go. "That's the way Mother was. I had to go to Hollywood come hell or high water." The studio found the girls a tiny apartment in a Spanish-style bungalow less than two blocks from Twentieth Century–Fox. Polly Woolsey, who owned the house, rented out all but the dining room, where she herself slept. Everyone had kitchen privileges and could use the living room. "I often wondered why I came," said Undeen, "because the studio had Tweedles so busy doing publicity and going out with different ones to nice dinner places where she could be seen. They had her out almost every night." Undeen worried that her sister wasn't eating properly and usually had supper waiting for her when she came home. More times than not, the studio would have notified Linda during the day that she was to pick something up from Wardrobe because she was going out that night, leaving Undeen alone.

"I was so homesick, it was terrible," Undeen recalled. For the first week she went over to visit the set, but that quickly became a bore. It seemed they spent more time setting up and deciding who was going to stand where than anything else. Undeen found watching her sister on the set difficult. "It was so unreal you just thought you were dreaming. I know Tweedles must have had a lot of qualms about these things, too, but she seemed to handle them well. Maybe that's what acting is."

Linda's business manager, Jonathan Smith, dropped by the apartment occasionally, and once he mentioned that Undeen should go into pictures, too, claiming she'd be great in westerns. "That was the furthest thing from my mind," said Undeen. "I couldn't act if I had to." Jonathan insisted she wouldn't have to act. "All you have to do is set a plate on the table or stand out at the gate and wave goodbye to a cowboy." He even made an appointment for her at Republic Studio, but she was too bashful to go.

Eventually Undeen found her way to the beach. The water was too cold to swim, but she walked from one end of the beach to the other, going back in time to fix Linda's supper. "Then she'd come home and wouldn't eat because she was going out someplace," her sister recalled. Polly Woolsey found Undeen in her room crying a couple of nights. "I was trying to cry quietly, because there were just French doors separating us from the adjoining room. I wouldn't turn any lights on so Polly'd think I was gone, but she heard me bawling. I wouldn't go out at night by myself because I didn't know where to go." Polly's solution was to find her a boyfriend, Harry Hunter, who worked with Polly's fiancé, and the four of them double-dated one evening. "That's how I met my husband," Undeen explained. "He was a blind date."

At four-thirty every morning Laraine, a hairdresser from the studio, arrived to wash and set Linda's hair. The studio had brought in a drier and makeup lights, setting them up in Polly's enclosed patio. "There wasn't any privacy," said Undeen. "There was another gal next to us, and a fella had the front bedroom. We had to get up early because Tweedles had to be at the studio ready to work by seven o'clock." Around five a manicurist came to do her nails, followed shortly by a Fox makeup man. Undeen would get up to make coffee and always had doughnuts waiting. "That was fun," she remembered. "We had a ball. Those kids really were nice. Sometimes a masseuse would come, and if I was lucky and she had a little time, I'd get a rubdown, too." Laraine would comb out Linda's hair, and off they went to the studio.

"I don't know about all this, Deen," Linda would say occasionally. "I love to act, but it sure is different from being in Dallas." Undeen reminded her, "You always said you were going to Hollywood." Linda would grin and answer, "Yes, I sure did." But Undeen warned, "If I ever see you getting high-hat and ignoring the little fella, I'm going to knock your block off."

Shooting on *Hotel for Women* was completed in June 1939. Darryl Zanuck realized even before the preview that he'd found a star. "Honey, you were just great," Zanuck assured Linda. "I'm going to find something else for you right away." Linda was walking on air. Zanuck soon told her he was taking Dorris Bowdon out of John Ford's *Drums Along the Mohawk* and putting her in. The film would be shot in Technicolor and required a trip to Utah for location work. Henry Fonda and Claudette Colbert were the leads, but Linda's was a strong supporting role. The period costumes and colonial hair pieces fitted for Dorris were quickly remade for Linda. "All the preliminaries had been done," Dorris recalled. "After *Hotel for Women* Darryl thought he had a star, and he didn't have another vehicle for her to go into right away. He wanted to keep her before the public. *Drums Along the Mohawk* was the next big production ready to roll. So a few days before filming started, I was taken out of the picture and Linda replaced me, which was very painful for me."

The initial shooting would be done on location, so Linda left for Utah, leaving Undeen at Polly Woolsey's. Since she would be working with the great John Ford, she was more terrified than ever. By the time they returned, however, Zanuck recognized what a sensation Linda was in *Hotel for Women* and decided it was a mistake to waste her in a subordinate role. Dorris was shortly called in and told she was going back into *Drums Along the Mohawk*. Since Zanuck had no intention of redoing the location footage, the part was sharply cut. All the scenes Linda had done in Utah with the principals had to be eliminated. Distance shots with Linda wearing Dorris's costume were used, but anything where Linda's face was visible had to be taken out.

Linda got back from Utah just in time to help Undeen prepare for the arrival of Pearl, Monte, and Cal. Roy had decided to remain in Dallas until he could arrange a transfer with the post office and sell the Hollywood Street house. Undeen and Laraine had become friends, and Laraine agreed to drive the sisters around to find a larger apartment. They finally located a place on Norton Avenue, still near the Fox studio. "We hated leaving Texas and all our friends," said Cal. "But Mother wanted the glittering prizes, the pearls, the fur coats, the chauffeurs, the maid, the big house. She was bound and determined to make her daughter famous."

Monte detested Los Angeles from the start. She found the people rude, asking all sorts of prying questions, teasing the family about their Texas accents and folksy ways. "We came out of Texas with hayseeds in our hair, mud between our toes, and snakes and frogs in our pockets," said Cal. "We were thoroughly naive. Linda was easily victimized, very easily hurt, and trusted everyone, because people down in Texas did trust one another. Your word was good enough there. You didn't have everything sewn up in a contract. That used to frighten Linda, all those business things."

Linda and Undeen moved into the Norton Avenue apartment with Pearl and the children. Dorris Bowdon stopped by one day to visit and was startled to find a rooster, the ubiquitous Weedy, in the living room. "I was so riveted on the chicken I didn't register much more," said Dorris. "I heard sometime later that the landlord would not permit the chicken any longer and they had to move." It was clear to Dorris that Pearl was "trying to find a footing in another life. There were references to Linda's father, but the father was never a very clear figure. I never heard her mother refer to the father, not even on that first trip out. I came to dislike her mother, because I could see she was a ramrod, forcing the girl and not very attractive in her methods. I was aware that Linda was overpowered by her mother's force. Her mother was proud of this golden egg that was hatching and saw in it the yellow brick road for herself."

Pearl vowed that Hollywood's loose morals would not rub off on her children. "She thought some dirty old man was going to get hold of us." said Cal. "We didn't know anything about sex really, except what we'd seen at Aunt Priscilla's farm. Mother had this terrible moral obsession, and I think it was from sheer frustration. I think that's why she found it hard to let go of us." Both Linda and Undeen were dating, but Pearl insisted they be home by 11:30 sharp.

One afternoon Pearl needed to go to the grocery in Westwood. Linda decided to tag along, wearing slacks and no makeup. The two of them did their shopping and were carrying sacks of groceries to the car, when Linda noticed Darryl Zanuck sitting in his limousine a few spaces away. The next day Zanuck called her into his office and laid down the law. "You are going to be a star," he informed her hotly, "and a star does not carry groceries! Whenever you go out in public, you dress to the teeth. You don't go around in slacks. You dress and look like a star."

"We were all caught up in Tweedles's career," Monte remembered, "because it advanced very fast. They worked her like crazy, but she loved every minute of it." At first Pearl and the children spent a great deal of time around the studio, with Cal usually taking along one of his pet snakes. But Pearl's unpopularity at the studio grew as she tried to tell executives how her daughter's career should be handled. "Mother could be so darn ornery," said Undeen, "and she really caused a ruckus over at the studio. She wanted to rule the roost. It was my mother up there on the screen; she really lived Linda's parts. They had quite a few squabbles over that."

Hotel for Women was previewed in Westwood, with the Darnell family in attendance. The trade journals found the movie old-fashioned, but agreed that young Linda Darnell had "charm, ability, and youthful freshness," displaying sufficient screen personality to justify her buildup. "Proudest woman in all Hollywood today is Mrs. Darnell," Jimmy Starr reported in the *Los Angeles Times*, "mother of fifteen-year-old Linda, who last night at the preview of *Hotel for Women* made her movie debut and, to put it mildly, created one of the greatest single sensations this always excitable town has seen and felt in many a year. I don't remember when so young an actress has made such an indelible first impression. It's a swell production and Linda Darnell is a sensation!"

Zanuck decided to premiere the film at the Palace Theater in Dallas, with Linda making a personal appearance. She arrived back home amid wild excitement four months after she left. Pearl insisted on going along, not wanting to miss any of the fun. Dallas rolled out the red carpet for the hometown girl who had taken Hollywood by storm. Linda's train was met in nearby Grand Prairie by her father, Dolly Elder, Oak Cliff officials, representatives from the Oak Cliff Lions and Kiwanis clubs, spokesmen from Sunset High School, the local press, and an estimated 2,500 onlookers. She accepted candy and flowers, giving the presenter a kiss on the cheek, repeating it until the photographers were satisfied. A twenty-mile parade brought Linda Darnell back home, moving through streets lined with smiling faces and waving hands. They drove past Sunset High and stopped at a reviewing stand in front of the Oak Cliff Bank, where Linda was officially welcomed.

"In less than the hundred days it took Wellington to conquer Napoleon," critic John Rosenfield wrote in the *Dallas Morning News*, "Monetta took the Twentieth Century–Fox studios of Beverly Hills." Aunt Cleo and Grandma Brown came down from Oklahoma for the premiere, and several of the Darnell aunts, uncles, and cousins were present. "It was bedlam," Pearl's sister Cleo recalled. "All of Dallas was in turmoil. I've never seen so many people and telephone calls. My sister was absolutely hilarious."

Outside the Palace Theater a crowd started gathering three hours before Linda was scheduled to appear, by nightfall jamming the street halfway down the block. The young star was introduced from a platform out front before going inside to be presented on the stage. She made a gracious speech of appreciation, after which *Hotel for Women* was screened. Rosenfield wrote, "The costume and makeup departments transformed an immature figure and a flashy face into a vision of full-blown beauty, refinement, and poise. Drama coach Florence Enright taught her to speak softly and from the throat without making too many faces. Handed the greatest movie break since Clara Bow's time, the fifteen-year-old Dallasite grabbed it, hugged it to her, and made one of the most successful starts in the history of talking pictures."

Linda signed hundreds of autographs while she was in Dallas and was sent 3,800 letters, 2,000 telegrams, and more than 150 floral offerings. Reading her fan mail, she discovered that at least seventeen babies already had been named for her in Texas alone. "Words fail me when I try to express my appreciation for the marvelous reception given me by Dallas," she said. "Everything was perfect and my only regret is that I can't stay longer." Linda and Pearl left in a state of euphoria, with the young star scheduled to begin tests on a new picture the following week.

The studio planned to cast her in *Johnny Apollo* opposite Tyrone Power, but when Henry Hathaway was borrowed to direct, he brought Dorothy Lamour with him from Paramount. It was then announced that Linda would star with Power in *Daytime Wife*, scheduled to begin shooting in the fall. The picture originally had been planned for Loretta Young, but Young balked at being given second billing. Nancy Kelly was next slated for the role, but once Zanuck realized Linda's potential, he took Kelly out. Linda would be costarring with Fox's top star, her screen idol, and the prospect thrilled her beyond words.

Meanwhile, *Hotel for Women* opened at the Roxy in New York,

Twentieth Century–Fox's major exhibition house. Frank Nugent wrote in the *New York Times*, "Nothing really need be said about the picture except that it introduces a newcomer, one Linda Darnell, who is as pretty as a model should be and probably will not be challenging Bette Davis's Academy title for quite a few years." Suddenly the country was blanketed with Linda Darnell stories and Linda Darnell photographs. She was selected sweetheart of Kappa Alpha at the fraternity's diamond jubilee convention, while Frank Orsatti, among Hollywood's most powerful agents, agreed to represent her.

At the studio Linda resumed her studies with Frances Klampt in September, but her life was far from that of a school girl. "Imagine studying in the studio school for ten minutes," she said, "and then being called to the makeup department. Next I will shoot a scene and then, with a few minutes to spare, rush back to class to split an infinitive." Miss Klampt found Linda an exceptional student, full of curiosity, especially gifted in art and composition. "If Linda didn't want a motion picture career," Klampt said, "she might be able to earn her living as an artist. She does lovely light things with pastels and her pencil sketches have real individuality."

The young star did a pastel of Tyrone Power during the shooting of *Daytime Wife* and came to like him enormously, although they saw little of each other off the set. Power had just married actress Annabella and viewed Linda as little more than a child. "That beautiful hunk of man!" sighed Undeen. "I met him and wouldn't wash my hand for a week. He was a doll. Tweedles really did like him, and they seemed to hit it off. They were just suited to each other."

Pev Marley, a close friend of Power's, was again Linda's cameraman, helping to perfect her image, while Zanuck's crony Gregory Ratoff once more directed. Making the picture was fun, although Linda was still extremely nervous. British actress Binnie Barnes was in the film and recalled that Linda bit her nails constantly. They had a scene together which had to be repeated time and again because Linda couldn't remember her lines. Finally she got them right, but Barnes was so astonished she blew hers. Linda's relationship with Pev Marley deepened, although Pev was fully aware how young she was. "I would be kissing Tyrone Power," Linda said later, "and the school teacher would come and tell me it was time for my history lesson. I never before or since have been so embarrassed."

Daytime Wife was completed on her sixteenth birthday, opening at the Roxy on Thanksgiving six weeks later. Bosley Crowther, reviewing for the *New York Times*, found the picture "a consistently light and superficial holiday comedy," and listed several other reservations. "Reservation Number 1 is that such a wife as Linda Darnell purports to be—so young, so beautiful, and at the same time such a patient, suspicious-free little sit-at-home—could obviously never exist in this world." At the Palace Theater in Dallas, Linda was awarded top billing over Tyrone Power. "Our Monetta takes about two steps backward and three forward in this, her second picture," wrote critic John Rosenfield.

Already she was working on *Star Dust*, Jessie and Ivan Kahn's script based on Linda's own discovery. "At first," Linda said, "everything was like a fairy tale come true. I stepped into a fabulous land where, overnight, I was a movie star. In pictures you're built up by everyone. On the set, in the publicity office, wherever you go, everyone says you're wonderful. It gives you a false sense of security. You waltz through a role, and everywhere you hear that you are beautiful and lovely, a natural-born actress. You believe what people around you say."

Yet the day of reckoning was near. Linda had lived on dreams, but a pretty face alone couldn't take her much farther. Even in a business that traded on beauty, meteors had a way of burning themselves out. For her career to develop, consolidation and growth would be essential, yet Linda's foundation was meager. She knew little about life and practically nothing about human relationships. From this point on Pearl was more a liability than an asset. Linda understood the difficulties that lay ahead no better than her provincial family did. She had no one to help her survive in a corporate world that placed power above talent. Instinctively she turned to Pev Marley, who was in love with her beauty, yet offered the strength Pearl lacked and still allowed her to remain a child.

Glory Girl

At sixteen Linda was already starring in an autobiographical film, her name alone above the title. Her studio contract had been revised so that she was making $200 a week, with bigger increments on the way. Much of her fame still seemed unreal. "When I wake up in the morning," she told a columnist, "I keep my eyes closed as long as possible. I'm afraid it will all fly away when I properly awake." Yet the giddy playground surrounding her did not encourage adolescents to grow up. Hollywood, the horn of plenty, was full of romance and happy endings, and it was easy to expect life to be equally flawless.

Linda's stardom was the stuff on which the Hollywood myth was based. If Lana Turner was the girl discovered sipping a soda at Schwab's Drug Store, Linda Darnell was the girl lifted from a hometown pep squad. Her story, and others like it, made the world spin for millions of teenagers, unfulfilled stenographers, and beauty shop matrons grown bored in a depression-ridden world. Fan magazines, fed by studio publicists, made the most of all opportunities. Even before the release of *Hotel for Women*, Ivan Kahn and his wife decided Linda's discovery was worth more than pulp coverage. They quickly devised a treatment, based not only on Linda's story, but on Dorris Bowdon's and Mary Healy's as well. In the initial draft of *Star Dust* the girls' first names were even used. Eventually Darryl Zanuck suggested the writers drop Dorris and combine her character with Mary's. Originally everybody in the story wound up happy, but Zanuck felt that didn't ring true. "One of the characters, Mary probably, should be a flop in pictures," he urged, "yet find happiness elsewhere. Only Linda emerges as a hit."

Eventually Linda's name was changed in the script to Carolyn, while *Twinkle, Twinkle, Little Star*, the working title, was shortened to *Star Dust*. Shooting on the picture began early in 1940, with Mary Healy playing her own part and John Payne as Linda's love interest. Walter Lang directed, an old-timer known for his screen musicals. Pev Marley again was Linda's cameraman. Lang decided to duplicate Linda's actual screen test in the film. She even wore the same clothes. "I had a little less accent and a little more poise," Linda said. "I think I was dazed when I played the [original] park bench test, but I was almost as scared in the *Star Dust* one, because by then I knew how much depended on it."

Mary got a chance to sing Hoagy Carmichael's title song, and the picture was previewed in Glendale in March. *Variety* found *Star Dust* entertaining and reported, "Miss Darnell displays a wealth of youthful charm and personality that confirms studio efforts to build her to a draw personality." Ultimately the film received a top B rating, playing not the major houses in most cities, but first-run theaters a notch below.

On March 18, 1940, Linda preserved her hand and footprints in cement in the forecourt of Grauman's Chinese Theater, just as she had at the end of her autobiographical film. Eventually her inscription would be surrounded by those of Jack Benny, Bing Crosby, George Burns, and Al Jolson. Later that month she received the first annual "Seein' Stars" award as the most promising actress of the year, a presentation the studio celebrated in grand style.

Linda was also the maid of honor when her sister Undeen married Harry Hunter. Roy came to California for the wedding, which was held in the First Christian Church of Alhambra, with Monte also an attendant. "Undeen was so pretty," Monte remembered. "She had the best figure of any of us. Her figure was a lot better than Tweedles's ever thought of being." Roy gave the bride away, and Linda assured the press that her father was at last reconciled to her career. "We send him letters in care of the Dallas Post Office," she said, "so he gets them before they're delivered."

Roy had saved vacation time so he could spend a month in Los Angeles, looking after Monte and Cal while Linda and Pearl went East on a personal appearance tour. It was Linda's first trip to New York, and they stayed at the Waldorf-Astoria Hotel. She appeared on Kate Smith's radio program and took in as many sights as possible, joining the Easter parade up Fifth Avenue and signing autographs for fans who recognized her.

Back in Hollywood, Linda had a few dates with Mickey Rooney, mainly as a pal. The two of them went to the amusement park in Santa Monica, and Monte recalled playing table shuffleboard with Mickey in the Darnells' living room while he waited for Linda. Through him, the young star met Dick Paxton, Mickey's stand-in, and the two of them became lifelong friends. "She made you feel like you were somebody," Paxton said. "You just wanted to gaze at her because she was so perfect, not star-conscious at all." Linda occasionally went out with Pev Marley, whom the press dismissed as her "devoted friend and escort," but their relationship was growing more complex. She actually was something of a homebody, partly out of shyness. "I'm not the nightclub type," she said early in her career. "The atmosphere of nightclubs is heavy, so I sneeze all the time. I don't believe any girl can be a success who spends her time jitterbugging."

Linda still bit her nails so badly that the studio made her wear vile-tasting gloves between takes. Shortly after Undeen married, Linda visited her sister in Alhambra, where Harry Hunter was a metal and supply salesman. It was Harry's birthday, and Linda insisted on buying him a present. The two sisters went to a men's shop, selected Harry's gift, then stopped by a dime store. "I need some false fingernails, Deen," Linda said. "You wait here, and I'll pick up some." She went into the store, but came out almost immediately, followed by a throng of fans. As she stood beside the car signing autographs, she whispered, "Deen, you'd better go over and get them." So while Linda signed autographs, Undeen went into the dime store and bought packages of fingernails. "I can't let my public know I wear false fingernails," Linda said as they drove off.

After the release of *Star Dust*, her salary rose to $500 a week. Already Twentieth Century–Fox was talking about starring her in three more pictures with Tyrone Power. Scheduled next was *Brigham Young—Frontiersman*, with Linda and Ty as the love interest added to give the film commercial appeal. Zanuck intended that the picture should be a frontier epic more than a treatment of Mormonism, and because of censorship, the polygamy question posed real problems for the writers. "As a spectacle the picture turned out okay," director Henry Hathaway maintained, "but I didn't like the characters much. I liked Brigham Young and the image of the church and their trip west, but I didn't care for that love story."

Hathaway had the reputation of being a tough director, especially difficult for women. He shouted, had a filthy mouth, even abused cast and crew members. "Being around him was like having a pet rattler in your pocket," said a stuntman who worked for him. Above all, Hathaway was a dedicated filmmaker who demanded that a job be done properly. He was instinctive in his ap-

proach, but a fabulous craftsman of the old school. Zanuck originally had intended to use stock footage for many of the outdoor
scenes in *Brigham Young*, but Hathaway insisted on location
shooting whenever possible. For three weeks his crew filmed at
Big Bear and Lone Pine, where the Sierra Nevada stood in for the
Rockies, and spent another six weeks in the Utah desert. "I made
the same picture that was on paper," Hathaway said, "but the locations made it big. If you could make it all on the back lot,
it would be a little picture. The only thing I changed was the
background."

Brigham Young would be the last grand spectacle filmed until
the foreign markets lost during World War II were regained. The
total cost ran over $2,500,000, and it was considered the most ex-
pensive picture Twentieth Century–Fox had yet produced. Since
Zanuck had decided on Broadway actor Dean Jagger for the title
role, the casting of the young lovers with screen names became
essential from the standpoint of box office.

Studio executives made it clear before the production crew left
for location work that they did not want Pearl Darnell tagging
along. There would be problems enough, and Hathaway wasn't
the kind of director to put up with Pearl's shenanigans. Since
Linda was under age, a chaperon had to be found for her, and she
was required to quit work every afternoon by four o'clock. "I really
don't remember her too well," Hathaway said. "She always fit into
the background. There was never any trouble. I don't remember
one controversy with her about anything. A sweeter girl never
lived."

When not needed on the set or busy with schoolwork, Linda
spent most of her time painting the western landscape. Tyrone
Power roomed with Hathaway, and she saw very little of him socially. It turned out that child actor Dickie Jones was also from
Dallas, and they struck up a temporary acquaintance. Linda quickly
found that outdoor shooting had its unpleasant side; apart from
the loneliness, it was hard, dirty work, and she was more than
ready to return home when the time came.

Brigham Young was completed in June and premiered in Salt
Lake City on August 23, 1940. Undeen and Harry kept Monte and
Cal so Linda and Pearl could be present. Tyrone and Annabella
Power were there, as were Darryl and Virginia Zanuck, Dean
Jagger, Gregory Ratoff, and an impressive number of Twentieth
Century–Fox stars. The premiere was preceded by a day of pa-

rades and celebration, and opening night the picture was simultaneously shown in seven different theaters. The next morning the *Salt Lake Tribune* devoted twenty columns to the premiere, while at least five hundred people lined up outside the Center Theater, waiting to buy tickets. "You were right," Tyrone Power wired Henry Hathaway. "It was sensational."

Most critics agreed that *Brigham Young* was a big picture, similar in texture to *The Covered Wagon*, and felt that Dean Jagger gave an outstanding portrayal of the Mormon leader. Power, as a Mormon scout, and Linda, as the non-Mormon he converts, were seen as little more than an incidental romance. Nonetheless, the *Los Angeles Herald-Express* claimed Linda "sparkles with a new brilliance."

She was becoming the darling of the Twentieth Century–Fox lot, even more with technicians and workmen than with top executives. She always had a smile, was always quick to thank everyone. "She was never anything but a lovable girl," a Fox gateman said. "I think she knew the first name of everyone on the lot." But Linda's popularity was earned despite Pearl's meddlesome ways. As a publicity woman remarked, "Linda's success went to her mother's head." Linda became increasingly embarrassed, as her own sophistication grew and her mother's antics became more outrageous. Pearl occasionally appeared at the studio wearing garish costumes, even bringing Weedy along. Once she showed up with a pet snake wriggling on her shoulders. "There were two things Linda could never manage," a close friend observed, "her mother and her money."

"I began to hear rumors of her mother's unpopularity on the Twentieth Century–Fox lot," remembered Dorris Bowdon. "She must have offended, irritated, or annoyed everybody she came in contact with. The record shows that every film Linda worked on, the people in charge had trouble with the mother." Finally Pearl was barred from the lot, forbidden to enter the studio gates. "You have to go to pretty extreme ends for that kind of result," said Dorris. "What she did was put a strait-jacket around this girl, creating conflicts that Linda couldn't handle."

When reporters asked Pearl if she missed her husband, she dutifully assured them, "In a choice between staying with my children or my husband, I choose my children." The family had recently rented a five-room house on Parnell Avenue, where Weedy had the run of the place. Linda bought her first car, a 1939 Buick convertible, to drive back and forth to work. The Darnells lived modestly, still with no servants and Pearl doing all the cooking. Linda spent most of her leisure hours sketching or painting at an easel in her bedroom. She did portraits of Walter Lang (her director on *Star Dust*), Pev Marley, and, later, Lana Turner and Clark Gable.

The family depended on Jonathan Smith to look after Linda's finances, since neither she nor her mother knew anything about money. Jonathan cautioned her to go over her books each month, making sure everything balanced, and encouraged her to have Undeen or Harry help her. "She didn't want to be bothered," her sister recalled. "If she'd have followed his advice, we'd all be rich today." After Jonathan died suddenly of a heart attack, Frank Orsatti remained her agent, but as Linda grew busier, she paid even less attention to money matters. "Mother and Dad never taught us about money," said Cal. "Father knew about it, Mother never did. If she had it in her pocket, she'd spend it. So would Linda."

Not that high-living ever appealed to her much. The Hollywood social whirl was foreign to the whole family. Eventually Linda would develop a small circle of friends, and enjoyed having a casual lunch or dinner with them, but never anything fancy. Whenever Pearl and the children went to parties, they didn't fit in at all. "I just thought all those people were very rude and ill-mannered," Monte remembered. "When we first came to California, we were over in Beverly Hills at one of these very exclusive afternoon garden parties with half of Hollywood there. What I thought spoiled that beautiful house and that gracious hostess were a lot of falling-down drunks. And this huge woman at least in her mid-forties, trying to look thirty, with heavy makeup and half of her hanging out, talking so loud you had to get ten feet away to hear anybody else." The woman put her hand on Monte's shoulder and asked, "Are you having a nice time?" Monte was miserable, but smiled politely. About that time a man came over and asked, "Who do we have here?" The woman turned and answered, "I can't remember her name, but she's Linda Darnell's sister. So be nice to her."

"I wish I had known Linda after she was an important Hollywood figure," said Dorris Bowdon, "before she became a tragic figure. It's just possible we could have had a friendship that might have been one of comfort. She couldn't have had pretenses with me—I knew Monetta too well. But I'm not sure Linda was close to anyone." Her best and only really close Hollywood friend was dancer Ann Miller, whom she met at a benefit on Catalina Island. Ann was under contract to Columbia at the time, having just left George White's *Scandals* in New York. The two had much in common and hit it off from the beginning. They were both from Texas, had started their careers when they were quite young, and lived with their mothers. Shortly Pearl and Ann's mother, Clara, became friends. Linda and Pearl frequently visited the Miller home up in the Hollywood Hills. "While the two mama hens clucked," Ann said, "we would gossip about our two studios and all the goings-on there."

In the summer of 1940, Linda began working with Tyrone Power on their third picture together, a remake of the Douglas Fairbanks classic *The Mark of Zorro*. The script had gone through revision after revision, but Zanuck felt the Spanish era in California could form the basis of a thrilling story if treated in a vein similar to *Jesse James*, a recent studio success. Power was the obvious choice for the Spanish nobleman turned Robin Hood, but Zanuck wavered between Linda Darnell and Anne Baxter for the role of Power's sweetheart. The brilliant stage director Rouben Mamoulian was brought in to direct. When he was a student in England, Mamoulian had seen *The Mark of Zorro* with Fairbanks and loved it. Mamoulian demanded additional script revisions, but Zanuck held firm. "I have to give Zanuck his due," the director admitted later. "He knew what was good and what was bad. Darryl was a tyrant, and he had his hand in everything, but he had a terrific eye." After considerable argument, Zanuck gave Mamoulian six weeks to make the changes the director wanted.

Most of the filming was done in the studio, with sun arcs used to simulate daylight. Practically every evening Linda came home laughing about some prank Ty had pulled during the day. "She was like spring," Mamoulian said, "young, sweet, and innocent. The whole crew behaved differently when she was on the set. There was a kind of innocence about her that was enchanting."

The prestige of working with Mamoulian and appearing in an expensive costume picture did much to enhance Linda's star status. *The Mark of Zorro* was first shown at Grauman's Chinese Theater early in November. The *Hollywood Reporter* felt it was "easily the best picture which has come from the Twentieth Century–Fox studio in many a long day. . . . Tyrone Power never has approached anything so fine as his brilliant and altogether engaging performance in the Zorro role, [while] lovely Linda Darnell has made outstanding a role which might have been quite secondary."

Already Linda was busy on *Chad Hanna*, playing Henry Fonda's young wife. Dorris Bowdon had tested for the part and thought she had an inside track, since Nunnally Johnson, whom she had recently married, was both scriptwriter and associate producer. Dorris and Nunnally were having lunch in the studio commissary one day, when suddenly her husband stood up and said, "Excuse me, I want to go over and congratulate Linda." When he returned, his wife asked, "Why the congratulations?" He said, "She just got a part in a film I'm going to do called *Chad Hanna*." Dorris was devastated. She stood up and left the commissary, vowing that their marriage was over. "I don't think it dawned on Nunnally until some time later that it was not the most diplomatic action." The couple made up, but not until there had been "a certain coolness" around the house for a while. Versatile Henry King, Zanuck's favorite director, was assigned to *Chad Hanna*, insisting the script be played against backgrounds that would keep alive the circus atmosphere of the film. Linda played Caroline, who marries Chad and eventually saves the circus by becoming a bareback rider. Henry King suggested they show Caroline trying to ride a horse for the first time, feeling the scene could be dramatically effective. Not only could Linda not ride, she was allergic to horses. Getting through the riding sequences was pure hell for her. In addition to coping with sniffling, watery eyes, and impaired breathing, she was supposed to jump on the horse and ride around a ring. A wire tied to her waist was to keep her from falling off, but as the horse ran faster, the wire lagged behind, pulling Linda up in the air. She had to practice for hours to get the timing right. "You should've seen me flying around that ring!" Linda told Undeen on the telephone. "It was hilarious."

Henry Fonda was not the easy-going person Tyrone Power was, but neither was he temperamental. After considering Hedy Lamarr and Ann Sheridan for the temptress role in the film, the studio again borrowed Dorothy Lamour to play the circus star who ultimately sends Chad back to his wife. Lamour spent considerable time with Linda, and they became friends. *Chad Hanna* would be Linda's first film in Technicolor, and in color she looked lovelier than ever.

Linda was not the only member of the Darnell family to appear in the film. Weedy, her pet rooster, was also given a part, perched on the back of a chair in Linda's introductory scene. Chad, played by Fonda, discovers Linda in a cabin, with her hair in pigtails, barefoot, dressed in gingham, with several chickens and dogs around for atmosphere. Like Linda, Weedy found picture-making no life of ease, for one of the dogs took after him with grim determination. Following some commotion and tears Weedy was rescued, having suffered only the loss of some tail feathers. The dog's trainer explained to a sobbing Linda that his charge had just spent seven weeks working on *Little Men* at another studio, during which his job had been to chase chickens.

The picture was completed shortly before Linda's seventeenth birthday and opened at the Roxy on Christmas Day. The *New York Times* found it slow-moving, "as full of hokum as a press agent's spiel, but bright as a circus poster and flavorsome as a winter apple." Linda was judged "brightly attractive," and the consensus was that she continued to show signs of improvement as an actress. Weedy, who always received his share of publicity, came in for another round at the time of *Chad Hanna*'s release, usually pictured in silk pantaloons. "That rooster is mighty important," Linda told the press, and claimed he had brought her all the good luck she had enjoyed in Hollywood. After watching Linda on the screen as a bareback rider, Monte, who loved horses, decided she wanted to become a stunt rider herself.

Linda's relationship with her mother had grown increasingly stormy over recent months. Feeling shut out of the career she had helped to mold, Pearl became more possessive than ever. Her anger seemed uncontrollable, much of it vented on her children. At times Pearl's screaming became so loud Linda had to lock her bedroom door to concentrate on her studies. Pearl never missed a chance to interject herself into Linda's fame, and the more public the occasion, the more eccentric and garrulous she was likely to appear. At one press conference she showed up in bedroom slippers with Weedy under her arm. Linda was mortified. At home she not only had to defend herself against her mother's tirades, but protect Monte and Cal as well.

The harangues grew worse when Pearl learned that Evelyn, her daughter by her first husband, had gotten into trouble and become something of a fallen woman, at least by Pearl's standards. Evelyn eventually would turn to drink and drugs and earn a scarlet reputation, dying in Florida at a young age. But early in her disintegration, she showed up at the Darnell home in Dallas look-ing for her mother. Roy was living alone there at the time and, soft touch that he was, allowed Evelyn to move in. Roy was work-ing nights, and one evening Evelyn made the mistake of asking a neighbor to buy some whiskey for her. The woman did, but im-mediately reported the episode to Pearl. So did the other neigh-borhood watchdogs, many of whom were envious of Pearl's al-leged success. In time Pearl's sister Priscilla became involved, and as the exchange of misinformation grew increasingly lurid, Pearl became convinced that Roy was having an affair with Evelyn.

Pearl, no stranger to the bottle herself, went on a rampage, ranting and raving against Roy, accusing him before his own chil-dren of incest. "It drove me mad," remembered Cal. Eventually Priscilla took Evelyn to her farm, but that only led to another round of accusations, this time involving Evelyn and Priscilla's husband, Lee. Pearl turned against Evelyn with a vengeance. "I think her imagination went rampant," said Cal. "Mother was a sexually frustrated woman. I think she possessed strong drives she couldn't gratify because of her religious background. That twisted her, and she thought there was incest in the family." Years later Cal asked his father if he had had an affair with his half sister. Roy answered simply, "No, son, I just felt sorry for the woman."

Roy's rumored relationship with Evelyn was a skeleton in the Darnell closet for years, and the family lived in terror that colum-nists Louella Parsons or Hedda Hopper would uncover the scan-dal and ruin Linda's career. In all likelihood it was a tempest over nothing. "Dad wouldn't lie to me," Cal said. "I believed him when he told me he felt sorry for Evelyn. He had no reason to lie." Yet Pearl chose to believe otherwise, using the incident to make Roy's life miserable, punishing him every chance she got. Eventually she made a hurried trip to Dallas to check out the situation there, and found Roy about to leave on a hunting trip. Nothing he could do ever convinced Pearl he was innocent. She became paranoid, convinced California neighbors were spying on her. "They're looking over here," she would say. "They're talking about us." She pulled her children in closer, smothering them with neurotic frustrations, trying to turn them against their father whom she plainly loathed.

Meanwhile, Linda appeared on one magazine cover after an-other, touted as an American princess. The studio assigned her Loretta Young's old dressing room and gave her Young's former stand-in and hairdresser. Fan letters poured in from all across the country, from England, Latin America, and South Africa, many of them asking for autographed pictures. Studio executives took note and soon boosted her salary to $750 a week. Advertisers sought her endorsement on product after product; she appeared in soap commercials, soft drink ads, anything that befitted her image.

Pearl decided it was time the Darnells lived in a manner consistent with Linda's fame, and rented a huge Spanish-style house on Sunset Boulevard in Pacific Palisades. "What a creepy place," recalled Cal. "It scared the bejesus out of me." Just before Thanksgiving 1940, Roy came out to look after the children, while Linda and Pearl flew to Mexico City for the premiere there of *The Mark of Zorro*, as well as second-unit work on *Blood and Sand*, Linda's next picture.

She was excited about visiting Mexico and seeing Jaime Jorba. Jaime had spent a vacation with the Darnells in Los Angeles the year before, and he and Linda had kept in touch through frequent letters. He was then twenty-two years old and studying to be a civil engineer. "He was really in love with Linda," said Undeen, "and she was quite smitten with him, too." The two of them spent days together in Mexico City, with Jaime taking Linda and Pearl to the pyramids, the floating gardens, and all the major attractions. Because of her coloring and fluency with the language, Linda fit comfortably into Latin culture, and her pictures had grown exceptionally popular throughout Mexico and South America. *Blood and Sand* was projected for even wider Latin American distribution, in part to compensate for the loss of European markets resulting from the war.

But Jaime had old world notions about marriage, which did not include having a wife in the public eye. Linda asked him to be patient, but gradually they drifted apart and their letters became fewer and farther between. "I had always expected one day to marry Jaime Jorba," Linda said a few years later. "But Jaime was discouraged with waiting. Just recently he married a girl in Mexico. I think I carried the torch for a while. At least I know how a broken heart can feel."

While Linda and Pearl were with Jaime in Mexico, Roy cooked Thanksgiving dinner in Pacific Palisades for Monte and Cal. A farmer at heart, Roy basically believed chickens belonged outside, and that included Weedy. Since the weather had turned cool, he put Weedy out in the garage with a box for a nest, but somehow Weedy got out and caught cold. By the time Monte and Cal found him, Weedy was a very sick rooster. "We doctored him," Monte recalled, "but he died in the middle of my bed upstairs. Dad, of course, felt awful." They called Pearl long distance and told her what had happened. Linda was grief-stricken, Pearl typically furious. They flew back to California immediately. Weedy was dressed in full regalia and buried in a pet cemetery near Calabasas. "He was the best-loved pet we ever had," Linda sobbed, with Monte and Cal joining in.

Since Linda had to be back for more exterior work on *Blood and Sand*, she and Pearl returned to Mexico City almost at once. The long shots of bullfight sequences were filmed in the Plaza de Toros, with Pearl maneuvering herself into one of the crowd scenes. They returned to California in time for Christmas, but Linda immediately resumed work on *Blood and Sand* at the studio, with Rouben Mamoulian again directing. Tyrone Power played the matador Juan Gallardos, a part Valentino had created, while Rita Hayworth was cast as the lusty Doña Sol. It was Linda and Power's fourth picture together and their last. Shot in Technicolor with a generous budget, *Blood and Sand* would prove the classic of Linda's early career. Mamoulian made the film one of the most visually exciting in motion picture history, while Linda was perfect in the role of the gentle wife.

Zanuck had such confidence in *Blood and Sand* that it was released without a preview. The picture opened at Grauman's Chinese Theater in May 1941, and at the Roxy a few days later. "As if he had all the gold of the lost Spanish galleons at his disposal," the *New York Times* said, "Darryl Zanuck has brought to the Roxy a prodigal new version of Ibañez's *Blood and Sand*, opulently Technicolored, resplendently caparisoned in the gold and pink brocades of Spain, and languid as midafternoon." Linda never looked more radiant, although Tyrone Power was judged "infinitely more believable as a threat to ladies than to bulls." Some critics, who had expressed reservations about Linda's acting in the past, now opened up with unrestrained enthusiasm, commenting both on her beauty and the vulnerability she projected. Carmen Espinosa is one of the roles for which she is best remembered.

But troubled times were ahead, and within a year the bubble had burst. "People got tired of seeing the sweet young things I was playing and I landed at the bottom of the roller coaster,"

Linda said later. "The change and realization were very subtle. I'd had the fame and money every girl dreams about—and the romance. I'd crammed thirty years into ten, and while it was exciting and I would do it over again, I still know I missed out on my girlhood, the fun, little things that now seem important." Yet without a girlhood, the woman stood little chance of normal emotional development.

Marriage

After the success of *Blood and Sand* the studio had difficulty finding another worthy vehicle for Linda. It was announced that she would costar with Claudette Colbert in *Remember the Day*, based on a play of a few seasons before. Then it was publicized that she had been cast as the female lead in *Swamp Water*, Jean Renoir's first American film, but the role ultimately went to Anne Baxter, who was considered a far better actress. Linda felt the disappointment, interpreting each lost role as rejection. "Right under your very nose someone else is brought in for that prize part you wanted so terribly," she said later.

For some months Linda was paid $750 a week to go to school and attend a variety of classes that the studio offered its contract players. She took acting lessons, singing lessons, dancing lessons, and lessons in posture, but the summer passed before another film assignment came along. She met practically everybody on the lot—not just stars, but electricians, grips, musicians, prop men, all the coaches. She found most people friendly, eager to help, a family really. There was a studio baseball team and a bowling team that played Metro and Warner Brothers, and Linda enjoyed the camaraderie. She was too naive to recognize the power struggles and studio intrigues, and rarely encountered Zanuck and the top executives.

In the Darnell home life had gone from bad to worse. The post office had promised Roy a transfer by fall, so he was busy selling the house in Dallas. The children looked forward to having their father again and needed him badly. Pearl was drinking heavily, brutalizing Monte and especially Cal in fits of anger. Weedy's place was taken by five baby ducks, a goose, two white rats, three Texas turtles, a desert tortoise, three guinea pigs, a skunk, some rabbits, a tank full of goldfish, a pet goat, and an alligator which had the bad habit of escaping from the premises and frightening neighbors. "It was really appalling," remembered Cal. "There were always ten thousand dogs around the house. Name it, it was there."

Linda still planned to return to Dallas and graduate from Sunset High School. "They've promised me that I could go back and graduate with my class," she said. "All my life I've looked forward to high school graduation like getting married." But in the end, school officials wouldn't permit it. Sunset High principal W. T. White wrote Linda that the school could not issue a diploma since she hadn't completed two full years in the Dallas school system. "I didn't tell her the real reason," Dr. White confessed later. "I could have put her on that platform if I'd wanted to. I didn't because those other children had spent eleven years getting there. Up to that moment it was the most important thing that had happened to them. If a movie actress had walked across that stage, people would have stood and clapped and yelled, and those other girls and boys would have been ignored. I couldn't permit that."

Linda was crushed. She sent a telegram to Dr. White asking him please to have Charloise Hufstedler, her cocaptain from pep squad days, pick up her annual and take it around for her classmates to sign. But the Sunset class of 1941 graduated without its most celebrated member. Her fame had excluded her. Linda Darnell went through commencement exercises at University High School in Los Angeles amid strangers. "I'm betting there's not a sweet girl graduate in the country who wouldn't change places with her," one journalist presumed.

There was talk that Linda would enter the University of California at Los Angeles in the fall, but her career made that impossible. In August the studio assigned her to a film adaptation of James Thurber's sketches *My Life and Hard Times*, which Broadway columnist Mark Hellinger was producing. Retitled *Rise and Shine*, the picture was at best a pleasant football romp. Jack Oakie starred as a mindless gridiron hero who has trouble staying awake, while Linda played a cheerleader and the daughter of an economics professor. Herman Mankiewicz devised a brisk, madcap script, while Allan Dwan, a former football player himself, directed. *Rise and Shine* won no prizes, and Linda's was anything but a demanding role. Still, for the first time, she played someone her own age and even sang a few bars, which the sound department dubbed.

The day before the picture wrapped, its cast and crew celebrated Linda's eighteenth birthday. "October 16 the jail doors opened for Hollywood's angelic beauty, Linda Darnell," claimed the *Dallas Morning News*. "The brunette starlet has served her juvenile term. She has bidden farewell to her teacher, also to the welfare worker who, with bulldog vigilance, kept a stopwatch on

Linda's every working moment." Now legally an adult, Linda looked forward to assuming responsibility for her own life. "At long last," she sighed. "I can now work longer on the sets every day. And I can marry without Mother's consent if I wish. But I can't imagine wanting to do that. Not for a few more years anyway."

Yet Linda's coming of age mattered little to Pearl, who remained the stern disciplinarian. She still demanded that Linda be home from dates by eleven-thirty, forbade smoking, frowned on short skirts, and preferred that her daughters not wear slacks. "Mother's a little old-fashioned," Linda explained to the press, but Pearl insisted she saw no reason to relax the rules just because her daughter was a famous movie star. "Every Hollywood home I know about serves liquor, but we don't," she announced piously, even as her own drinking problem grew increasingly serious.

Linda's dating was never extensive, and was most often masterminded by the studio's publicity department. She did see press agent Alan Gordon, whom she liked a great deal, occasionally went out with Johnny Hyde (later the agent instrumental in Marilyn Monroe's success), continued to pal around with Mickey Rooney and Dick Paxton, and was sporadically seen at Ciro's or the Mocambo with one wealthy playboy or another. Cameraman Peverell Marley remained a close friend, proudly escorting Linda anytime an opportunity arose, seldom arousing much comment.

The Darnells had recently moved to Brentwood Heights, taking along their menagerie. The family continued to live simply, with only an occasional cleaning woman to help out. Linda's wardrobe was neither large nor expensive. Most of her fancy clothes came from the studio. Despite all her inner tensions, studio publicists painted her as a paragon of tranquility. "She is a thinker," reports assured. "She knows what she wants to do and when and how she's going to do it. Although she got into pictures on her beautiful face, she's getting on by using her head." As always, Linda tried to please, be what was expected, conform to whatever ideals were imposed on her—until the stress became unbearable.

No sooner had she turned eighteen than some of the kindly uncles at Twentieth Century–Fox began making advances. Darryl Zanuck led the pack, calling her into his office shortly after her birthday. He watched her walk toward him, then inched his chair closer as they discussed a part he had in mind for her. His talk seemed more risqué than usual, and Linda wondered if he was purposely trying to shock her. She understood all too well when he invited her into his inner sanctum, a secluded bedroom behind his desk. Linda made it clear she wasn't available. Zanuck never bothered her again, but neither did she get the part they had been discussing.

Pearl grew more convinced than ever that Hollywood was full of dirty old men. She accompanied Linda on a personal appearance tour of the East Coast in conjunction with the opening of *Rise and Shine*, reluctant to allow her daughter out of her sight. Meanwhile Roy had moved into the house in Brentwood, soon going to work in the Beverly Hills post office. He made a curious figure on the Hollywood scene, with his rimless glasses and mild manners, avoiding the limelight so far as possible, content to hunt and fish much as he had in Texas.

Two days after *Rise and Shine* opened in New York, the Japanese bombed Pearl Harbor, thrusting the United States into global war. Linda and her mother learned the news in their Manhattan hotel suite. They finished the publicity tour and, as quickly as possible, returned to California. The Darnells spent Christmas that year, like the rest of the nation, in a state of shock. Undeen, Harry, and their son Wendell drove over from Alhambra, but the holiday was a tense one with all the talk about a possible bombing of the West Coast. Immediately Linda threw herself into the war effort, working for the Red Cross, selling defense bonds, becoming a regular at the Hollywood Canteen. She wrote letters to hundreds of servicemen—friends, acquaintances, total strangers. To some she even mailed cookies. Eventually she would be named Service Beauty of the Month and was a constant volunteer for hospital work.

Early in 1942 Linda made a tour of eastern army camps with comedian Joe E. Brown, returning to Los Angeles just in time to begin *The Loves of Edgar Allan Poe*. Again it was not a plum assignment for her. The property was one producer Bryan Foy had brought with him to Fox from Warner Brothers, and Zanuck gave it slight attention. John Shepperd played Poe, while Linda was one of his three loves. The *New York Times* claimed the film might serve a useful purpose in the classroom, but as an adult drama about a complex man of letters it proved "a postured and lifeless tableau."

Linda realized that although she was making $1,000 a week,

plus income from commercials and various endorsements, since *Blood and Sand* her career had been on a downhill glide. The bloom of her Cinderella image seemed to be gone, and her talent wasn't deep enough for her to develop into a dramatic actress, as Elizabeth Taylor and Jane Fonda did as they matured. Linda knew Darryl Zanuck didn't especially care for her—not so much because she'd refused to go to bed with him, but because he didn't find her exciting either as a personality or as an actress. She was rarely his first choice for parts, but Zanuck remained short on stars, and Linda had caught on with the public as an innocent beauty. How many times she could repeat that role and still keep audiences interested was another matter, and Linda sensed correctly that Zanuck had doubts.

She always harbored reservations about her own acting ability, and invariably panned her performances, certain she was never good enough. She had come to hate the Hollywood social scene, finding it nauseating—the gossips, the meddlers, the endless opportunists. Linda was aware people were using her. "She was a very deep feeling person," her Dallas school friend Dolly Elder assured, "and she admitted in letters it was a hard, hectic life. She seemed to handle it, at least on the surface. Her life never did seem really happy, but I'm not sure she had much choice. Once you're in it you sink or swim, and her instinct was to swim."

Upon completion of *The Loves of Edgar Allan Poe*, Linda was scheduled to go into *Orchestra Wives*, opposite George Montgomery. She was unhappy about the role from the start, protesting to Darryl Zanuck that she was hardly the jitterbug type. When he insisted that she accept the assignment, she resolved to make the best of it, but after twelve days of shooting, Zanuck replaced her with Ann Rutherford. "Linda Darnell and Twentieth Century–Fox aren't on the best of terms at the moment," the press reported.

Linda was plagued by worries, physical problems that undermined her confidence as a woman. She was eighteen years old and still had not had a menstrual period. Doctors told her she might never be able to have children. It was a tremendous psychological blow. Pearl refused to discuss the matter, increasing the burden on Linda. She felt unworthy, unlovable, guilty. How could she possibly think of marriage when she was not a complete woman— merely a shell, a bigger fraud than the worst Hollywood phonies?

She felt isolated, unable to share the secret that was ripping her apart. Whenever she brought up the subject, Pearl flew into a rage, causing Linda to sink into deep depression.

"There's something in the Darnell blood," said Cal, "It was all screwed up." Monte couldn't have children either, and as a boy Cal suffered tremendous glandular problems, spending years under the care of an endocrinologist. He suffered cravings for sweets and food in general, and took shots until he was driven nearly frantic. "I was a mess glandularly," he recalled. "If you offered me another life, I wouldn't have it on a bet if I had to go through all those injections and diets and wild cravings again."

Nor was life any easier since Roy had rejoined the family, for he and Pearl fought incessantly. "They didn't just battle up until eight o'clock," Cal said. "They battled all night long. I mean loudly. The old girl literally used to throw eggs around, not to mention picking up a knife or two, which she did once or twice when she was drunk." Cal would go off to school the next morning barely able to stay awake. The boys tormented him unmercifully, making Brentwood Grammar School absolute hell for him. Linda and his mother didn't approve of his wearing blue jeans and plaid shirts like the other boys, so he never became one of the gang. He was effeminate and sensitive, and the other children branded him a sissy, laughing at his Texas accent and goading him into fights, in part because Cal was Linda Darnell's brother. Monte found school so unpleasant she refused to attend, claiming complications from the rheumatic fever she had as a child. For a while she had private tutors. In his quiet way Roy saw what Linda's career was doing to his children, yet could do nothing to stop it.

Linda stayed away from home as much as possible, for she and Pearl also fought bitterly. While the studio searched for a suitable role for her, Linda busied herself with war work, selling bonds, and traveling wherever she was needed. Pearl usually went along, freer to enjoy the limelight outside the studio's control. Servicemen greeted Linda with whistles and shouts, making her feel warm and appreciated. She insisted on eating with the enlisted men rather than the officers and strenuously objected when she found out they had to pay to see her perform.

The war news during 1942 was anything but good, and the West Coast felt particularly vulnerable. In the midst of the turmoil the studio called in the FBI when two extortion letters were discovered in Linda's fan mail, threatening the young actress and her family with bodily harm unless $2,000 was immediately paid. The notes came after an announcement of Linda's recent salary increase. The extortion threat created quite a stir. FBI agents not only put a watch on the Darnells' house, but on Undeen and Harry's place as well. A few weeks later a seventeen-year-old high school student was arrested in Salt Lake City and charged with writing the letters.

Despite all the commotion, Linda still impressed casual observers as a shy, sensitive girl. Broadway actress Carol Bruce, who had recently scored a hit in Irving Berlin's *Louisiana Purchase*, was under contract at the time to Universal. Carol met Linda through her manager, and the two of them ate lunch together one afternoon on Wilshire Boulevard. "I was absolutely enchanted with this girl," said Carol. "I couldn't take my eyes off her. I had never seen such a face and such a complexion and such sweetness. And those eyes! They wouldn't quit—simply two deep, dark pools of absolutely luminous beauty." Linda had brought Cal along and seemed quite protective toward her brother. "Apart from her beauty," Carol Bruce continued, "she was no more anyone's concept of a movie star than anything. Here I was the city gal, with all the worldliness of New York; she was the little country gal. She belonged in a small town—not in this jungle. Obviously she was propelled by a force greater than herself."

Privately Linda was beginning to resent that force and Pearl's sledgehammer determination to control her life. She and her mother had rows at least once a week, with Linda becoming more outwardly aggressive. One night she came home exhausted from the studio to find Pearl and Roy in a fight. Pearl was drunk, shouting and throwing things everywhere. "It was absolutely frightening," said Cal. "Linda left that night, taking Monte with her, and moved into an apartment on Doheny. She never came back, not to live. I was relieved for Linda. She and I would stand up to Mother, not quietly like Monte and Undeen, who were more like Dad. We just fought filthily—it was dreadful."

Linda had rushed from the house, taking no luggage. A few hours later she received a message at the studio from a local mortuary, saying they had been told to contact her regarding instructions for picking up her mother's body. Linda hurried home, only to find that Pearl had arranged the call. "I have left home, and I shall never go back again," Linda told fan magazines. "The situation was becoming more and more difficult. I had been thinking of moving away for some time. I hadn't been happy for months. I felt stifled. I couldn't even paint or read without interference." She rented a four-room apartment with a tiny swimming pool in her backyard for $165 a month. "When I told Mother I was going to get an apartment," said Linda, "she hit the ceiling, as I expected. She argued I wouldn't be able to take care of myself. But I feel freer and happier than I have ever before in my life."

For a week or two Pearl called every night, demanding to know whom her daughter was seeing. "She didn't want Linda to step out of line at all," said Cal. "When Linda left home, Mother wanted to ruin her. I remember her telling Clara Miller, Ann's mother, that she had made her and she could break her. She was going to do it. Of course, she was raving drunk." Linda tried to explain to reporters, "Mother is hurt. She was a great help to my career when it was starting. For this I owe her, and give her, appreciation and gratitude. But it seems to me mothers, like everyone else, must learn that the time comes when their job is done." The media made her sound like a spoiled, ungrateful child, turning her back on her family once she had attained success, and a storm of public indignation followed. The studio warned Linda about bad publicity, which confused and hurt her. Through it all Pev Marley remained her best friend, her devoted shadow, offering sound professional advice when she needed it most.

Linda still helped her family financially and saw them once or twice a week, although her visits usually ended in a spat with Pearl. She learned to do her own cooking and spent a great deal of time alone, writing letters or reading. She dated more once she could set her own curfew. Alan Gordon remained a steady escort, and friends thought him to be her favorite. At one point she was said to be serious about Kay Kyser, only to be seen later with Eddie Albert, George Montgomery, Jackie Cooper, and others. For a time Vic Orsatti, Ann Miller's agent, was in love with her, and the two of them almost eloped, getting as far as Albuquerque before Linda asked him to take her home. Gradually she became known as filmland's most eligible bachelorette. "I am concentrating on my career," Linda said. "When I do marry, I intend to retire from the screen. I want a large family—at least four children. But that won't be for years yet."

Linda adored going places with her pal Dick Paxton until he was drafted. They went ice-skating, to football games, boxing matches, basketball games, wherever Dick's wallet would permit. "She could relax when she went out with me," he said, "wear slacks and skip the makeup—a fact that pleased both of us. Although I was head over heels in love with her, I knew in my heart nothing would ever come of it. But Linda and I had a lot of fun." She wrote Dick regularly when he went into the army, and the two remained fast friends long after both had married.

In an effort to mend her relationship with Pearl, Linda made a trip in May 1942 with her mother and Ann and Clara Miller, driving to the Grand Canyon, Carlsbad Caverns, and ending up in Texas. Linda and Pearl visited Aunt Priscilla, while Ann and Clara stayed with relatives in Nacogdoches. Pearl introduced herself in hotels and restaurants as Linda Darnell's mother and adored traveling with another celebrity.

Later that summer Linda was with Alan Gordon in a Los Angeles nightclub when they ran into Lana Turner and Stephen Crane, who was a friend of Alan's. Lana and Steve told them they planned to elope the next day and invited Linda and Alan to come along. "I had never double-dated with Lana," Linda said later, "but was thrilled to be her bridesmaid when she asked me." The four of them flew to Las Vegas, where Lana and Crane were married. Linda was photographed standing beside the couple as Lana cut their wedding cake. When reporters asked if she and Gordon also intended to marry, Linda said definitely not. "When the right boy comes along and I fall desperately in love—then I will marry," she told them. "I want to be very sure."

Since Linda and Twentieth Century–Fox remained at odds, Darryl Zanuck decided to loan her out, partly as punishment. In August she reported to Columbia Pictures for what proved an unimportant budget picture, *City Without Men*. It was her first loan-out and a new experience working at another studio, even though Columbia was a lesser company. She found people saying, "I've always hoped to meet you, Miss Darnell!" At Fox she was still treated like a child. "Everybody seems to forget that children grow up," she complained.

City Without Men was Linda's first serious acting role, and she showed up on the set with a phonograph and records to help put her in the mood for her scenes. During the filming, character actress Rosemary DeCamp, also in the picture, got to know Linda well. "She was a lovely lady," DeCamp remembered, "very polite. She was young and laughed a lot and was so beautiful to look at."

Linda occasionally visited Rosemary's home in Beverly Hills, where she came to adore the actress's baby. "She would hold my daughter on her lap," DeCamp recalled. "I was very flattered, because she was a big star, always elegantly dressed. We'd have a meal or sit out in the patio, and she loved my daughter—holding her, counting her toes, playing games with her. I'm sorry she couldn't have children of her own, because she'd have been a wonderful mother."

Linda spent most of her free time with Ann Miller. "Those girls didn't have any adolescence," Cal remarked. "They were always working. When Sunday came, they just collapsed or stayed in bed. Linda didn't have much social life." Occasionally she, Pearl, Ann, and Clara would take off for Palm Springs, Santa Barbara, or the mission at San Juan Capistrano. "Linda was very kind to Mother," Cal said. "California, after all, was a strange place to us."

Nevertheless, Linda and Pearl's fights grew more serious. "My mother and I are very decided people," the young actress told the press, "and as independent as the devil. Naturally there has always been a certain amount of conflict." Her career seemed to have an adverse effect on the entire family. Roy continued to find the Hollywood scene ridiculous. "He didn't like it at all," said Cal. "He wasn't used to a daughter making that kind of money." Monte grew up in Linda's shadow and found life difficult. "I was very shy," she recalled, "and here was my sister, this fantastically beautiful woman. I felt so ugly. I hated to look in the mirror, hated to go outside. People don't understand what it's like to grow up with a famous name in the family."

Even Undeen, pregnant with her second child, tried to keep it a secret that she and Linda Darnell were related. "You really got some strange questions," Undeen said. "Stars used to be put on such a pedestal. Some people were nice and wanted me to bring them autographed pictures, but I used not to tell anyone Tweedles was my sister." Undeen's daughter Jan was born in 1943, and although Undeen was always supportive of Linda's career, she and Harry stayed in the background by choice.

Although closer to the battlefield, Roy led his own private life. For over ten years he worked at the Beverly Hills post office and sold avocados from the Darnell's yard to fellow employees. Roy had a romantic life as well, for Cal once found a package of contraceptives underneath the floormat of the car and assumed his father had a girlfriend. "Mother would never have agreed to a divorce," said Cal. "But I wish they had. I truly wish they had."

By then Linda had bought her parents a home in Brentwood on Avondale Avenue. It was a corner lot, which Pearl turned into a floral riot, with a wall of roses around the back, bougainvillea beside the garage, begonias and succulents in the shady areas, and an arbor of morning glories. "Mother was a lousy housekeeper," said Monte, "but she had a green thumb that wouldn't quit." The Darnells eventually bought an acre lot a block up the street, where Roy planted a Victory garden. Pearl acquired a Shetland pony from friends, which the family named Texas Jim and kept in the backyard. Around five-thirty every morning he came up to the kitchen and started to whinny. Pearl usually was up by then and would hand him buttered toast through the window to keep him quiet, since the neighbors often complained. Whenever she went to Texas or Oklahoma, it was Monte's job to awaken early and make the pony his morning toast.

The war years were halcyon days for the American film industry, a time when almost any picture shipped to theaters was assured box office success. Musicals and escapist fare were especially desired, but the public was hungry for entertainment of all kinds. In April 1943 Linda was put into a big Technicolor musical, initially called *The Girls He Left Behind Him*. The film was directed by Busby Berkeley and starred Alice Faye and Carmen Miranda. Later its title was changed to *The Gang's All Here*, but by then Linda had been taken out. Although her absence theoretically was due to an ankle she had sprained during a dance sequence with Tony DeMarco, in actuality she was placed on suspension.

Without consulting her family, Linda and Pev Marley had eloped to Las Vegas, where they were married on Sunday, April 18. Justice of the Peace Paul O'Malley performed the ceremony, with Ann Miller as Linda's maid of honor. Marley was a sergeant in the army at the time, stationed in Culver City. He had been married twice before—first to actress Lina Basquette (Sam Warner's widow), then to dancer Virginia McAdoo. When Linda married Pev, she was nineteen years old; he was forty-two. All of their friends expressed shock, and Darryl Zanuck was furious. Twentieth Century–Fox executives claimed Linda had damaged her image by marrying a man more than twice her age and that their investment was in serious jeopardy. Even close acquaintances swore they had not expected the marriage; no one had seen Linda and Pev as anything more than friends.

Linda maintained that it was when Pev went into the service four months earlier that she realized how much she depended on him. The Friday evening prior to their marriage, the couple had been at Ann Miller's house. Pev had a three-day pass and proposed to Linda on the drive back to her apartment. "I wasn't even remotely shy," she said. "I accepted him right off." They telephoned Ann and told her their plans. "Can you leave for Las Vegas with us tomorrow?" asked Linda. Ann explained she was working the next day until four o'clock. "We'll pick you up at the studio at four sharp!" Linda told her.

Linda packed a white wool suit she had recently bought for the ceremony, while Pev asked Private Bill Heath to serve as his best man. The wedding party drove to Las Vegas on Saturday afternoon. Later Linda said she always knew in her heart that she and Pev would marry. "He's what I want," she told reporters. "I need an older, experienced man to guide me. I know what I'm doing. Our marriage will be a success." Pev admitted he had been in love with Linda from the start, but realized she was too young for romance. Over the past eight months they had seen each other regularly, so Linda claimed she was not surprised when Pev proposed.

Immediately after the ceremony, the wedding foursome rushed back to Los Angeles, where Ann and her mother gave a reception in the Miller's Laurel Canyon home. Pearl heard the news and went into a rage. "You could hear that old girl screaming and raving against Linda and Pev from a block away," said Cal. "'The son of a bitch' this, 'the unholy bastard' that. It was appalling. . . . She was throwing clothes, vases, kitchen utensils, everything out of the house and yelling at the top of her voice. She went on for a couple of hours. I mean she emptied the house. It looked like a tornado [had hit]. Out in the front rose garden, with a flagpole in the middle, were clothes, pots and pans, broken things, eggs, garments, sofa cushions, the whole lot. It was a horror."

Pearl was drunk and crying when Clara Miller called to invite her to the reception. "She's married," Clara told her. "There's nothing you can do about it. They've been joined in holy wedlock." That sobered Pearl a bit. "Clara brought God into it somehow," remembered Cal, "and my mother was afraid to talk back to God. So she behaved herself at this bloody reception." Pearl pulled herself together, went to her closet and began rummaging through dresses. She came to a black one with great red strawberries on it and yanked the dress off the rack. "Come on, Big Strawberries," she snorted, "we've got to say hello to my new son-in-law, that son of a bitch!"

So off they went to Ann Miller's house. "My God," thought Cal, "this is going to be folly. But Mother went in there and stood in front of the cameras and the newsmen and behaved herself—weeping, of course, her hair streaming behind her like a witch. But she behaved rather well." With the exception of Linda and Ann, no celebrities were present. Most of the eighty guests were close friends or relatives. Linda wore an orchid on her white wedding suit, while Ann's outfit consisted of a blue suit with a large matching hat. "They practically frisked Mother for butcher knives when we walked in," recalled Monte. Linda talked to her mother, and Pearl agreed to pose with the wedding party, although she refused to kiss the bride.

"That was a wild time," said Undeen. "Mother was upset because Tweedles was marrying such an older man, and Dad just sat there on a couch not saying anything." Finally Pearl began enjoying the party. The Millers had an open bar, and Undeen, who seldom imbibed, started drinking cuba libres. "We were sitting there talking, and when I started to get up," said Undeen, "I began weaving. My head was just spinning." She sat back down and said, "Harry, is Dad still over there on the couch?" Harry told her he was. "I think I'm drunk," she said, "and I don't dare walk across that floor and let Dad see me looped." So Undeen drank another cuba libra while they waited for Roy to leave. Harry eventually asked Cal to come get his dad so that Undeen could get off that bar stool. "It took me a whole week to get over that," she said. "I was so thirsty the next morning and drank some ice water. That room just started spinning. I was drunk all over again!"

Linda received only three wedding gifts: a glass dish from her agent, a dressing gown from her older sister, and an electric bread warmer from Dolly Elder. Nothing arrived from the studio, nothing from her parents. Few thought Linda was in love with Marley. He was the father figure she needed. "It was an understandable marriage," said Dorris Bowdon. "Linda was in terrible need of getting away from her mother. Pev was a very kindly man, and he must have been completely entranced by her beauty. As a cameraman, he was particularly sensitive to beauty." Certainly Roy had never been the strong force any of his children needed. "All of us

Darnells were looking for a father figure," admitted Cal. "Dad was sort of a shadow; he was a ghost flitting around. All he did was suffer from the old girl. I think Linda asked Pev to marry her because she wanted to get away from Mother. I think Linda needed a father figure, and Pev was an older man who was trying to protect her." Pev seemed the settling ingredient Linda craved. "She turned to him," Dolly Elder said, "as a stable element in all that false tinsel world. He had befriended her, and he became a father figure. He felt protective toward her."

The Tuesday following the wedding Linda showed up for work on *The Girls He Left Behind Him*, only to be told she had been taken off the picture and suspended. Twentieth Century–Fox publicists announced that the studio was granting her six weeks off for a honeymoon, but not even Louella Parsons was fooled. "What looked like storm clouds brewing over Linda Darnell's honeymoon in the form of a suspension," the columnist wrote, "is now officially explained as 'just a leave of absence' for the bride. Maybe so. But the fact remains that Linda is out of *The Girls He Left Behind Him*. Linda claims she hurt her leg and asked for a leave. But there are persistent rumors that Linda's elopement with cameraman Pev Marley may have had something to do with upsetting the applecart."

With Pev back at his army post, Linda filled her hours with volunteer work at St. John's Hospital in Santa Monica. She went as Monetta Darnell, although everyone recognized her. "I know there's a shortage of nurses," she told authorities at St. John's. "Surely there must be something I can do. I'll do anything at all to help, including washing bedpans." It was hard, dirty work. She saw suffering and pain, but felt needed. "Linda was doing penance," Cal said later, "scrubbing up placenta, because she felt guilty, about what I don't know."

Linda insisted that she and her husband planned to go on their honeymoon as soon as he received a furlough. Meanwhile she moved into Pev's spacious house at 901 N. Amalfi in Pacific Palisades. He promised that she could redecorate the house anyway she liked, and Linda soon turned it into a showplace.

Fellow workers remembered Pev as an outstanding photographer, pleasant on the set, coarse in private conversation, a bit on the mischievous side. "He was fun," said Rosemary DeCamp, "but you never knew where you stood with Pev, because he played games. He'd draw you out and then reverse himself and show you

you were wrong." According to film composer David Raksin, "He was one of those birds who verged on having style without actually having it. There used to be a certain tradition in the studios which was adopted by guys who didn't come to this naturally. In other words they didn't have a heritage of wealth, but they learned style from those who did. Pev Marley was a guy who didn't have the physique to make it."

Article after article appeared in fan magazines under Linda's byline justifying her marriage. "I'm Glad I Married an Older Man," she announced in *Photoplay*, followed some months later by "Should Young Girls Marry Older Men?" Linda's answer was invariably, "I like him—and age doesn't matter. I feel people meant well when they busybodied around about me marrying Pev. It's just that they couldn't know the truth." But the studio remained hostile, awaiting a verdict from fans, while Pearl and Pev were like two lions, pacing for the kill.

"Little Linda Darnell deserves happiness," Louella Parsons dictated from her column, "for she hasn't had the easiest time in the world these last few months." Sympathy for Linda appeared to be mounting. Eventually Twentieth Century–Fox recanted, primarily because they needed her. A quarrel had arisen over one of their major productions, *The Song of Bernadette*, for which Jennifer Jones would receive an Academy Award. Director Henry King wanted the Virgin Mary to appear on the screen, whereas scriptwriter George Seaton definitely did not. The question was resolved when Linda was brought in to play the vision. She would receive no billing, and hers was at best a cameo role. Seaton grew so upset when he saw the scenes of the Madonna, with Linda in blue, that he showed them to the author, Franz Werfel, who exploded with rage. "If you release the picture with the girl in blue," Werfel said, "I will write a letter to the *New York Times*." The scenes were reshot with Linda appearing in a creamy, misty light.

Linda's Virgin Mary made an indelible impression on audiences, and hundreds of letters poured in when the film was released. Exonerated by the public, the studio had little choice but to acquiesce. "Every time I saw that picture I cried," said Monte. "Tweedles was so beautiful as the Lady, and the part fit her so well. In spite of all her tantrums, I always thought that was the real her."

The studio already had cast her as the second lead in William Wellman's *Buffalo Bill*, playing the part of a young Indian woman who teaches in a frontier school. Linda resumed work early in June, radiant and happy to be back on salary. She began costume fittings, while the Fox publicity department announced that Linda was perfectly cast, since she had "a few drops" of Cherokee blood in her veins. Joel McCrea was featured as Buffalo Bill, with Maureen O'Hara playing his wife, Thomas Mitchell as Ned Buntline, and Anthony Quinn as Yellow Hand. Director William Wellman began with the idea of showing Buffalo Bill as "the fakiest guy who ever lived." Wellman and writer Gene Fowler worked on a script for three months and came up with what they thought was an absolutely truthful account. Then a few days later, Fowler called Wellman, obviously drinking, and asked to see him. "Bill," Fowler said as Wellman walked into his house, "you can't stab Babe Ruth. You couldn't kill Dempsey. You can't kill any of these heroes our kids worship, and that's what we're doing. Buffalo Bill is a great figure, and we can't do it. Let's burn the goddamn thing." So the two of them sat in Fowler's home, drinking continuously as they tossed page after page of their script into the fire.

By the time *Buffalo Bill* was finished, the studio had already loaned Linda to Arnold Pressburger for *It Happened Tomorrow*, an absurd comedy-drama released through United Artists. Clearly Zanuck's confidence in his star had not been fully restored. Linda began to think her looks were standing in the way of her getting better assignments, and she poured out her fears to her husband when she saw him on weekends.

Upon the completion of *It Happened Tomorrow*, Linda returned to Twentieth Century–Fox, still feeling unappreciated by her home studio. She began to think that perhaps she had been there too long, that Zanuck and his producers were never going to give her a chance to develop as an actress. She longed to play a bad girl for a change, someone of real dimension. Instead the studio put her in a musical featuring Benny Goodman, a piece of fluff called *Sweet and Low Down*. Thin on story, the picture's main attraction was the Goodman orchestra. Linda played a young Park Avenue socialite with a fondness for swing, while Jack Oakie was a would-be trombone player who never quite makes the grade. During costume fittings Linda grew close to designer Yvonne Wood, whom she had met preparing *Orchestra Wives*. "We got along like peas in a pod," said Wood. "She had a fantastic sense of humor, and I can get kind of silly, too. That's one reason she was so fond of me." They would remain friends, with Yvonne a constant pillar of support.

During the shooting of *Sweet and Low Down*, cinematographer Lucien Ballard was out briefly, keeping a medical appointment he couldn't change. Pev Marley was borrowed for a few hours to photograph his wife in a kissing scene with James Cardwell. It was one of the last times Pev worked on the Twentieth Century–Fox lot. Angry over his marriage to Linda, the studio did not renew his contract. After the war he moved to Warner Brothers, where he filmed a number of important pictures—*Pride of the Marines*, *Night and Day*, and *Life with Father*, among others. Later he worked on Cecil B. DeMille's *The Greatest Show on Earth* and *The Ten Commandments*.

If Pev's marriage to Linda did nothing to help his reputation with Darryl Zanuck, *Sweet and Low Down* did little for his wife. Bosley Crowther found the picture "weak and weary." Of its two beauties, Linda Darnell and Lynn Bari, Dorothy Manners in the *Los Angeles Examiner* said, "Lynn comes off the best because she has more of a chance to shine. Linda just doesn't have enough to do—but looks beautiful doing it."

There it was again—beauty, never talent. As the war appeared to be winding down, neither Linda nor Pev had much reason for jubilance over their careers. Linda had been reduced to second leads and mediocre starring roles, while her husband had no job awaiting him. She was only twenty, but after five years in Hollywood she felt like a veteran. "When I first came here," Linda said, "I was way up in the clouds. I dreamed of a big house, servants, two swimming pools, a car a block long, and as many fur coats as I wanted!" Now she had the big house, the fur coats, and most of the rest, but knew that her dream—Pearl's dream—had imprisoned her. The only thing to do was fight, beat Hollywood at its own game. "You have to get Hollywood quick," she said, "or Hollywood gets you."

Vixen

Linda's standing at Twentieth Century–Fox had fallen to such a low ebb that there was serious doubt the studio would pick up her next option. Then two things that happened almost simultaneously turned the situation around. Early in 1944 *Look* magazine sponsored a contest to determine who was the most beautiful woman in Hollywood. While the vote was indecisive, ending in a four-way tie, Linda was named one of the four. The others were Hedy Lamarr, Ingrid Bergman, and Gene Tierney. All four stars were prominently displayed in a magazine layout, and Linda's selection was considered a major accomplishment.

Linda's stature as a beauty was beyond question; her capacity to project a screen personality was another matter entirely. Darryl Zanuck found her range limited. Shortly before the *Look* contest, however, an agent sent Linda the script of *Summer Storm*, adapted from Chekhov's story "The Shooting Party," suggesting that she might be interested in playing the seductive peasant girl who takes three men to their ruin before she herself is murdered. Susan Hayward was also being considered for the part, but Linda begged Fox executives to loan her out for this mature role. Zanuck had reservations, but since his studio had nothing for her at the moment, he eventually consented. "I was told that such a violent change of type might ruin my career," Linda said later, "but I insisted on taking the chance."

Scheduled for release through United Artists, *Summer Storm* was directed by Douglas Sirk. Filming began in the spring of 1944, with *The Wicked and the Weak* as a working title. Linda got on well with Sirk, although things didn't always progress smoothly. One particularly bad day, the director had shot sixteen takes of an important scene in a greenhouse. Linda grew tired, embarrassed, and was almost in tears. Finally Sirk ordered, "Everybody take a breather." Putting his arm around Linda's shoulder, he said, "Now I want you to relax." Suddenly he yanked her across his knee and spanked her hard. "Now you go out there and do that scene right!" he snapped. The spanking so shocked and infuriated her that she went back on the set and made the scene one of the best in the picture. "After that, Sirk and I got along better than ever," she said.

The gamble paid off, and Linda quickly claimed that the Russian woodcutter's daughter was the role she liked best. It provided her with a whole new screen image. A photograph of her sitting voluptuously in a haystack with a tight blouse and scant skirt drew wide attention. "I never did cheesecake before," she said. "I like it. For five years I played a sweet little girl. I didn't want to be a little cheesecake dame. Now I've grown up." Word leaked out that demure Linda Darnell had gone bad with a vengeance in *Summer Storm*. "This is one picture on which I am setting much store for the future," she claimed. "For eighteen months I did nothing in pictures. I pleaded for something to do, but nothing happened. The character in the Chekhov film is a wild sort of she-devil, which any actress would go miles to play. She's devil mostly—at times angelic—and perfectly fascinating to interpret. I'm counting on my Russian girl to give me a new start."

The picture was completed in May, but would not be released until the following fall. Linda continued to feel unappreciated by her home studio, which shortly loaned her out again. This time she was sent to Bing Crosby Productions for *The Great John L.*, a film biography of prize-fighter John L. Sullivan. Although director Frank Tuttle did his best to capture the flavor of the times, *The Great John L.* provided more tedium than excitement. Linda's portrayal of showgirl Anne Livingstone, to whom John L. was unhappily married, was a fairly rewarding assignment for a star in need of a new image. She wore plumes and garters, mouthed a couple of sultry songs, and died in the end, paving the way for Sullivan's marriage to his boyhood sweetheart. "Never before have Miss Darnell's legs appeared on the screen," reported the *Los Angeles Citizen News*. "This has been a serious loss. Hidden assets, they are."

Linda already was battling a weight problem and had been forced to trim down before *The Great John L.* went before the cameras. Darryl Zanuck meanwhile saw a cut of *Summer Storm* and began hunting for a vehicle that would capitalize on her vixen demeanor. Louella Parsons urged Twentieth Century–Fox to give Linda the break she deserved. "I do all these loan-out pictures," she told Parsons, "and have such wonderful parts, and my own studio forgets I am alive." But the tide was soon to turn. Even before *Summer Storm*'s rave notices, Zanuck decided to cast her in a succession of parts that took her to the height of her fame.

With *The Great John L.* wrapped in September, Twentieth Century-Fox rushed Linda into *Hangover Square*, in which she played Netta Longdon, a woman who ruins the lives of all who come in contact with her. Linda returned to her home studio with renewed confidence, aware she had been given a choice part. Zanuck had originally wanted "a very sexy woman, possibly a foreigner" for Netta, someone with the allure of Marlene Dietrich. When the censorship office objected to some of her low-cut costumes, Linda was flattered. "They've never paid much attention to me before," she claimed. "I've had to act, appear, and behave older than I was ever since I came to pictures. The main difference is that now I'm old enough to know how."

With *Hangover Square* completed, *Summer Storm* finally opened at the Gotham in New York on October 20, 1944, to almost universal praise. Audiences across the country sat up and took notice of both Linda's histrionic abilities and her newly revealed physical attributes. Twentieth Century–Fox rushed *Hangover Square* into the Roxy early in February. Again Linda's reviews were excellent. "Miss Darnell will soon become, if she is not already, Hollywood's most rousing portrayer of unhousebroken sex," *Time* magazine said.

With Linda's triumph in *Hangover Square* assured, Zanuck decided to take her out of *Don Juan Quilligan* opposite William Bendix, in which she was to repeat her familiar ingenue role. While the studio looked for another bad girl part, Linda went to Canada on a bond drive and made a tour of American army camps. She was hostess for a group of servicemen at a Los Angeles Jive Jamboree and continued working regularly for the Red Cross and the Hollywood Canteen.

Pev was home more as the war progressed, and the Marleys sometimes invited friends in for a poker session or a dinner party at their house on Amalfi Drive. Neither Pev nor Linda cared much for the Hollywood social whirl, preferring to entertain quietly. Pev drank a great deal, although he could hold his liquor without showing it. Linda often came home from the studio tired, and Pev's solution was for them to have a drink. "This will relax you, kiddie," he'd tell her, handing her a shot of whiskey. He showed her how to drink liquor straight, the whole shot at once, then wash it down with water. "Pev got Linda onto booze," said Cal, "and I shall never forgive him. He taught her to drink. That's where it started." Pev encouraged her to match him drink for drink. If she refused, he became nasty-tempered, more cutting than usual. That generally led to a fight, with Linda fully capable of erupting like a volcano, much as her mother did.

Certainly life with Pearl and Roy was no bed of roses for Cal and Monte. Trudi Dieterle, a friend of Cal's from junior high on, was a frequent visitor in the Darnell home. "The first time I walked in that house was a shock," Trudi recalled. "Two or three of the bedrooms were furnished very expensively, but tastelessly—lots of satin, velvet, and mirrors, almost like a Hollywood set out of the 1930s." Chickens and ducks walked through the house at random, and there were animals all over. By then Texas Jim and the goats had eaten most of the flowers and shrubbery. "There were animal droppings everywhere," Trudi continued, "in and outside the house. And fleas! That was fine for Pearl. She was well fortified with Southern Comfort and things didn't seem to bother her. She did a lot of yelling at her kids. And Roy, a sweet old man, didn't say anything." Once Trudi entered the kitchen to find Roy housecleaning. "I guess the chicken poop got too much even for him," Trudi commented. The kitchen floor was vinyl, surrounded by rooms that were carpeted. Roy, who had a bucket of water and a mop, took the full bucket and threw its contents across the floor, sending water sloshing onto the carpeted areas. Trudi gasped in amazement, "That's an odd way to mop a floor!" Roy muttered, "If it's good enough for the U.S. Navy, it's good enough for the Darnells."

Pearl always wore an apron. Trudi never saw her cook, but she always wore the same apron, and it was invariably dirty. Someone once commented, "Gee, Pearl, that apron looks like it's really had it." Pearl looked down and said, "Well, I reckon." With that she took it off, turned it around, and put in on backwards so the clean side showed. She became increasingly convinced neighbors were spying on her, gossiping about her family, snickering behind their backs. One day, roaring drunk, she defiantly brought Texas Jim into the house, while a group of astonished Brentwood neighbors looked on.

Trudi Dieterle found Pearl fearsome. "She would periodically explode," Trudi said, "not at me, but at Cal or the world at large, and I never knew when these explosions would come. They were irrational and made me uneasy." There never seemed to be food in the house, nor did Pearl seem to care whether Monte and Cal had clothes. So far as Trudi could tell she was always drinking. "She never appeared drunk. She never slurred her words. She never stumbled. I never saw her sleepy. But I think she was functioning in a state of semireality." Nor did Pearl seem concerned any longer about her children's whereabouts. "I was envious," said Trudi. "I thought it was wonderful to have parents like that, where you could come and go as you pleased and not have a curfew. At this point Linda's career was so successful that Pearl didn't have anything more to do. Maybe that had something to do with her drinking. There was nothing more she could manipulate."

Roy and Pearl appeared to be strangers. "I don't remember them ever discussing anything," said Trudi. "They seemed to shift independently of each other." Roy faithfully went to work at the post office, and he did a lot of driving, taking Pearl wherever she wanted to go. "They had this absurd vehicle," Trudi remembered. "It was a big, black limousine with a glass divider between the driver and the back seat." That was the way Pearl went shopping, with Roy driving her. "Mother abused the old man terribly," said Cal. For two years she insisted that Roy sleep in a tent up on the vacant lot. It was an old Boy Scout tent, set up amid fir trees, close to a shed. "He slept out there until Monte and I finally said something to him," Cal claimed.

The children's hatred for Los Angeles grew stronger as their lives became increasingly miserable. Both Monte and Cal longed for Texas, to be back among friends. "I liked running around with snakes and frogs in my pocket," said Cal. "I liked the South and the rural life there. California was quite mad. I learned to distrust people out there. People would be nice until they got to know Linda, then they had no time for you. And the boys at school would bully me to give them money. I hated it." He also hated baseball and football and was a terrible athlete, causing his peers to heckle him all the more. "I was always out in left field," Cal recalled, "staring into the Western sun, and I could never see the ball. I couldn't catch it or hit it. One time I caught the ball all right and turned and ran as if fifty demons were after me. Suddenly these twenty-one gargantuans were running at me, and I had the beastly football! So I turned and ran the wrong way and made a touchdown for the other side."

As Cal entered adolescence, school became even more of a torment. With no strong father as a role model, he seemed effeminate and sissified to his peers, and was known only as Linda Darnell's brother. "And he was pretty," Trudi Dieterle insisted. "He wasn't handsome, he was pretty. It was very hard for him. He was a wonderfully crazy, mixed up guy. We were two of a group of perhaps ten or twelve youngsters who were all misfits. There was not one of us that was a conventional teenage kid. None of us seemed to fit."

One morning Cal showed up at school with a boa constrictor around his neck, frightening the girls. He was extremely knowledgeable about science and, like Monte, had a way with animals. Another time, at the end of a school day, Cal, Trudi, and several of their friends were standing on the steps in front of Emerson Junior High, waiting for somebody's mother to pick them up. They were swatting each other, hitting one another with books, when the vice principal walked up. He grabbed Cal by the shoulders and shook him. "Darnell," he said, "life's going to be a lot easier for you when you decide whether you're going to be a boy or a girl." Forty years later Cal admitted how much that remark hurt.

Pearl still worried that Hollywood decadents would corrupt her children. "With us Darnells," Cal said, "I think it was the other way around. We were more likely to get hold of the dirty old men." Clara Miller once suggested Pearl tell her children about sex, let them know what life was about. Pearl's solution was to take them to see Ken Murray's *Blackouts*, which in 1944 was considered a risqué stage show. "Mother thought she was showing us the whole works in one sweep," said Cal. "But it was really like Sunday school, certainly nothing worse."

Somehow Monte remained cheerful, although growing into a stubborn personality. One night, after a particularly bad harangue, Pearl slapped her youngest daughter for something Cal had done. It so infuriated the boy that he struck his mother, knocking her to the floor and tearing her dress. "She showed the whole neighborhood where her son had bruised her," said Cal. "And I had. I didn't mind so much if she hit me, but I couldn't bear for her to hurt my sister. Mother was a coward that way. Linda was too. If you stood up to them, they backed down." Linda was becoming as hot-tempered as Pearl, especially when things failed to go her way. Placid as she was on the surface, she had become a star, privately as well as on the screen. Although she relished her celebrity, career frustrations repeatedly led her to lash out at others, whom she tended to blame for the trap she found closing in on her.

Shortly before Christmas, Pearl was drunk and raving at Roy, swearing she was going to commit suicide. "She'd done it so often," Cal said, "always picking up a knife or saying she was going to kill herself." Roy got the children out of the house, taking them to buy a Christmas tree, with Pearl still threatening to do herself in. On their way back home an ambulance was clanging down a nearby thoroughfare, headed for St. John's Hospital. Cal thought, "She's in there. She's tried it." Sure enough, Pearl had put on a satin negligee and all her diamond rings, made up her face, loosened her hair, and taken sleeping pills. She called the police, who arrived to find her unconscious.

Roy drove the children to St. John's Hospital that evening, where Pearl was resting in a private room. Monte burst into tears and left, and Roy went to comfort her. Pearl opened her eyes, peering at Cal through the hair that hung down over her face. "You silly old bitch," he said angrily. "Why didn't you do it? You didn't intend to for one minute." Suddenly Pearl was awake, hearing it all. Cal walked to the window and threw it open. "There," he shouted. "If you really want to kill yourself, go ahead and jump. I'm not going to stop you. The window's open." Pearl screamed and rang for the nurses. "Mother never tried that again," said Cal. "Neither would she let herself be alone with me. I think she was afraid. If you stood up to Mother, or if you stood up to Linda, you could survive."

Monte was ill for three weeks and went to stay in Linda and Pev's guest room. During that time she learned that her sister's marriage was far from happy. "There was a lot of friction," Monte remembered, "and they argued a lot. Pev knew how to needle, and he liked to needle. He'd sit there and watch Tweedles's eyes flash and then go over and deliberately say something he knew would set her off." But Pev helped polish Linda and guided her through various crises in her career. "There's no doubt he helped her fantastically," said Monte, "in acting and everything else. It was a good professional marriage, but it wasn't a good personal marriage."

Pev meanwhile urged the Darnells to become more sophisticated, not always with the desired results. "We were really stupid, clod-hopping Texans," Monte admitted, "and the Great LD, as Pev called her, needed to have the right background." Yet he pushed so hard that the Darnell children sometimes revolted. "I never wanted to play bridge because Pev kept insisting I learn," said Monte, "and his lectures were never less than two hours long. I can imagine what Tweedles went through."

Hollywood may have found Linda and Pev an oddly matched couple, but those who knew them well understood her need for reinforcement. Gradually they became accepted. Linda's drinking added to her weight problem, and there was still the trauma of her not having physically matured. Hormone shots had done nothing for her condition, and it was now certain she could never bear children. For all her full-blown beauty, privately she felt like a fragment of a woman.

Late in January 1945, Linda learned her next studio assignment would be *Fallen Angel*, with the Viennese tyrant Otto Preminger directing. Linda would play Stella, a mercenary waitress eventually killed by a blow on the head. Dana Andrews was cast as the male lead, and Darryl Zanuck coaxed Alice Faye out of retirement to play a dramatic role with no singing. *Fallen Angel* was the first of four pictures Linda would make with Otto Preminger, whom she learned to dislike intensely. The director had scored a huge success with *Laura* the year before, but Linda found him stubborn, humorless, terrifying on the set. "Preminger was a sadistic monster," one studio worker said. "It was a sickness with him." In later life the director remembered Linda as a girl who was serious about her acting, but "a rather colorless personality."

Linda looked upon her role in *Fallen Angel* as a challenge, even working as a waitress in the studio coffee shop a few hours to gather experience. She played the tramp with gusto, and almost everyone agreed it was her finest acting yet. "Linda Darnell was the best thing in the picture," said costar Dana Andrews. "The scene I had with her was at least showy." There was even talk of her receiving an Academy Award nomination. David Raksin, who wrote the score, vividly recalled seeing Linda on the set: "My impression was that she was learning her profession as she went along. She had a sexy beauty. There was something lusty about her without any overt attempt to seduce. I realized she was there not because she was a schooled actress, but because she was beautiful. That meant there would be a more or less sophisticated competition for her in the studio, which apparently developed. Little girls like that were sort of fair game."

Crew members continued to find Linda cooperative and

friendly. Hairstylist Gladys Witten came to know her well over the years. Since Witten had recently arrived in Hollywood from an ordinary Kentucky background, the two girls had much in common. "Linda always said what she thought," Witten maintained. "She was very down to earth—fun, happy. She was loved by everyone." The two of them spent hours sitting on the floor of Linda's dressing room telling jokes. Linda was never much for Hollywood gossip, but she welcomed a good laugh. "She was the highlight of my studio work," Witten insisted.

World War II was officially over one month before shooting on *Fallen Angel* ended. Twentieth Century–Fox decided to premiere the melodrama at the Majestic Theater in Dallas, in conjunction with the Victory Bond drive, with Linda heading the celebration. She arrived at Dallas's Love Field in November, and was greeted by Dolly Elder, former Sunset classmates, her high school principal, and a host of officials, friends, and teachers. Acquaintances were disappointed to find that her personality had hardened, that she was no longer the gentle girl they had known earlier. She seemed cynical, and her vocabulary had become downright salty. Friends noticed there was a drink in her hand most of the time.

Critics in Dallas received her film enthusiastically. "*Fallen Angel* is not as original, chic, or moody as *Laura*," John Rosenfield wrote in his review. "But Preminger gives it style with adroit and not too self-conscious camera work. . . . Although a nonsinging Alice Faye is the titular heroine, Linda Darnell has the major assignment. And she demonstrates quite a bit of still inchoate histrionic power. She is big enough for several seething sequences."

Already the studio was planning to cast Linda as Catana, the peasant spitfire in the screen adaptation of Samuel Shellabarger's *Captain from Castile*, scheduled to go before the cameras within two years. Laid against the tapestry of the Spanish Inquisition and Cortez's conquest of Mexico, the picture was to reunite Linda with Tyrone Power, who was slated as the swashbuckling hero. Catana was an ideal part for Linda, taking advantage of both her Latin looks and her newfound powers as an actress. She felt the part would give her a chance to make her strongest impact yet, and she looked forward to the picture, convinced it would be her masterpiece.

Linda and Pev Marley celebrated their third wedding anniversary at the Tropics in Beverly Hills. Although she had just signed another seven-year contract with Twentieth Century–Fox, fan magazines insisted Linda put her marriage before her career. "I shall retire from the movies when I'm twenty-five," the twenty-two-year-old Linda Darnell told columnist Sheilah Graham. "I shall have been in the business for ten years. And that's enough. When I'm twenty-five, I'll be home when my husband is home." Since the war Pev had worked steadily for Warner Brothers, having recently photographed Humphrey Bogart and Barbara Stanwyck in *The Two Mrs. Carrolls*. He and Linda were seldom between pictures at the same time, but neither seemed to mind. The distance between them appeared to be growing. Close friends suspected Pev was indulging in some philandering on the side. As for Linda, she spent most of her free time at home painting, sculpting, or reading. She had taken up smoking, ran a casual household, and still leaned toward being an introvert.

While *Captain from Castile* was in preparation, Darryl Zanuck assigned her to two pictures filmed almost simultaneously. First she played Tuptim, the doomed harem girl in *Anna and the King of Siam*, immediately followed by the sultry sister in Otto Preminger's musical *Centennial Summer*. Since *Fallen Angel* she had ballooned in weight, so even with rigorous dieting, Tuptim's midriff appeared somewhat heavy. For the title roles of Anna and the King, Zanuck wisely chose Irene Dunne and Rex Harrison. Sets alone cost over $200,000, the most exquisite Twentieth Century–Fox had built since before the war. The city of Bangkok, as it appeared in the 1860s, covered ten acres of the studio's back lot. At the Academy Awards celebration that year, *Anna and the King of Siam* took Oscars for both art direction and cinematography.

Tuptim was a brief, but effective part for Linda, who was rapidly becoming the most-often-killed actress in Hollywood—shot in *Buffalo Bill*, stabbed in *Summer Storm*, strangled and burned in *Hangover Square*, bludgeoned in *Fallen Angel*, and burned at the stake in *Anna and the King of Siam*. Ironically, Linda had a deep fear of fire dating back to childhood and harbored the premonition that she would die by burning. During the filming of the cremation scene for *Anna and the King of Siam*, while her hands were tied, the flames did come dangerously close, so close that Linda was slightly singed. "Next time," she confessed, "I prefer being shot or stabbed. At least that kind of dying is painless."

Filming on *Centennial Summer* began before *Anna and the King of Siam* was finished, although Linda and Pev did manage a brief trip to New York with Howard Hughes, as part of a group aboard the maiden flight of the Constellation. Warner Brothers almost immediately called Pev back, but Linda stayed on, returning just in time to change into period costumes for her role as the flirtatious Edith. *Centennial Summer* was set in Philadelphia during the Exposition of 1876 and was Fox's attempt to equal Metro's recent success with *Meet Me in St. Louis*. Jerome Kern supplied the score, but did not live to see the project finished. Preminger's direction did little to invigorate the musical, so that the picture possessed neither vitality nor warmth.

Linda had no sooner started work on *Centennial Summer* than the eccentric Howard Hughes, a multimillionaire who had dabbled in films, called to invite her to lunch. She refused, seeing no point in being polite. Hughes discovered she was taking golf lessons and, although an excellent golfer himself, enrolled in the same class. Linda felt flattered. "Why are you so difficult?" he asked. "What harm could there be in the two of us having lunch together?" Eventually Linda consented, insisting that her agent, Bill Schiffrin, come along. Hughes arrived for their date promptly in his old Chevrolet, and drove Linda and Schiffrin to his company's airfield in Culver City. Waiting for them was a Constellation, among the largest planes then in use. They boarded to find no pilot, no copilot, no one but the three of them. "We are going to lunch," Hughes announced. He took over the controls and flew the plane to San Francisco, where a car stood waiting. They were driven to the Fairmont Hotel to find that Hughes had rented an entire floor. A buffet was laid out and a small orchestra played, while waiters served with great solicitude.

Linda was overwhelmed, as she had never experienced such treatment. She was aware Hughes was courting practically every actress in Hollywood, yet she liked his quiet charm, found his tall, lanky looks attractive, and was impressed by his persistence. Gladys Witten, who was assigned to Linda on *Centennial Summer*, recalled fixing the actress's hair every morning in the stars' building. Betty Grable and Tyrone Power had dressing rooms downstairs; Linda was upstairs across the hall from Gene Tierney. Witten and Linda would hear the phone ring across the hall and notice Tierney talking to someone. Then shortly Linda's phone would ring, and Witten would answer. Invariably it was Howard Hughes making his morning rounds. Eventually Linda agreed to have dinner with him, assuring friends that he never so much as laid a hand on her.

Centennial Summer wrapped in May, and opened at the Roxy in July to cool reviews. By then Linda had already finished *My Darling Clementine*, a John Ford western, with its famous gunfight at O.K. Corral. Linda played Chihuahua, the Mexican mistress of Doc Holliday, and again she died, this time from Holliday's botched operation to remove a bullet. Henry Fonda played Wyatt Earp, while Victor Mature was the consumptive Holliday. The film meant a trip to Monument Valley, where most of the exterior scenes were shot. Linda had worked with Ford on the location footage for *Drums Along the Mohawk* early in her career, but now recognized him as a master filmmaker. Since Chihuahua was a saloon entertainer, she was heard singing in a throaty contralto, wearing an off-the-shoulder blouse throughout. Upon its release in the fall, the picture was favorably compared to Ford's *Stagecoach* and has since become a classic.

Linda had no sooner returned from Monument Valley than her telephone started ringing. Howard Hughes called time and again, asking her to have dinner with him. They had been seen out together before she left, dancing or talking alone at a secluded table. Life with Pev Marley had become increasingly strained, and Linda had had time on location to fantasize Hughes into a hero he never was. The wealthy playboy even gave her flying lessons, and they actually came down in a field once (fortunately neither was hurt). Linda found Hughes a strange man, wrapped up in himself, yet she was fascinated with him. Ann Miller insisted that Linda fell madly in love with him and that her friend was probably "Howard's biggest crush since Billie Dove."

They began seeing each other regularly. Linda dismissed gossip saying, "Rumors don't bother me. I learned long ago to disregard them." Hughes was a Texan, experienced with women, and showered Linda with the gifts she and Pearl had dreamed about. He took her to exclusive restaurants and all the fashionable clubs, and called her constantly. She talked with him just hours before an experimental plane he was testing crashed in Beverly Hills, almost killing him. Hughes was rushed to Good Samaritan Hospital, where he battled for his life. His chest had been crushed, his left lung had collapsed, and he suffered multiple fractures, extensive burns, and severe shock. Linda arrived at the hospital soon after the accident, to be stopped by an armed guard outside his door. She nervously asked questions and fended off photographers as best she could, until Lana Turner and other celebrities arrived and the press made staying impossible. Few thought Hughes would live, as telegrams poured in from around the country.

A week later, with *My Darling Clementine* completed and Hughes's condition improving, Linda announced that she and Pev Marley had separated. "Divorce proceedings will be filed soon," a Twentieth Century–Fox spokesman told reporters. "We intend to remain the best of friends," said Linda. "We have agreed to disagree. I'm moving in with some friends—I won't say who. And I'm going to file for a divorce—I can't say when." The separation came as no surprise to those close to her. As Linda matured, the father figure Pev had always been gradually lost its charm, and friends had watched their relationship wearing thin. "There was simply too much difference in their ages," Gladys Witten said. "Linda was growing up."

Linda convinced herself that she and Hughes would marry, and her heart became set on it, even though Hughes began backing off. Pev was still begging her to come home, but she was certain Hughes was serious. Ann Miller broke the news to her. Hughes had called Ann shortly before his crash, telling her he had a problem with Linda. He didn't want to hurt her, he explained to Ann over dinner, but neither was he planning marriage. "I think the world of Linda," he said. "I know that she's becoming very serious and really thinks I'm going to marry her. I haven't encouraged her in this at all because I don't want to get married." He also mentioned to Ann that Pev Marley had asked for a substantial sum of money before he would agree to let Linda go. "I'm not going to let any man do that to me," said Hughes. "It has sort of turned me off. I want no part of it."

Ann talked to Linda the next day, attempting to soften the blow, but Linda became hysterical. A few nights after Hughes was released from the hospital, Linda and Pev were invited to his house in Coldwater Canyon to talk. In the course of their discussion, Pev said to him, "I'll let her go. I'll go ahead with the divorce for $25,000 a year for life." Linda drew herself up and said, "Who the hell do you think you are? You're discussing me like a ham. You can both go straight to hell." And that was the end of whatever serious relationship she had with Howard Hughes.

About this time *Life* magazine asked Henriette Wyeth Hurd, the sister of painter Andrew Wyeth and wife of southwestern artist Peter Hurd, to go to Hollywood and paint certain stars. Linda was one of them. "I loved her at once," Henriette said, "but she had no idea of what was reality in life." The artist planned a portrait of Linda wearing a white Mexican blouse, similar to the one she wore in *My Darling Clementine*. "The portrait came to nothing," Henriette explained, "because by 10:30 Linda was beginning to drink brandy and milk, and she'd be just a blur. I can't work under those conditions."

Henriette quickly realized how lost Linda was, and although they gave up on the portrait, the two women became intimate friends. When the painter prepared to return to New Mexico, Pev's Aunt Mildred suggested Linda go with her. Ahead was *Forever Amber*, Linda's biggest screen challenge, but she didn't have to report to the studio until September. A vacation, away from everyone, might prove her salvation. So the kindly artist brought the unhappy actress home to the Hurd Ranch. They drove with Henriette's Hollywood hostess in a big Buick roadster, loaded with art supplies and luggage. They had at least three blowouts on the trip, and the heat grew unbearable. Near San Antonio, New Mexico, the car broke down completely, and they checked into an old hotel around two o'clock in the morning. Linda said to Henriette, "Bini, I hope I like your ranch!" And she did. She loved it from the start, and eventually bought property nearby.

Linda spent several weeks with the Hurds, came to adore Henriette's husband, Peter, and the Hurd children, and found a haven in the rustic setting. The Hurds worried about her constantly. She drank too much and laughed a great deal, but spent much of her time in New Mexico alone, trying to sort things out. Professionally she was at her peak, yet she was more miserable than she'd ever been in her life. She knew she'd made a fool of herself over Howard Hughes and felt terribly isolated. Pev had disappointed her, but already she missed his support. "I'm grown up now," she insisted publicly. "I can't stay a sweet little thing all my life. Life doesn't treat you that way. There comes a time when you learn what it's all about."

Celebrity

"Motion pictures have probably been more responsive to the corrupt ethic which governs American life than almost anything else," observed film composer David Raksin. "The effort is to separate oneself from everyone else who is clawing to be separated and be noticed apart from the throng. People who shouldn't give a damn are like that. That's the thinking when the Hollywood Mama has to separate her daughter from everybody else. The children of such parents get a peculiar idea of the world."

Linda reached her greatest separation, the height of her celebrity, shortly before she left with Henriette Wyeth Hurd for New Mexico. With *My Darling Clementine* finished and Linda's rift with Pev Marley made public only days before, Darryl Zanuck announced that she would step into the title role of Fox's much awaited, multimillion-dollar production of *Forever Amber*. Kathleen Winsor's bestselling novel of Restoration England had been hailed during the final months of World War II as the raciest book in years, and Twentieth Century–Fox paid $200,000 for the screen rights, primarily for the title. The studio was prepared to spend $5 million on a Technicolor epic, making it the most costly film Fox had produced. For Linda, Amber was the chance of a lifetime, the most coveted screen role since Scarlett O'Hara.

Shooting on the picture had begun four months earlier with British actress Peggy Cummins in the part of Amber St. Clare. Not quite twenty, the pert blonde had practically no acting experience, but had won the role because Zanuck liked her. After five and a half weeks of filming under John Stahl's direction, the production was shut down. "The footage so far shot," Zanuck declared, "fails to measure up to the high standard of quality originally planned. We will have to review this footage and determine afterwards what changes will be made when production is resumed." Although Stahl was later replaced, the major problem rested with Peggy Cummins, who simply was too inexperienced for the central role. "Peggy flashed her two expressions for thirty-nine days," explained actor Cornel Wilde, who played Bruce Carleton in both versions. "At the end of thirty-nine days Zanuck finally admitted she just couldn't do it. He finally gave up and had the negative and all the prints burned, so that nobody would ever rake that up and show what a horrible mistake he had made."

By the time Linda was announced as Cummins's replacement, the studio had already invested over $1 million in *Forever Amber*, and pressure had built to make certain the film was a financial success. Otto Preminger was selected to replace Stahl as director, while Zanuck insisted that the cast—with the exception of Wilde as the male lead—be altered. Schedule conflicts for Linda ruled out her playing Catana in *Captain from Castile*, the role she had counted on for two years. "To get the best part of my life, Amber in *Forever Amber*," said Linda, "I had to give up Catana. I guess you never quite get everything you want." Jean Peters, who ironically married Howard Hughes later, would make her screen debut in *Captain from Castile*, while Peggy Cummins was shifted to a less demanding role in *The Late George Apley*. Meanwhile Linda realized that her future rested on the success of a film already in trouble.

Zanuck, normally so adept at selecting the right story and putting the proper talent together, had purchased Kathleen Winsor's 972-page novel convinced that its controversial title alone would assure screen success. "It was a terrible book," said screenwriter Philip Dunne, who worked on the script for nearly a year. "It was an amateur book, but somehow it caught on. It was a dollar catcher. It was supposed to be raunchy, and of course here were the censors looking at us like, 'Don't you dare make a move.' I wanted to make a spoof out of it. But Zanuck said, 'No. It's a bestseller. Let's go with it.'"

Dunne remained convinced the only way to save the project was to turn it into a satirical comedy. After several weeks of uninspired work, the writer turned in what he considered "a dreary, dutifully sanitized script," which Zanuck judged an improvement over the previous attempt. When director Otto Preminger was called in to salvage the project, another rewrite was ordered. Preminger had wanted no part of *Forever Amber*, telling Zanuck, "I read the book when it was sent around by the story department. I found it terrible." After the director saw what John Stahl had already put on film he was more negative than ever. Zanuck reminded Preminger that he was a highly paid member of the Fox production team and insisted he had an obligation to salvage the picture. "I won't blame you if it doesn't turn out well," Zanuck supposedly told Preminger. The director demanded that he be allowed to bring in a writer of his own choosing, Ring Lardner, Jr. "For a few hilarious hours I thought I was free of the whole sorry mess," Philip Dunne wrote. But Zanuck didn't want Preminger to gain complete control of the project and asked Dunne to stay on. So Dunne and Lardner were thrust together on a script neither liked. "I thought *Forever Amber* was essentially worthless," Dunne confessed. "Ring shared my contempt for the material, so we worked well together."

When Cornel Wilde learned Otto Preminger had been assigned to *Amber*, he wanted off the picture himself. The two had worked together on *Centennial Summer* and were barely on speaking terms. Wilde resented the director's sarcasm and tyrannical behavior and from the beginning had found the script of *Forever Amber* pompous and static. But Wilde was a popular star at the time, and Zanuck needed his name on a production already headed for trouble. Linda, on the other hand, viewed *Amber* as a golden opportunity, as did nearly every other actress in Hollywood. Her selection for the plum role came as a huge surprise, especially to Linda herself. "I was practically living and breathing Catana when I got word I was to play the new Amber," she said. "Naturally it was the most thrilling surprise that has ever come to me. I thought I was the luckiest girl in Hollywood."

During lunch at the commissary, a procession of dignitaries walked over to her table to offer congratulations. Suddenly she felt like queen of the lot. Salutations poured in from writers, producers, and top executives. When she walked around the studio, gazes were fastened on her from sources that counted. Instinctively she knew this was her moment, her chance for superstardom.

When Linda reported for work in September, after returning from New Mexico, she was immediately placed on a rigid diet. Next it was decided she would work with Constance Collier, the distinguished British actress and coach, in an effort to affect something of the speech of an Englishwoman. Since *Forever Amber* involved forty-two costume changes, Linda spent hours in fittings, working out the elaborate wardrobe that made Amber's role so dazzling. A big question arose over whether she should become a blonde for the part. Finally her brunette tresses were bleached in stages, each lighter than the one before. Gladys Witten, on tour with actress Vivian Blaine, received a phone call asking her to return to the studio at once. Thirty-four hairstyles had to be worked out.

Linda celebrated her twenty-third birthday as a blonde, surrounded by more publicity than she had ever received in her life. Most of the top journalists wanted to interview her, and her portrait in Amber's costumes appeared prominently in all the fan magazines. *Esquire* artist Alberto Varga painted her in a Grecian gown, while publicists assured the public that "Kathleen Winsor herself could scarcely have picked a better person for the intriguing character of Amber than talented Linda Darnell." Articles outlined how Linda's career paralleled Amber's, coming as they both did from humble backgrounds and working their way up. "My first seven years in Hollywood were a series of discouraging struggles for me," Linda told a reporter. "For a while it looked as though the Darnell-versus-Hollywood tussle was going to find Darnell coming out second best. The next seven years aren't going to be the same."

Suddenly she was given better tables in restaurants and spoken to endearingly by Hollywood moguls. When asked about her relationship with Howard Hughes, Linda refused to comment. Since their separation, she had been seen out with Pev Marley, and she now told reporters that the chief source of their difficulties was that she and her husband didn't have time for each other because of the demands of their work. With *Amber* in preparation the studio wasn't unhappy over her current talk of divorce. Since Linda was to play an immoral character, the last thing the Fox publicity office wanted was to have the star happily married. A slightly bad reputation at the moment could even help out at the box office.

Meanwhile Cornel Wilde was still trying to get out of the picture. "The whole thing was a bad experience for me," the actor explained. "I'd had enough with the Cummins footage and didn't want to work with Preminger." But Zanuck's head was on the block with his New York office, and he needed Wilde's name on the marquee. "They thought I was holding out for more money," the actor said, "and agents did get me a huge raise to $200,000 a year for forty weeks, which was the third highest salary on the lot."

Filming resumed in mid-October and would continue for 125 days. For Linda this meant getting up at 4:30 A.M. and racing to the studio, where she spent an hour and a half having her hair done and another hour each morning with the costumer. She normally finished work around eight o'clock in the evening, although the picture involved a great deal of night shooting. Soon the strain took its toll. Linda looked worried, and bit her nails constantly. Frequently she called Pev to ask his advice on scenes. "I had dinner with Pev last evening," she told a columnist. "I was tired and he massaged my neck. It seemed just like the old days."

Otto Preminger did nothing to make her burden easier. "Otto liked to break actors down so that he would be in control," Cornel Wilde said. "He would do cruel things, mostly to little people." Linda, who had disliked Preminger earlier, came to loathe him. "Tweedles was not one to dislike many people," her sister Undeen assured, "but Preminger she couldn't tolerate. He was a good director, but a mean SOB. She hated him."

On November 11, the production suffered another setback when Linda was sent home with a fever. Her physician, Dr. Samuel Alter, diagnosed the illness as mastoiditis, although the strenuous dieting she had undergone contributed to her condition. "Linda is a very sick girl," Louella Parsons announced in her column. "Twentieth Century–Fox may have to start calling it 'Forever and Forever Amber.'" A week later Linda was back before the cameras, feeling miserable. Her doctor ordered plenty of rest, that she not drink, and that a nurse be with her at all times to supervise her diet.

With Linda sick, the studio decided they would have to shoot around her and rearranged some dueling sequences between Bruce Carleton and another of Amber's lovers. Preminger wanted the look of an early morning fog in an English countryside setting. They first tried dry ice, which quickly vaporized and failed to hold the effect. "So they got Nujol," Cornel Wilde remembered, "an oil mixture which was a laxative. They sprayed huge quantities of that stuff up in the air, and the lights would catch it and it would look pretty. Then it would settle. Half the cast and crew got diarrhea, breathing and swallowing it. The grass, of course, was slippery, just like slime."

Before long Wilde caught a cold, actor Richard Greene tripped over his sword and bruised himself, and another player suffered a wrenched back when he fell from a horse. The fire sequence, which had required days of preparation, was shot at three in the morning, with traffic blocked off for a mile around the Fox lot. Nonetheless the simulated burning of London resulted in scores of telephone calls to the local fire department, which assured callers that the studio had fire trucks standing by. The only casualty was Linda herself, who got burned, although not badly. "She just escaped death," cinematographer Leon Shamroy recalled, "because during the Great Fire a roof caved in. I pulled the camera back, and she just got out in time. She was terrified of fire, almost as though she had a premonition."

Linda grew convinced that Otto Preminger was holding her back in the part. She gave up on an English accent, but was seen at parties with her coach, Constance Collier. Her only dates during the making of *Forever Amber* were with Pev Marley. "You know, at this moment," she said, "I am more in love with Pev than any other man. I'm having cocktails with him tonight. He's the best friend I have in the whole world."

As filming progressed and the pressures mounted, she began relying more heavily on Pev than ever, turning to him for counsel her family couldn't provide. During Christmas Linda found living alone unbearable and spent the holidays either with him or his Aunt Mildred. Linda and Pev celebrated the New Year together and three weeks later announced that their trial separation was over. "We know now that we're really in love and always have been," the actress said. "There never was anyone else for either of us." The couple informed the press that as soon as *Forever Amber* was finished, they would take the honeymoon they had never had. "I had to separate from my husband to save our marriage from going on the rocks," the fan magazines quoted Linda. No mention was made of Howard Hughes.

Linda moved back into the house on Amalfi Drive, finding her clothes exactly as she had left them. Part of the Marleys' agreement was that they would adopt a baby, and negotiations for an adoption soon began in earnest. Linda was wildly excited, Pev initially less so. "I have long wanted to adopt a baby," she said, "but Pev wasn't sure it would be a good idea. An only child, he isn't used to babies. Now he's as enthusiastic as I am."

Fan magazines turned Linda into an expert on how to save crumbling marriages. "It frightens me to think how close we came to missing the wonderful thing we have today," she reputedly wrote after their reconciliation. "I learned a lot during the time I was separated from my husband. But it was all mixed up with misery and emotion. Not until we were back together did I have the detachment to analyze what had happened to us."

Yet life on Amalfi Drive was never so sunny. The making of *Forever Amber* continued to be a draining experience for Linda, while Pev was busy at Warner Brothers shooting *Life with Father*, for which he would receive an Academy Award nomination. Their relationship never reached the happy tranquility chronicled in the fan magazines. More and more Pev let Linda have her way, yet he continued to needle her. As she grew older, Pev's lecturing became increasingly annoying, and the bickering soon started again, more intense than ever.

Occasionally Linda dropped by her parents' house while she was making *Forever Amber*, but her visits were becoming less frequent. Although the Darnells' neighborhood was quite conservative, the notorious gangster Mickey Cohen lived around the corner from them. Somebody threw a bomb through his window and caused a fire, and although no one was hurt, the neighbors drew up a petition to oust Cohen. When they approached Pearl, she refused to sign it, and wrote a letter of protest. Mr. Cohen, she insisted, was a "mighty fine" neighbor: he was quiet, kept his property up, and never had loud parties. Cohen called Pearl to thank her for her support. "That cracked me up," said Cal's friend Trudi Dieterle, "because if the neighbors had had more guts, they'd have done something to get Roy and Pearl and their roosters out of there, too."

Cal was still trying desperately to be one of the boys. Someone dared his group to try shoplifting, and he accepted the challenge, going with Trudi and some other friends through the stores of Beverly Hills. "I just leaned over and picked up a gold cigarette lighter," he later admitted, "put it in my pocket, and gave it to a friend for his graduation present. That was being one of the gang." Four of them walked into Saks Fifth Avenue on Wilshire Boulevard one day. A girl in the group picked up a pair of gold-plated glasses and put them on, while Cal stole a compact. They were leaving the store when a house detective stopped them and ushered all four into the manager's office. When the management discovered Cal was Linda Darnell's brother, they let the teenagers go home without notifying the police.

Monte meanwhile had won the championship for Roman riding

at the Los Angeles Horse Show. As a result she had been offered a contract with an equestrian troupe, but Pearl insisted she finish high school first. After graduation she began working with a rodeo, the same show that had exhibited Emperor Hirohito's horse. By late 1947 she was riding for Mark Smith during the opening of the Polo Grounds in New York, where Roy Rogers and the Sons of the Pioneers were headliners. Monte's specialty was riding two horses at once bareback. With her youngest daughter's career taking off, Pearl assumed something of a new lease on life, since she insisted on traveling with Monte and supervising her life as much as possible. "She's having more fun with Monte than she ever did with me," Linda remarked thankfully.

Throughout *Forever Amber*'s interminable shooting schedule, Linda alternately dieted and declared she was eating her last fattening meal until the picture was finished. As the production entered its fifth month, her exhaustion neared a breaking point. "It went on and on," wrote Otto Preminger, "the longest shooting schedule I ever had. Zanuck was determined that this would be the biggest and most expensive and most successful film in history." With three days left on the picture, its star collapsed on the set and had to be taken home. The next day she returned, only to collapse again. Officially *Amber* was completed on March 11, 1947, but Linda and Cornel Wilde were called back for retakes when the censorship office objected to Linda's "heaving bosoms." In the end the picture cost $6 million.

Linda left for Europe as soon as the film was finished, arguing already that *Forever Amber* had been ruined by Hollywood censors. Exhausted, she sailed for Paris, determined to combine travel with rest. Pev had planned to make the trip with her, but commitments at Warner Brothers forced him to remain behind. Linda found herself uncomfortable in Europe, and later claimed the trip had proven to be a nightmare. She was ill much of the time, had little appetite, and lost twelve pounds. She visited art galleries, attended film festivals, and had brief sessions in Zurich with psychologist Carl Jung, which she found personally revealing.

She arrived back in Los Angeles in August, in time to celebrate her husband's forty-eighth birthday. Since neither Linda nor Pev had an immediate assignment, they made a whirlwind trip together to Cuba, aboard the S.S. *Quirigua*. Upon their return Linda invited a few friends in to preview *Forever Amber* and was deeply disappointed, sensing that the picture could never measure up to its publicity. Everyone agreed that she looked marvelous, yet Linda knew what the critical reaction was likely to be.

The picture opened at the Roxy Theater in New York on October 22, greeted by record-breaking crowds. Bosley Crowther found Kathleen Winsor's "remarkable harlot" considerably cleansed on the screen, her lovers reduced in number, and the details of her affairs less boldly told. "It doesn't spare the innuendos," the *Times* critic conceded. "You have to be awfully innocent not to gather what's going on." The film, Crowther felt, ran about an hour too long, with the London plague sequence the most impressive episode. "Certainly a more becoming Amber could hardly be conceived than the firm, luxurious creature that Linda Darnell makes," the critic concluded. "Costumed in a wealth of brilliant dresses and perilously low-cut gowns and armed to the teeth with makeup, she parades herself in truly sensual style. Moderate exception might be taken of her conventional performance as a tramp, but the part doesn't offer subtleties."

Still, the picture topped all previous attendance at the Roxy and did a land-office business throughout the country at road show prices. Financially the film was a success, returning $8 million during its first year, although it was never the blockbuster Zanuck hoped for. While Linda had acquitted herself admirably, she could not save a project that was artistically doomed from the outset. Although the picture by no means proved a disaster in Linda's career, neither did it bring her the superstar status she longed for. Her prestige as Amber brought her good roles for the next few years—a string of sultry sirens she played well—yet the parts did not allow her to become a cult figure.

"Amber didn't do right by her men—or me," the disappointed star said. "Somehow or other we fumbled the ball." Whenever she mentioned the picture to friends later, she referred to it as "Forever Under." Within the industry there was respect for her, mainly because with no experience she had started in films and built herself into the star of a multimillion-dollar production. Yet scriptwriter Philip Dunne remained convinced that *Forever Amber* deserved the lumps it took from critics, insisting it was a movie that should never have been made. "Linda Darnell was certainly far better than Peggy Cummins," Dunne said, "although the title carried the picture. It became a conversation piece. But *Forever Amber* was a national joke."

Publicity photograph of Linda Darnell during her later television and
stage work. (General Artists Corporation)

Margaret Pearl
Brown as a girl.
(Courtesy of Cleo
Brown Johnson)

Roy, Pearl, Undeen, Monetta,
and Monte Darnell on a family
outing to Glen Rose, Texas,
1929. (Courtesy of Undeen
Darnell Hunter)

Calvin Darnell, Linda's
brother, with Spot in
Dallas. (Courtesy of
Cal Darnell)

Monetta Darnell in her "Alice Blue Gown," late in her elementary school years in Dallas. (Courtesy of Undeen Darnell Hunter)

Monetta in Dallas shortly before talent scout Ivan Kahn discovered her. (Courtesy of Undeen Darnell Hunter)

Linda visiting Fort Ord, California, 1942. (Courtesy of Undeen Darnell Hunter)

Linda and J. Peverell Marley at the time of their marriage, 1943.

Linda and Tyrone Power in a scene from *Blood and Sand*. (Courtesy of the Academy of Motion Picture Arts and Sciences)

Linda Darnell at fifteen, with her first film behind her. (Photograph by Frank Powolny, Twentieth Century–Fox Film Corporation)

Linda Darnell arriving in
Dallas for the premiere of
Hotel for Women, 1939. (Cour-
tesy of Undeen Darnell
Hunter)

Roy, Linda, and Pearl at the homecoming ceremonies during the premiere of *Hotel for Women.* (Courtesy of Undeen Darnell Hunter)

Undeen and Linda at Santa Monica, May 7, 1939. (Courtesy of Undeen Darnell Hunter)

Mickey Rooney and Linda at the amusement park in Santa Monica, 1940. (Courtesy of Undeen Darnell Hunter)

Linda and Tyrone Power on the set of *Blood and Sand,* 1941. (Courtesy of the Academy of Motion Picture Arts and Sciences)

Linda in *Chad Hanna*, 1940. (Courtesy of Undeen Darnell Hunter)

Linda in *Buffalo Bill*, 1944. (Courtesy of Undeen Darnell Hunter)

Linda in *Fallen Angel*, 1946. (Courtesy of Undeen Darnell Hunter)

Linda in *Forever Amber*, 1947. (Courtesy of Undeen Darnell Hunter)

Linda, Monte Darnell, and Linda's hairdresser, Gladys Witten, at the time of *Forever Amber*. (Courtesy of Gladys Witten Cox)

Linda, Gladys Witten, and Gladys's mother, sister, and nephews on the set of *Forever Amber*. (Courtesy of Gladys Witten Cox)

Linda, Ann Sothern, and Jeanne Crain in *A Letter to Three Wives,* 1949. (Courtesy of the Academy of Motion Picture Arts and Sciences)

Linda and Paul Douglas in *A Letter to Three Wives.* (Courtesy of the Academy of Motion Picture Arts and Sciences)

Linda and Rex Harrison
in the original version of
Unfaithfully Yours, 1948.
(Courtesy of the Academy of Motion Picture
Arts and Sciences)

Linda and Richard Widmark in *Slattery's Hurricane,* 1949. (Courtesy of
Undeen Darnell Hunter)

Linda, Philip Liebmann, and Linda's six-year-old daughter, Lola Marley, shortly after Linda's second marriage. (Courtesy of Undeen Darnell Hunter)

Linda, Gale Edlund, and Ann Lee in the star's first stage appearance, *A Roomful of Roses* at the Sombrero Theatre in Phoenix, 1956. (Courtesy of Undeen Darnell Hunter.)

Calvin Darnell standing before a poster for his sister's Broadway debut at the Playhouse Theatre, 1956. (Courtesy of Undeen Darnell Hunter)

Linda's third marriage, to Merle Roy Robertson, March 3, 1957. (Courtesy of Undeen Darnell Hunter)

Linda and Thomas Hayward during their nightclub tour, 1960–61. (Courtesy of Undeen Darnell Hunter)

Linda with Rory Calhoun and director R. G. Springsteen on the set of her last film, *Black Spurs,* 1964.

Linda Darnell as Lora May in *A Letter to Three Wives,* her best role.
(Courtesy of the Academy of Motion Picture Arts and Sciences)

Back Street Affair

The studio instructed Linda to keep her hair blonde until *Forever Amber*'s London premiere. Because of a new tax in England on American films, the opening of the picture there was postponed, so the star went into her next assignment, *The Walls of Jericho*, with light tresses. Linda felt she looked better as a brunette and knew that the bleach was ruining her normally thick head of hair, yet the prattle around Hollywood was that Linda Darnell had been miraculously transformed. "I don't know any girl who has developed in personality and sophistication as Linda has this past year," wrote Louella Parsons. "She used to be such a mousey Miss—beautiful but uninteresting. Recent reports from European capitals are that she has become a dazzler."

Beyond question Linda's being cast as a slut rather than a virgin made her a more interesting property both for her studio and for gossip columnists. She had come to accept that the only way to survive in Hollywood was to be tough. To simulate a tough facade her language took on bluer shades, while liquor gave her the courage to unleash some of the fury raging inside. On the screen she became a model of hard-boiled determination, playing ambitious women using their wiles to scheme and conquer. Personally she was much less successful, remaining too softhearted and loving to internalize the image she hoped would protect her.

The role of Algeria Wedge in *The Walls of Jericho* was typical of the parts Linda would play over the next five years. The project was a favorite of director John Stahl, who had called the Paul Wellman novel to Darryl Zanuck's attention even before his aborted attempt at *Forever Amber*. "In the years I have been on the lot there have been few story properties that I have gone out of my way to mention," Stahl wrote the story department, "*A Tree Grows in Brooklyn, Leave Her to Heaven,* and now *The Walls of Jericho,* which I feel is a story that has some swell characters and will make a great picture."

Screenwriter Lamar Trotti also thought the Wellman novel, while no literary masterpiece, had great pictorial possibilities, and it became Linda's twenty-third picture in eight years, marking the beginning of her career as a serious actress. She looked fresh and thin in *The Walls of Jericho,* although the picture itself received tepid reviews when it opened in August 1948. Linda was considered effective as the scheming villain, although most of the acting plaudits went to Anne Baxter as a lawyer and Ann Dvorak for her portrait of an alcoholic.

While *The Walls of Jericho* was still before the cameras, Linda and Pev were busily decorating a nursery for their long-awaited adopted child. The baby was born on January 5, 1948, and arrived at their Amalfi Drive home on January 11, two days before *Jericho* wrapped. Named Charlotte Mildred for Pev's mother and aunt, respectively, the blonde baby girl was called Lola. "Dear Monetta," Pev wrote on a card the day Lola was born. "You'll be the best, wonderful mother a girl ever had. I love you." He took a series of pictures of Linda, her blonde hair in a chignon, holding the child. "Your first day at home," Linda wrote beside the snapshots in Lola's baby book.

The child's arrival was not made public for another ten weeks, when the press reported that the Marleys had received the baby from Chicago. Presumably there was concern that Lola's birth mother might discover who the baby's adoptive parents were. "The simple truth is, I can't have a baby," Linda told reporters, "and that's more painful for a woman to face than any childbirth." Linda wanted to see her baby's natural mother and arranged to wait outside a Westwood ice cream parlor for the young woman to come out. The mother was with her older child and had no idea Linda Darnell had adopted her recently born daughter, since Linda didn't introduce herself. "Mother was always very open with me about my natural mother," a mature Lola said. "She told me that my mother was very young and not married and that I look very much like her."

Within the Darnell family it was rumored that Pev was Lola's biological father. Monte was certain that with the couple's reconciliation and decision to adopt, Pev had agreed so long as the child was his. "They made one of those harebrained Hollywood pacts," Monte claimed. "Pev wanted to be the father. And Linda agreed because she had wanted a child, and there was no way she was going to [conceive one]. As it turned out, Lola looked exactly like Pev. He couldn't have denied her." Undeen and Cal both admitted they always thought Pev was Lola's biological father, but quickly added that nobody ever told them that, certainly not

Linda. "I don't know anything more than that it's a rumor," Lola herself said. "It doesn't matter to me one way or the other. If my father is in fact my father, that's fine. If he's not, that's okay, too. I don't think Mother really cared whose child or what child. I think she simply wanted a child."

Since Lola's adoption was kept secret until March, Linda was already busy on her next picture before friends at the studio could give her a shower. She returned to her dressing room at lunch hour one day during the making of *Unfaithfully Yours* to find Gladys Witten, her stand-in, and about a dozen others gathered with gifts. Linda was ecstatic, showing off pictures that Pev had taken of their baby daughter. "As soon as Lola is old enough to understand, I'm going to let her know that she's more than a daughter who happened to me," Linda said. "I think 'adopted' is the wrong word—I always substitute 'chosen child' instead." She insisted that she and her husband planned to adopt a boy within a few years so that Lola would have a playmate.

Lola's nurse wrote Linda regularly whenever the actress was away from home, telling her about her daughter's first tooth, first step, all the happenings most mothers know from daily contact. "There are special things between parents and child you can't get in a letter," Lola said later. "Maybe that's why Mother and I never were really close until I was older and we could approach each other on a more adult level. But we missed all the fifteen years before, and I think that's sad. Mother deserved better than that. It wasn't her fault; she had to work and couldn't give what I needed most. Anybody can get pregnant, but it's taking care of a child that makes you a parent. I feel sorry Mother missed that."

Unfaithfully Yours allowed Linda to stay in Los Angeles for the first few weeks of motherhood, since it was shot entirely at the Twentieth Century–Fox studio. Written, produced, and directed by Preston Sturges, the sophisticated black comedy was under-rated until years later, even by Darryl Zanuck. In 1983 the story was remade with Dudley Moore in the role Rex Harrison created, but the idea of combining humor with symphonic music was con-sidered to be over the heads of the average audience in 1948, when the original version was released. Zanuck had agreed to film the script mainly for the prestige of having Preston Sturges on the lot. Linda proved perfect in the part of Daphne, the young wife of the conductor who thought her unfaithful. Many found it the best acting she had done, certainly her most subtle.

During the shooting of *Unfaithfully Yours*, Linda's hairdresser, Gladys Witten, introduced her to Jeanne and Richard Curtis, Linda's best friends from that point on. The Chicago couple were in California for a visit, and the three of them immediately became close. Jeanne was pregnant with their daughter Patty at the time. "Honey, you have your duck in the oven," Linda said when they met. "Linda was very outgoing, but also a very private person," said Jeanne. "She was knowledgeable, well-read, very intelligent. She had gained a lot of knowledge through her travels, and she was a very warm person. But she kept to herself." Jeanne possessed the business sense Linda lacked, and the star considered Dick a refreshing change from the Hollywood phonies she had come to despise.

When *Unfaithfully Yours* wrapped in late April, Linda enjoyed a few weeks at home with Lola before beginning *A Letter to Three Wives*, her best film. "You were very fond of chewing on Mommy's turquoise beads," the actress wrote in Lola's baby book. "Mommy started to do a head of you in clay, but you couldn't be still long enough, so I never finished it." The Marleys had planned a trip to England, but Pev's involvement with *Look for the Silver Lining* at Warner Brothers ruled that out. Conflicting work schedules always seemed to interfere with their personal plans.

While Vera Caspary and Joseph L. Mankiewicz tightened the script Linda would be filming that summer—first from five, then to four, finally to three wives—the actress managed a whirlwind vacation alone to the Hurd ranch, staying in the guest house. She loved to go without makeup and spent much of her time in New Mexico drinking. "After three days of great fun and marvelous good humor, she would not show up for breakfast or for lunch," Henriette Wyeth Hurd recalled, "and this became worse and worse. Yet Linda had a kind of exquisite dignity in spite of her drunkenness. She'd behave badly sometimes, but no one really disliked her or even blamed her. She was like a little girl in shackles."

Linda frequently tied up the Hurd's telephone talking with her agent or the studio. "Out of that waxen skin and those exquisite lips," Henriette Hurd maintained, "came a stream of profanity that was really quite imaginative." Eventually the local operator asked, "Mrs. Hurd, will you tell Miss Darnell to try to control her language?"

The star returned to Los Angeles determined to buy a ranch as near the Hurds' as possible, where she could build an adobe house. She planned to live there between pictures and felt it would make an ideal place for Lola to grow up. She seemed more content than she had been in months. "Funny how a husband can also be one's greatest friend," she wrote on a postcard.

More and more the timid girl from Texas was giving way to a spirited, no-nonsense woman—honest, good-natured, yet not beyond playing the prima donna for fun. She tried to camouflage her insecurities with a foul mouth, but few were fooled. Gradually her taste in food and clothes improved. She developed a sense of which wines went with which dishes, liked big band music, and had a passion for perfumes and scented lingerie. Yet she preferred informal wear, peasant blouses and comfortable, loose fitting dresses, and adored Mexican jewelry. Pev's Aunt Mildred helped develop Linda's sense of style, and Pev contributed more than his share. But no one could teach her how to protect herself in the Hollywood jungle that would soon consume her. "Mother's little Frankenstein monster was helpless and never could defend herself," assured Cal. "She thought she could. But she was as helpless as Mother, who couldn't even protect herself against me. Linda was tragic."

Linda's role in *A Letter to Three Wives* was easily the best of the trio of leads. She had risen in Darryl Zanuck's estimation after *Forever Amber*, and perhaps for the first time he felt she was a solid gamble in an earthy part. *A Letter to Three Wives* was shaping up into a script of quality, which Zanuck was confident would also be good box office. Although Zanuck privately found Joseph Mankiewicz an "arrogant bastard," he had faith in Mankiewicz's genius, both as a writer and as a director.

Even in the first draft Lora May, the part Linda played, was viewed as a masterful portrait of a hard-boiled, cynical gold digger with a tender heart. Paired with Linda was veteran radio actor Paul Douglas, making his screen debut after a huge success on Broadway in *Born Yesterday*. They matched each other scene for scene, with Linda revealing a remarkable sense of comedy. Lora May's classic line came in response to an older friend's suggestion, "If I was you, I'd show more of what I got. Maybe wear somethin' with beads." Linda replied, "What I got don't need beads."

The part quickly became Linda's *tour de force*. Joe Mankiewicz had endeared himself to her early in the production, when they were filming a scene in which Lora May eyes a photograph of Addie Ross, the common nemesis of the three wives, sitting on a grand piano. To elicit the necessary look of disgust from the actress, Mankiewicz had substituted a portrait of Otto Preminger in a Nazi uniform. Linda thought the prank was hilarious and began to relax with the director, even though she considered him an intellectual, which she clearly wasn't.

Much of the outdoor filming on the picture was done on the Hudson River, so that Linda was away from home for several weeks, spending most of her time in the East with Gladys Witten. "We were staying in an old hotel in Connecticut," the hairstylist remembered, "and our beds were straw." One night Joe Mankiewicz said, "I think we should get away from here." So he, Gladys, Linda, and their makeup man went into New York City by limousine. "We had a delightful time," Gladys recalled. "We were all just crazy about Mankiewicz." They ate in a marvelous restaurant and caught the Dean Martin-Jerry Lewis nightclub act, which was then the rage at the Copacabana. Mankiewicz teased Linda about her southern accent. "What do you expect?" she told him. "Here I've been working on my voice for years, and now I have a maid from New Orleans and a hairdresser from Kentucky!"

For nine straight days it rained in New York, forcing work on *A Letter to Three Wives* to stop. While the studio fumed about needless expenses, the director waited for the weather to clear. Mankiewicz had developed a reputation as a Pygmalion, since his leading ladies invariably seemed to fall in love with him, despite his being a married man. He and Gene Tierney had had a romance during the making of *Dragonwyck*, and his affair with Judy Garland had been emotionally wrenching for the unstable singer. Now it was becoming apparent that Linda Darnell had fallen in love with the genius responsible for the best performance of her career. She talked about him constantly, always full of glowing respect, but her love for him was obvious.

Fourteen years older than Linda, Joseph Mankiewicz had been born in Wilkes-Barre, Pennsylvania and raised in New York City. The son of an academic father and the brother of Herman Mankiewicz, the brilliant author of *Citizen Kane*, Joe grew up a fiercely ambitious boy, always in the shadow of his father and older brother. He graduated from Columbia University at age nineteen, and shortly sailed for Europe. There Mankiewicz became fascinated with the theater, celebrated actresses, and the company of distinguished artists. He soon married Elizabeth

Young, a union that lasted two and a half years, and then met actress Rosa Stradner, a beautiful, statuesque blonde who had been a star of Max Reinhardt's theater in Vienna. Stradner was brought to Metro-Goldwyn-Mayer while Mankiewicz was a writer there, and the two married during the summer of 1939. Rosa's hold over her husband and her psychological miseries were clear from the outset. His life with her was never a happy one, for she made things dreadful, repeatedly threatening to kill herself. "He was actually physically afraid of Rosa," Mankiewicz's friend Dr. Marc Rabwin said, "as she could be violent. Joe is a very forceful person and can be pretty dominating. But where Rosa was involved, he would accede to anything just to keep peace."

They had two sons, and when Rosa was not indisposed, the couple made fabulous hosts, noted for their fine cuisine and sparkling conversation. During the early 1940s Mankiewicz moved to Twentieth Century–Fox, where he collaborated with Nunnally Johnson in adapting *The Keys to the Kingdom* for the screen. Then in 1945 he replaced Ernst Lubitsch as director of *Dragonwyck*, a screenplay he himself had written. "Joe was very bright and very able," said writer Philip Dunne. "And he was extremely talented. His big mistake, I think, was that he tried to do too much." Certainly Mankiewicz's ego was tremendous, although he seemed to have the wherewithal to back it up. He excelled with verbal touches, little darts and innuendoes, while he consistently proved a fascinating raconteur. Around the Twentieth Century–Fox lot Mankiewicz became recognized as the house wit—a brilliant phrasemaker who could write dialogue better than almost anyone. He was equally competitive on the softball field, where he played second base for the Fox team, and bragged that he had slept with the leading lady on every picture he had made.

A Letter to Three Wives marked Mankiewicz's breakthrough, elevating him into the big league. He hated the glitter and social climbing of Hollywood, while his overriding strength was an ability to give substance to a script without destroying its commercial appeal. *A Letter to Three Wives* was not only a psychological comedy, but also a critical look at contemporary society—examining money, sex, middle-class mores, and class consciousness in postwar suburban America. "Joe Mankiewicz was a Svengali type of director," said studio executive Howard W. Koch. "He would really get into the soul of somebody, especially women. Joe really hypnotized the ladies. He mesmerized them. They all fell in love with him because he was a handsome, virile, dashing kind of guy. They were awed by his ability, and he controlled them."

When the *Letter to Three Wives* company returned to Los Angeles, Mankiewicz's romance with Linda Darnell was no secret on the Twentieth Century–Fox lot. Their private lunches in her dressing room scarcely escaped notice, and it was soon known around the studio that "she was his girl." Friends recognized how deeply in love Linda was, and most of them feared repercussions. "Joe Mankiewicz was an interesting and complicated man," composer David Raksin observed. "He looked a lot more innocent than he was. Joe was renowned for ripping off the ladies." One of the girls in the publicity department made a practice of calling Mankiewicz and talking to him at length in a seductive voice, just to put him on. "This very sophisticated man got hooked by this young girl," Raksin continued. "She really ran a number on him. But Joe, I guess you could say, ripped off Ms. Darnell. It's astonishing how many of the most beautiful women in Hollywood, the so-called love goddesses, were actually victims who got ripped off by guys left and right."

On July 15, 1948, with three weeks of shooting left on the picture, the press confirmed that Linda Darnell and Pev Marley had again separated. No mention was made of Mankiewicz, but Linda said she intended to file for divorce. The separation was a brief one, with Pev insisting they be sensible about their situation. Mankiewicz clearly had no intention of leaving his wife, and the Marleys had Lola to consider. When *A Letter to Three Wives* was completed in August, Linda was back at the Amalfi Drive house, although her relationship with Joe Mankiewicz would continue for another six years. She assured Jeanne Curtis and others close to her that he was, and always would be, the great love of her life, referring to him later as her "back street affair." Old enough to be a father figure, dashing enough to be a lover, cultured and intellectual enough to serve as mentor, Mankiewicz represented the perfect combination Linda sought in a man, and she was willing to risk everything.

Joseph Mankiewicz never talked about Linda, not even to his biographer, except to say that he "adored" her and that "she was a marvelous girl with very terrifying personal problems." He had a record of persuading women who fell in love with him that they were in serious need of psychiatric treatment. Judy Garland had been one, Linda became another. On her lover's advice she entered psychoanalysis. "After she got involved with Mankiewicz," director Henry Hathaway recalled, "she became a little exotic. I think he was the one who turned a simple girl into what came damn close to being a neurotic."

When *A Letter to Three Wives* was released early in 1949, it brought Linda the most unanimous acclaim she ever received, providing her with the undisputed triumph *Forever Amber* failed to deliver. The film opened at the Radio City Music Hall, indicating peak enthusiasm. Critics agreed it was the Darnell-Douglas segment of the film that proved explosive. *Theatre Arts* maintained, "Linda Darnell suddenly emerges as an actress after years as a face and figure," while *Time* contended, "Miss Darnell, who can be a temptress without even trying, has never shown so strikingly that she can be an actress as well."

Elated by what she knew was an excellent performance, Linda left with Pev and their friends Gloria and Arthur Jacobson on a Central American vacation shortly after work on *A Letter to Three Wives* ended. Proud as she was of Lora May, what mattered most to Linda was her relationship with the force that had elevated her beyond her natural limits, both as an actress and as a woman. Dreams of Joe Mankiewicz crowded her mind, fantasies of a charming knight who could lift her toward sophistication and culture. To those around her, she appeared distant and vacant, while inwardly she suffered loneliness as never before. To fill the void she drank more, trying to hold onto the euphoria she had glimpsed, but would never claim. As deeply as she loved Mankiewicz, she was also trying to salvage her marriage—out of gratitude to Pev, but mainly for Lola. The adoption agency had taken a dim view of the couple's recent separation, and above all Linda was determined not to lose her child. The conflict of loyalties was more than her uncomplicated nature could handle, and the resulting tensions eroded what stability she had left.

Wherever the vacationers went, discreet telegrams from Joe Mankiewicz awaited Linda. They arrived in New Orleans to find a message at the hotel: "Dearest Linda, I have written Roark and Mary Bradford to expect a call from you. He is the famous author of *Green Pastures*, and she is the uncrowned queen of New Orleans. I know you will all love them. My very best to Gloria, Pev, and Artie. Dillinger has a sunburned nose and looks like a banana split. Love, Joe." In their communications, Mankiewicz often referred to himself as an outlaw, apparently enjoying the image of himself as an adventurer, stealing someone else's property.

Linda returned to Los Angeles to find herself suddenly taken seriously as an actress. Her telephone rang as never before with all kinds of offers. "You can always tell how you are doing in Hollywood by whether your phone rings," she said. She wanted the title role in *Pinky*, a story about a black girl who passes for white, but lost out because Darryl Zanuck thought audiences might think Pinky had a touch of Amber in her. Jeanne Crain, Fox's Miss Homespun, was awarded the part instead. "Linda had the taint of the adventuress," said Philip Dunne, the film's scriptwriter. "Pinky could not be an adventuress. She had to be whiter than white."

Instead, Zanuck assigned Linda to *Slattery's Hurricane*, a tumble from the height she had reached with Joe Mankiewicz, and her anger toward the Fox production head deepened into lasting bitterness. Freed by psychotherapy and encouraged by Mankiewicz, who thought Zanuck was holding him back also, Linda was at last able to vent the hostile emotions that had been building since childhood. Even more than Pearl, Zanuck became the target for her fury. He was her captor, the slave merchant, the villain in her private melodrama, and she railed against him at every turn.

Linda celebrated her twenty-fifth birthday in New York, where Mankiewicz was shooting exterior locations for *House of Strangers*. He had flown up to Boston, where his wife was rehearsing *Bravo!*, the Edna Ferber–George S. Kaufman play in which she attempted a comeback. He wired Linda on her birthday: "Darling, I have a call in for you and I haven't slept. I am just as eager as you and love you for wanting to try to come, but I can't let you take so many chances with so much at stake for both of us. Please talk to me as soon as you can." Four days later he telegraphed from New Haven: "Everything under control, but I can't call. Think I can spend most of Sunday in New York. Will try to call tomorrow. Love, Joe." Rosa Stradner opened in New Haven, but was replaced in Boston by Lili Darvas. She never appeared on stage again, refusing even to audition.

Linda flew directly from New York to Miami, where most of *Slattery's Hurricane* was filmed. Gladys Witten was already there, as were director Andre De Toth and most of the cast, which included Richard Widmark and the director's wife, Veronica Lake. The company hoped to be back in California by Christmas.

"Dearest Baby, Missing you," Pev wired Linda. "Forgive the lateness of this. I've had everything go wrong. Are you my girl? Well, then get your ass home. I love you." The *Slattery's Hurricane* company was a congenial one, although Linda missed Lola and longed to be back in Los Angeles, where Mankiewicz by then was shooting *House of Strangers*. "Darling, I couldn't get through tonight on account of election," he wired the night Truman was reelected. "Will try again tomorrow. All my love and I miss you terribly, Joe."

Filming ended in Florida on December 11, with Linda and Veronica Lake stopping briefly in Dallas on their flight to California. Pev took charge of selecting Lola's first Christmas tree, filling it out with additional branches and seeing that the tree was decorated to perfection. "Your very first Christmas," Linda wrote in Lola's baby book, "and did we have a time keeping you away from those glittering packages."

Slattery's Hurricane made no lasting impression, but did well at the box office and brought Linda satisfactory notices. Six days before the picture's completion on January 25, Linda went to court, accusing her former business manager, Cy Tanner, of fraud. Singer Andy Russell and his wife, Della, were there to make the same charges. Linda claimed that an examination of her financial records revealed a shortage of $7,250 between 1946 and 1947, when Tanner had handled her finances. He had appropriated sums from her salary, which passed through his hands as her manager, and had withdrawn money from her bank account. Eventually he admitted embezzling the funds and two months later was sent to San Quentin. "What a blow," Linda said. "I'm lucky that this happened while I'm young and have most of my earning span ahead of me—it could have been so much worse!"

To capitalize on the successful combination of Paul Douglas and Linda Darnell, Zanuck quickly teamed the two stars again in *Everybody Does It*, a remake of the 1938 film *Wife, Husband and Friend*. Zanuck's production formula relied heavily on remakes and sequels, on the premise that a good thing was worth doing again. Nunnally Johnson reworked his earlier script, and Linda portrayed a famous opera singer in the film, another femme fatale. Douglas played a rough-hewn wrecking contractor who suddenly discovers he has a voice powerful enough to shatter glass.

Having made five pictures in eighteen months, Linda was ready for an extended vacation. She made a quick train trip to New

York, ate more Mexican and Italian food than she should have, and continued her psychotherapy when she returned, determined to deepen into a truly fine actress. But most of her vacation was devoted to Lola, making sure the adoption agency approved of conditions within the Marley household. She also worked on plans for a new home in Bel Air, a "motley modern" house, as she called it, designed specifically to suit her tastes.

In March Joe Mankiewicz won Academy Awards for both writing and directing *A Letter to Three Wives*, thrilling Linda as if she had been awarded the Oscar herself. It was rumored that she would make a film in England, but the studio ultimately cancelled that. She wanted to play Lola Montez on the screen, a part full of temperament and fire, yet she could not interest Darryl Zanuck in the project. On June 9, Linda and Pev became the legal parents of their seventeen-month-old daughter. "She is *ours!*" Linda wrote, underlining *ours* twice. "She's our first baby, but not the last, we hope," the actress informed reporters. Soon she added, "We have our application in for another baby. We don't care whether it's a boy or a girl. We think Lola should have a playmate."

Mankiewicz was busy all that summer working on the script of *No Way Out*, an intense melodrama dealing with racial prejudice, more hard-hitting even than *Pinky*. Linda saw less of her lover during the weeks she was away from the studio, but they managed to talk on the telephone several times a day and arranged frequent rendezvous. Emotionally it was a bad time for her. She seemed to live increasingly in her own world and continued drinking heavily.

As fall approached, Linda grew bored with homemaking and was ready to go back to work. Zanuck had spent the summer looking for a script for her, but hadn't found anything suitable. Then in October came the best news possible. Anne Baxter would not be able to finish *A Ticket to Tomahawk* in time to star in Mankiewicz's *No Way Out*, and Linda had been selected to replace her. It was a dramatic, deglamorized role, the kind Linda dreamed of playing, and she would again be under her lover's direction. "I'm a female bum in *No Way Out*," she said enthusiastically. "It's a good role. I do everything—get drunk, go on a couple of crying jags, and get slapped around by Richard Widmark. A pal of his even beats me with a chain."

No Way Out was beyond question the most honest depiction of racial prejudice yet put on film, and the cast approached their assignments enthusiastically. Linda's admiration for Mankiewicz showed during every take. He was low-key on the set, speaking softly, but she absorbed each word he uttered. "The way he writes!" Linda marveled. "I can read the part once and get the whole gist of it. You don't find that often. With Joe, I read it over two or three times and I've got it all. And he's such a grand director, too!" Thrilled to be in daily contact with her idol and convinced they were filming a vital story, Linda gave an outstanding performance, certainly her most dramatic. "Honey," she told Henriette Wyeth Hurd, "that's the only good picture I ever made."

One morning while driving to work, Linda's car mysteriously exploded. For a few moments it appeared that she was trapped in the flaming vehicle, but she managed to escape with only slight burns and a cut hand. A passing school bus driver put out the fire with a portable extinguisher, but not until the car engine was completely destroyed. Linda arrived on the *No Way Out* set forty-five minutes late, badly shaken. For a third time fire narrowly missed claiming her life.

No Way Out was completed in December 1949, just in time for Linda to finish the family's Christmas shopping. It would not reach the theaters for almost a year, in part because of censorship problems. Linda frankly hated to see the picture end, knowing that Mankiewicz's new project, *All About Eve*, would take him away from her and that in all likelihood their schedules would never again mesh.

Later Linda admitted that she felt so despondent during the 1949 holiday season that she was on the verge of suicide. In love with Mankiewicz, yet sensing nothing permanent could ever come of their relationship, she fell into a depression that the yuletide festivities merely exaggerated. Her affair with Mankiewicz would last another four years, although the agony persisted the rest of her life. "Romantically, it was the bitterest pill she ever swallowed," Linda's friend Richard Curtis said. "That was really the tragedy of her life," agreed designer Yvonne Wood. "She never got over it. I never knew a time when she wouldn't have just walked off if the guy had asked her."

One night during that troubled Christmas season, Linda was alone in the house with Lola and seriously considered reaching for the sleeping tablets, all but ready to take enough to end her unhappiness. "All the years I had spent in Hollywood crowded in on me like so many nightmares," she said later. "I had lost the will to continue what seemed to be a futile rat race. Millions of people pictured me as living like Cinderella. But I felt desperate, and the rest that I needed was only an arm's length away." Suddenly she bolted up in bed. "Monetta Darnell," she heard herself say. "What on earth are you thinking of?" The sound of her voice jolted her to her senses. "What I felt," she said, "was the realization that somehow all my problems hadn't befallen my real self, but a sort of synthetic, unreal self known as Linda Darnell. It makes me shudder to think how close I came—or perhaps I should say how close Linda came." But with the struggles ahead, Linda and Monetta became one, even when she struggled to keep them apart. Gradually the suffering eroded the facade, revealing that the angel and the hellion had finally merged.

Alone

"I remember Mother was very unapproachable at that time," Lola said, recalling her first impressions of the Amalfi Drive house. "She was working and gone so much. A very early memory I have is that she was getting dressed—they were going somewhere. I came in, like a two-year-old, probably with stuff on my hands, and she said to me, 'Don't touch me!' My earliest memory is that she was so beautiful and smelled good. She always wore this perfume called Femme, and that's the scent I associate with her. But Mother was away a great deal, and I really didn't see her that much." The girl's early memories of her father were even fewer.

As a child, Lola had frequent nightmares. Her French nurse, whom she called Zellie since she couldn't say Mademoiselle, told her that when she had a bad dream she should think about happy things. So whenever Lola woke up in the night frightened, she would say, "I'm in my room, I'm in my bed, there's my book, there's my bear," until she stopped crying. "It seems to me I have been on my own emotionally most of my life. I never really had a family. A governess is not a mother."

"I think Linda tried to be a good mother," Jeanne Curtis maintained, "but she wasn't a mother that was always there. She tried to be a disciplinarian and went overboard on that. She didn't want her child getting into trouble like the kids of other Hollywood stars had. She was concerned and wanted her daughter to ride a straight path, which sometimes made her look like not such a good mother. But she tried to be."

Lola grew up thinking her Grandmother Pearl was the most fascinating person in the world. "I didn't know anyone else who was as interesting and as different as my grandmother," the girl remembered. Linda often told her daughter about Pearl's showing up on the set with a snake wrapped around her and getting thrown off the lot. "Mother was horrified," said Lola, "as I would have been if my mother had showed up with snakes. But to a kid, finding out that your grandmother had done that was marvelous.

I had visions of snakes wrapped around her arms and coming out of her hair like Medusa! I loved it."

Monte had had an accident during the summer of 1949, while attempting to ride through a flaming hoop, which ended her rodeo career. She soon married Dr. Daniel Wilson, a Burbank obstetrician, so Pearl was home more, with little to do. Once in a while Linda would leave Lola with her mother, which the girl loved, especially as she grew older. "There were no maids, and we ate strange stuff like oleomargarine," said Lola. "I sat in the kitchen with a relative, not a servant. Most of my meals at home I ate with servants. And there I got to eat with my grandmother. I was allowed to roller-skate to the corner store and buy bubble gum with baseball cards, and we'd drink Dr. Pepper. My grandmother had a trunk full of squaw clothes, and I was allowed to play in them. Nobody I knew lived like that. Everybody else had maids and nurses and Chinese gardeners, and here was my grandmother who walked to the store. Her place was wonderful, and *it was messy*. We never had any mess because we had a fleet of servants to pick things up." Lola considered her grandmother a real clown and very approachable. "She's probably the reason why I like older people today."

Pearl loved "The Grand Ole Opry" and radio mysteries, and later she enjoyed the hair-pulling and eye-gouging on television wrestling. Lola and Undeen's daughter Jan both liked watching television with her. "We'd stay up and watch all the gangster movies and any of the scary ones," recalled Jan. "I didn't get along with Lola that well, because to me she always acted like she was better than everybody else. But the rest of us kids had parents who were home all the time, which Lola didn't."

Cal began to see more and more of his mother in Linda. "She began tying her hair in a knot," he recalled, "not bothering to make herself pretty, unless she had to for a party or was going out. She just didn't bother." Friends noted that Linda was not her usual obliging self, and those closest to her realized she was brooding over the affair with Joe Mankiewicz. "I've begun to think there's something to the law of compensation," she told a columnist. "I've had all of the good things any woman could ever desire—and most of the bad things no woman wants."

Construction had begun on the ten-room home in Bel Air that Linda had helped design. On a clear day the new house would offer a view of Catalina Island, and she would have her own studio for painting, with plenty of glass and natural light. Lola's room would be a large one divided by an accordion partition, so that her governess could sleep nearby. The master bedroom would have a fireplace, a king-size bed, and a mirrored dressing area.

In April 1950 Linda left Los Angeles for six weeks in New Mexico, where most of her next movie, *Two Flags West*, would be shot. It was her first outdoor picture since *My Darling Clementine*, and she had misgivings, particularly about her colorless role. Jeff Chandler was borrowed from Universal-International for the role of Linda's brother-in-law in the picture, while Cornel Wilde was chosen to play a Union captain and Joseph Cotten a Confederate colonel. Robert Wise, the distinguished editor of *Citizen Kane*, was set to direct, his first assignment for Twentieth Century–Fox. Wise found Linda more than adequate in her role, but not an exceptionally skilled actress. Linda, on the other hand, genuinely admired Wise, finding him unpretentious, the kind of director she could discuss scenes with, and recognized in him a man of unusual cinematic abilities. Linda wrote Pev from New Mexico, "This director is just grand. I hope that five weeks or possibly more of this type of living and working conditions doesn't make everyone too disgruntled. Perhaps Mr. Wise will be able to keep us all on an even keel."

Two Flags West was shot near the San Ildefonso reservation, some fifteen miles northwest of Santa Fe. The company lived in what had been a camp for construction workers, and for about ten days straight they were plagued with sand storms. The crew sat around playing poker waiting for the dust to clear. "What do you know?" Linda wrote Pev. "A whole week, and I'm still alive. It hasn't been too bad actually. The little cabins are as comfortable as can be expected, with my own shower and johnny, and the food is really excellent quality, but pretty starchy and heavy. I really have to watch it. My costumes are getting tight on me already. The wind has been something ferocious, and the dust has been murder. I have such a chronic case of hay fever that I wonder if I'll ever get over it. Fortunately the girl double for me is excellent, and I have not had to do very much riding so far."

Linda hated making westerns, particularly since she was allergic to horses. Gradually the crew came to refer to the picture as "Two Fags West," as tempers began to flare. "Cornel is seemingly trying to be halfway decent," Linda wrote, "but I still avoid him as much as possible. Joe Cotten is an awfully stuffed shirt, and a lush to boot, but Jeff Chandler is a dreamboat, good actor, and a real down-to-earth guy." The studio sent out her record player and records, allowing the company to have "music, music, music," as Linda put it.

She rented a car and visited the Hurd ranch, but as the weeks of location work dragged on, nerves became jangled. "I want you to write me, you stinker," Linda wrote Pev. "I want to hear how you all are and what Lolita has been doing and saying." Shooting on the film finally ended early in June.

Linda returned to California and quickly became absorbed in the building of the Bel Air house, pleased that work had progressed so nicely during her absence. Constructed of stone and wood, the $250,000 home had scenic windows all across the front, giving a panoramic view of the ocean. Linda's friend Dick Paxton made a hand-tooled copper top for the bar in the den, which became her pride and joy. Although the backyard was not deep, there would be a stretch of grass and room enough for Lola to have a swing set and a lamb. Time and again Linda and the contractor disagreed, but she held firm on what she wanted. At the height of her career, she was determined to have her dream house.

Then on July 19, six weeks after the completion of *Two Flags West* and with Joe Mankiewicz vacationing in Europe, came the announcement that Linda and Pev Marley had definitely separated. It was reported that Linda would move with Lola into the new house in Bel Air, while Marley would remain on Amalfi Drive. The split had been planned for months; it came without recriminations. Although the couple were not ready to discuss divorce, friends knew this time their parting was final.

Darnell family members claimed Pev realized there would be a divorce as soon as Lola's adoption became final. He supposedly told his wife he would agree to a quiet settlement, with no mention of Mankiewicz, for a payment of $125,000. It was rumored that Pev himself had been stepping out with other women, but Linda could never prove adultery. Scraping together the $125,000 her husband demanded took everything she had—the trust funds she had set up for her brother and sisters, her bank account, everything. "There went all of her money again," said Undeen, "and she had to start over." Pearl never knew Linda paid Pev for the divorce. "But Linda told me about it," Cal said. "I don't think she dared to tell Monte or Undeen."

It now became essential for Linda to work. She shortly renegotiated her contract with Twentieth Century—Fox, adding a nonexclusive clause that permitted her to do outside pictures. Darryl Zanuck informed her in July that her next assignment would be *The Thirteenth Letter*, with her old nemesis Otto Preminger directing. The star's lack of enthusiasm could be heard all over the studio. Her role, however, was that of a lame woman, another interesting departure from her usual glamour roles.

In September Linda left with Lola for Canada and location shooting on *The Thirteenth Letter*. Much of the film was shot in Saint-Denis, with Charles Boyer and Michael Rennie also heading the cast. To suggest a limp, Linda wore one built-up shoe. She appeared frequently in Montreal nightclubs, telling reporters that 1950 marked the year of radical changes both in her private and public lives. "Look at Darnell," she said quietly, "she's a very different girl!"

The Thirteenth Letter was finished on October 20, just four days after Linda's twenty-seventh birthday. Almost immediately Zanuck scheduled her to play the hard-bitten other woman in *The Man Who Sank the Navy*, opposite Paul Douglas and Joan Bennett. She felt she had done so many similar parts that she at first refused. Zanuck was determined to bring together the winning combination of Darnell and Douglas for the third time, but Linda stood her ground and consequently was placed on suspension. She was furious, resolved to change the pace of her screen characterizations. She had specialized in shady ladies for so long and was eager to play a "nice" girl again, yet her financial situation didn't permit her staying on suspension long.

The Bel Air house still lacked most of the basic furnishings when she moved in and would even years later. Linda referred to the new home as "my California farmhouse," since her design allowed each room to amble into the next. She wanted the place to be "comfy and roomy," but her taste often seemed dubious. There were an abundance of overstuffed sofas and chairs, and much of the mishmash she had bought at a local Akron store that specialized in job lots from manufacturers who had gone out of business. Linda herself described the furnishings as "early Akron," and there was no style anyone could identify.

The only rooms completely furnished were the den, which Linda called her "cantina," and her own bedroom. The den was magnificent, with a fireplace, a huge television set, and Dick Paxton's copper bar, always well stocked. The master bedroom, where Linda spent most of her time, was gigantic—complete with another large television set and push-button draperies. In the bathroom there were paper stars on the ceiling, one of several *déclassé* touches. Rather than a grand staircase, there was a narrow stairway in front, designed by another friend—curved, hard-carved, beautifully done, but inappropriately small. There was a second stairway in back, leading down to an eating area off the kitchen.

By November, with expenses mounting, Linda was willing to accept the part in *The Man Who Sank the Navy*, now called *The Guy Who Came Back*. The picture marked Linda's return to glamour on the screen. Her wardrobe included a silver-blue mink coat that designer Renie fashioned especially for her, a black fox stole, and a wool coat trimmed with six fox skins. She again balked when the studio asked her to bleach her hair for the part, and finally Zanuck let her remain a brunette. Once that was resolved, director Joe Newman found Linda "a charming, efficient, cooperative and competent actress, despite the fact that she had not wanted to do the role. She was exceptionally gracious about it and was a director's delight—agreeable, intelligent, and with great natural talent and charm."

The picture was completed in December, opening in New York the following August. Most reviewers said Darnell and Douglas were again convincing, but that the stars were not enough to make *The Guy Who Came Back* a winning combination. If Linda's marquee value was slipping, so was that of virtually every other star in Hollywood, as they became expensive commodities for studios losing audiences to television.

On February 19, 1951, Linda won her divorce from Pev Marley. At the time he was fifty-three, she was twenty-seven. She told Judge Thurmond Clarke during the five-minute hearing, "On numerous occasions my husband was extremely rude to my friends and to members of my family and caused me great embarrassment. He used to go to bed while guests were still in the house and refused to attend affairs given by my fellow film workers. He would promise me he would change but he never did." She testified that the humiliation and mental anguish had reached a point where her "health deteriorated and she became nervous and rundown." Linda informed the court that she had been under a doctor's care, claiming her husband was sometimes so rude she had to "hold back the tears."

Pev filed a denial, but did not appear to contest the action. The judge granted the decree on grounds of mental cruelty, since by 1951 California law, a "no fault" divorce was impossible. Under the property settlement Linda received custody of Lola and seventy-five dollars a month child support, but no alimony. Pev retained the home in Pacific Palisades, two of their four cars, and some oil leases, while Linda kept the other two cars, her furs and jewelry, and the house in Bel Air.

Joe Mankiewicz made news when he won double Oscars for the second time in two years, an unequaled coup. In 1951 he received an Academy Award for writing and directing the internationally acclaimed *All About Eve*, bringing him to the peak of his celebrity. Mankiewicz's name was never mentioned publicly during the Marley divorce. All Linda ever told the press was that, in addition to her other troubles, she had suffered "a disappointment in love," which "is always most important for a woman," and that everything together had her "on the verge of a complete breakdown." Friends privately admitted that Pev had become difficult, inclined to say belittling things to his wife in front of other people. Eventually he would remarry Virginia McAdoo, his second wife, but that marriage also ended in divorce.

On March 21, Linda signed a contract with Universal for her first picture as a free-lance star. The film,`The Lady Pays Off*, would commence in April, with Linda receiving $7,500 per week for a minimum of ten weeks. Douglas Sirk, who had worked marvels with her on *Summer Storm* years before, had specifically asked producer Albert Cohen to consider Linda for the part of an attractive schoolmarm who works as a governess to pay off her gambling debts. According to Louella Parsons, Linda arrived on the Universal lot looking "prettier than I have ever seen her. She seems to have taken an entirely new lease on life." The star liked the script, found it an appealing change of pace, and eagerly awaited the reunion with Sirk. "It's wonderfully flattering to have people fussing over me again," the actress said exuberantly.

On the fifth day of shooting, Linda collapsed on the set when she learned of the death of Ivan Kahn, the talent scout responsible for her discovery. Distraught, she was sent home for the day. She missed another day's work to attend Kahn's funeral, putting *The Lady Pays Off* behind schedule and slightly over budget. That meant working doubly hard to catch up, since an executive committee kept an exact record of where each picture on the lot stood at any given point. Then early in May, Linda was out with a case of flu and co-star Stephen McNally was in the hospital recovering from an emergency appendectomy, forcing the company to shut down for two weeks.

The Lady Pays Off was completed in May, only four days over schedule and $26,000 over budget, despite the delays. Linda appeared to like free-lancing. "I am happier than at any time in my screen career," she said. "You have no idea how wonderful it is to pick and choose your roles." Many free-lance stars felt similarly, not yet realizing the loss of security that came with the demise of long-term studio contracts.

When *The Lady Pays Off* opened in December, Linda's reviews were excellent. Six months later she went to Jamaica for location work on *Saturday Island*, taking Lola with her. Directed by Stuart Heisler and made partially with British money, the film was released in the United States as *Island of Desire* and marked the beginning of Tab Hunter's career as a teenage heartthrob. The crew was half British, half American. Heisler, whom Linda found an exceptionally warm director, had engaged a suite for her at the Shaw Hotel in Jamaica. She found the tropical vegetation breathtaking, even though the mosquitoes and West Indian summer heat became practically unbearable. On June 30, she wired Pev: "Darling, impossible to keep Lola. She has had bad tonsil trouble and is too hard to handle. Am stark raving mad. Please arrange to have her picked up in Miami by a competent husky nurse. Hope it is soon. Am broken-hearted, but cannot work under such strain."

A maid escorted Lola to Florida, where she was turned over to her nurse and flown back to California. Two weeks after Lola left, Linda received a cablegram from Joe Mankiewicz, who was traveling in Europe: "Airmail in Turkish means get lost. Leave tomorrow for Rome. Then to Los Angeles, flea-bitten, exhausted, but always your boy and all love. Pancho Villa." She was still carrying his cable in her billfold at the time of her death, fourteen years later.

In July a hurricane hit Jamaica, and all communications were cut, as wind and rain pounded the island. "I'll never forget it," said Linda. "It was horrible. The sound of it, the awful deafening roar of the winds. The trees crashing to the ground, the walls shaking. It was terrifying." Gladys Witten, who was working with Linda on the picture, remembered, "They couldn't get in touch with us, and everybody was worried. There were headlines in all the papers." Actually the cast and crew were relatively safe, boarded up in their hotel on the north side of the island, but the south shore suffered severe damage. Linda wired Pev as soon as she could: "Your cables received tonight. First word from outside. Communications now restored. Am still thanking God for everything. Will phone. Kiss Lolita."

Opening and closing scenes of *Saturday Island* were shot in England. Because of union regulations Gladys wasn't permitted to work in Britain as Linda's hairdresser, so they arranged for her to go as the star's secretary. The two friends stayed at the Savoy Hotel in London and had great fun taking in all the sights. Linda no sooner finished the picture than she became ill with jaundice contracted in Jamaica. She spent five weeks recuperating in a London hospital, observing her twenty-eighth birthday quarantined in a sick room. She wired Pev: "Darling, two more weeks in hospital. Very depressed. Please call before Lola goes back to school." When released by the doctors in mid-November, she told the British press that she had had her fill of living alone and was looking for a new love. "There's no happiness like being in love," she said. "I just hate to be alone."

Before leaving London she was contacted by Italian producer Giuseppi Amato about the possibility of her making a movie for him in Rome. She returned to New York, only to suffer a recurrence of the jaundice and be confined to her hotel suite. Since Joe Mankiewicz had taken up permanent residence in a Park Avenue apartment, Linda decided to lease a suite in the nearby Warwick Hotel in Manhattan as her second home.

She arrived back in Los Angeles just in time for Christmas with Lola, having lost sixteen pounds over the past three months. She still ran a fever and had been forbidden to drink anything alcoholic, although she repeatedly violated doctor's orders. Linda returned to the Warwick Hotel early in January to discover that her suite had been burglarized. Thieves had ransacked everything, making off with jewelry and a $3,000 mink stole.

She flew back to Los Angeles, where she was met at the airport by Lola and Pev. She was still feverish and informed her agent that she would not be able to work until she felt a great deal better than she presently did. Stuart Heisler wanted Linda for another picture, but she had to turn his offer down. She saw very few people, spending most of her time with Lola.

Roy Darnell had recently retired from the post office, after forty-one years of service, and spent most of his time traveling. He fished, hunted, and camped, sometimes for several weeks at a time. Frequently he took off for Texas, with Pearl eventually going after him. Lola remembered seeing her grandfather only twice. Both times he just appeared without Linda's knowing he was coming. "He sort of lived in his car and camped around, following the fishing season," Lola said. "He seemed happy and never seemed to want much from anyone. I would ask Mother about him, and she would say, 'Daddy was a postman,' which I thought was neat."

Eventually Roy left California, settling near Hamilton, Texas, where he knew Pearl could never find him. He kept in touch with his children, but refused to tell his wife where he was. "I was glad when my father left my mother," assured Cal, "because she gave the man no peace. I told him to go. I loved him very much and knew Mother was never going to change." Roy spent the last twenty years of his life in south Texas, away from the Hollywood socializing he had detested. "He just messed around and lived kind of a lonely life," his nephew Glenn Darnell said. "He lived in different places, hitting all the little towns. Hunting and fishing were his life. Finally my dad kind of looked after him."

So Pearl was alone in the Brentwood house. Cal took a job with a radio station in Flint, Michigan, and only her grandchildren occasionally visited. In her loneliness Pearl rambled on about Linda and Dallas, spinning the same stories again and again. Linda saw her mother rarely, although her own life was filled with more than its share of isolation, too.

Saturday Island opened in London on March 14 to unenthusiastic notices. Critics agreed that the Jamaican locations added color to the film, but dismissed the story of a Canadian nurse and a young marine marooned on a desert island during World War II as fairly contrived entertainment.

Under Linda's revised contract with Twentieth Century–Fox, she still had to make one film a year, and reported to the lot in March 1952 for what was to be her last picture for the company that had been her professional home for thirteen years. The film, a psychological melodrama called *Night Without Sleep*, also featured Gary Merrill and was directed by Roy Baker. Linda played a cinema queen who meets and briefly romances composer Merrill in a series of flashback sequences. After the picture was completed, Darryl Zanuck decided Gary Merrill's characterization was wrong.

"Once he meets Linda and straightens up, he becomes a very attractive, interesting man," said Zanuck, "but up to that time you are bored and a little fed up with him." The critics couldn't have agreed more.

Still Linda remained optimistic about her future. She wrote Bill Langley, the Dallas photographer who helped launch her career: "Have just finished my one picture a year commitment for Fox, a psychological murder mystery called *Night Without Sleep*, and am now madly preparing for a new one at RKO, called *Blackbeard the Pirate*. I should be finished with it around the first week in July, at which time I'll fly to Rome for about a month and try to get a house or villa for me and Lola and my maid, when we return there in September to do a picture for a very charming Italian producer." She was excited about the prospect of working abroad, since "I'm footloose and fancy-free now and love to travel. I've never seen Italy, so it promises to be a very exciting summer."

Linda was feeling better, although still not up to par, and tired easily, which was to be expected after such a long illness. She promised Langley that she was "on the wagon, except on a special occasion, and that helps the ol' liver a lot," but failed to mention that special occasions occurred with great frequency. Her major worry seemed to be her lack of a romantic interest. "I'm bored with not being in love," she informed the press. "I'm looking for a steady boyfriend. Being in love is the most wonderful thing that can happen to anyone."

Then in September came the news that Twentieth Century–Fox had cancelled her contract. At the time she was relieved, since the cancellation involved only one film a year and freed her to make pictures in Europe. "She was actually very glad when it was over with," her sister Undeen assured, "because she could freelance and go to Italy and not infringe on anything over here. She said she'd never sign another long-term contract. She wanted to be free to branch out." That same year Metro-Goldwyn-Mayer dropped Clark Gable's contract. Betty Grable, once the number one star on the Fox lot, left the studio in 1953, while Jeanne Crain soon received her pink slip, along with Anne Baxter, Gene Tierney, Mitzi Gaynor, and Terry Moore. Studios all over Hollywood were eliminating their contract players in a panic over the competition from television. Like Linda, most actors initially felt they had been pardoned from a prison sentence. Later they would look back on the ease and protection they had enjoyed under the big studios and regret the passing of a golden era. Linda did state at the time her Fox contract was terminated that she felt "like a girl leaving home for the first time." Without Darryl Zanuck to pilot her career, shrewdness—a quality Linda definitely did not possess—would be essential to stay on top. She was a creation of the big studio system and was all too quickly viewed as a has-been by the new breed of filmmaker that soon took over Hollywood.

The entire entertainment industry was in the throes of an upheaval nothing could stop. Hollywood would quickly become a different town, emerging with a new product. Already many of the old attitudes and methods seemed outdated. Once the studios had been divested of their theaters, production heads drastically cut back on schedules, turning out fewer and fewer pictures. The movie business never recuperated from the blow. Soon only specialized films were made, which stood some chance of drawing audiences out of their homes and away from television sets. Gradually Zanuck's approach came to be derided as "Sixteenth Century–Fox." To modernize and better compete with television, the studio announced in the spring of 1952 that henceforth all of its features would be photographed in CinemaScope, but the widescreen process proved little more than a fad. By 1955 the once-glorious Fox back lot was in a state of decay, full of ghosts of thousands of pirates, cowboys, and warriors who had sprung to life there.

In 1956 Zanuck resigned as Twentieth Century–Fox's chief of production, naming Buddy Adler his successor. "I don't think the situation is going to improve," he told Philip Dunne. "It's going to get worse. In a short time, the business will be completely dominated by the stars and their agents. We made the stars, but they've forgotten that. Faces, that's all they are, just faces. It's been good, working with people like you and Nunnally and Jack Ford and Henry King. Perhaps it was just too good to last."

Darryl Zanuck immediately formed his own company, negotiating a contract with Fox that gave him carte blanche to produce the films he wanted and spending most of his time in Europe. During Zanuck's absence Spyros Skouras, who was a great politician but no picture maker, moved to the helm at Twentieth Century–Fox. In July 1962, at the height of the *Cleopatra* disaster, after the back lot had been sold off to form present-day Century City and Zanuck had enjoyed a comeback with *The Longest Day*, the former production boss was brought back to save the studio from financial ruin.

By then the Hollywood Linda Darnell had known was gone, and many of its former stars were feeling like aging orphans, wondering from day to day if they would ever work again. For many the future looked dark, with no big studio system left to guide them. "Suppose you'd been earning $4,000 to $5,000 a week for years," Linda said a decade after her Fox contract ended. "Suddenly you were fired and no one would hire you at any figure remotely comparable to your previous salary. I thought in a little while I'd get offers from other studios, but not many came along. The only thing I knew how to do was be a movie star. No one expects to last forever in this business. You know that sooner or later the studio's going to let you go. But who wants to be retired at twenty-nine?" From here on Linda would have to go it alone— without Pearl, without Pev, without even Darryl Zanuck. The prospect terrified her. With no studio contract to support her, the house of cards began to fall, and the future was plainly written in spades.

Out of Control

Work on *Blackbeard the Pirate* began at RKO in June 1952, with veteran director Raoul Walsh in charge. Linda spent hours in costume fittings, since her role required elaborate seventeenth-century gowns with layer upon layer of petticoats. A lusty, romantic swashbuckler filmed in Technicolor, the picture had her playing the adopted daughter of Sir Henry Morgan, Blackbeard's mortal enemy, who is kidnapped by the famous buccaneer. Linda's character maintained her virtue even though, as Linda said, "the poor woman I play is chased by one pirate chief after another."

Raoul Walsh was a stupendous action director who kept the set laughing between takes. In one scene Walsh had Linda clouting a drunken pirate over the head with his own bottle. She caught the spirit to such a degree that she knocked the poor actor dizzy, despite a heavily padded hat. Most actresses enjoyed working with Walsh, although Linda was on edge most of the time and thought he favored the men in the cast.

Mainly she was eager to have the picture finished so she could leave for Italy. "We are so far behind schedule on this stupid pirate picture," Linda wrote photographer Bill Langley. "I won't finish until the end of July or first week in August! Heaven only knows when I'll be able to get away." She was excited about the prospect of living abroad for a year. "I'm so fed up with this town and everyone in it, including myself, that a change will probably be like heaven. I'm a damned gypsy anyway, and hate sitting in one place for very long. And, just for your information, Uncle Willie, I'd LOVE to find me a charming Italian!"

Producer Giuseppe Amato had flown to Los Angeles in May to finalize negotiations on the picture he and Linda would make in Rome. Immediately there were rumors that he was the new romance in her life. "Every time I go out with a man they say I'm in love with him," Linda complained. Joe Mankiewicz was in Hollywood during the summer *Blackbeard the Pirate* was filmed, working on *Julius Caesar* for John Houseman at MGM. Linda saw little of him, even though he was still much in her thoughts.

Blackbeard was not completed until October, but Linda finished her part earlier, and flew to Europe in late August. She took Lola with her, plus enough luggage to fill two cabs. Amato met their plane and escorted his star to a nightclub the evening of her arrival, although the two continued to deny any romantic involvement. Amato was married with three children, yet he spent the first week of September vacationing with Linda on Capri. The press pointed out that the producer's last name in Italian meant "loved one" and that the couple had been in each other's company almost constantly since Linda's arrival in Rome.

Before leaving Hollywood Linda had studied Italian and learned to speak the language reasonably well. She fell in love with Italy immediately. "The Italians are so natural and free," she declared. "I want to learn their technique. After thirteen years at the same studio, I'm ready for something completely new. And you can't blame an old crone of twenty-nine for trying." With a diet rich with pasta and wine, she quickly began gaining weight, maintaining she could lose it easily before shooting on the film began.

Amato offered her a two-picture deal, giving her a choice of three scripts. She decided first on *Donne proibite*, ultimately called *Angels of Darkness* in English, which would begin filming no sooner than February. Once their basic agreements were settled, Linda was free to turn the next six weeks into a holiday. "Lola and I are vacationing here in this heavenly country," she wrote her Grandmother Brown. "I'll make two pictures here in the future, and I'm sure they will be the best I've ever made. We love the people here so much, and the country is beautiful beyond words."

Linda returned from Italy in November, after an affectionate send-off in Rome by Amato. She changed planes with Lola at Idlewild Airport in New York, greeted by a bevy of newspaper reporters. The actress repeated that she was looking for a steady boyfriend and complained, "There's no romance in Hollywood for me." In Bel Air she spent most of her time alone, drinking constantly. "She was left without a lot of true friends," Jeanne Curtis said. "Whether it was of her own making or just the way things happened I can't say, but I know she was a very lonely person. When you've been at the top of your profession and then drop off, you hate to face your peers and contemporaries. You go into a shell, and that's what Linda did. She went into a deep, depressive shell. She avoided the whole Hollywood scene."

Dick Paxton, whom she had met years before through Mickey

Rooney, had just finished a small part in a picture for a director with whom he discussed Linda. Dick told him he had "a movie star friend, a wonderful girl, who drinks too much, spends too much time alone, and cries too much. Everyone would love to date her, but they all think she's so beautiful there's no chance. So nobody calls." The director had been married for over ten years, and his wife was terminally ill. Upon Dick Paxton's urging he finally telephoned Linda, who suggested he stop by for a drink. He accepted her invitation, returning maybe a half dozen times over as many months. Invariably he found Linda drunk, an empty bottle or two of gin on the bar and another one open. After offering him a drink she would pour half an inch of gin into a tall glass for herself, adding more every fifteen or twenty minutes. She drank her gin straight, always in that tall glass with no ice. "Sometimes it would come down and splash all over her," he remembered. "She'd just smile and pour herself another drink."

They talked about sports, especially baseball, but mainly about the movie business, which Linda seemed to know inside out. The director found her bright, articulate, and astute in her observations, yet she seemed somewhat uncomfortable with him because of his Ivy League background. She had seen most of the current pictures, including his, evidently attending them by herself. She was curious to know how he handled actresses and was intrigued by his approach to direction. "We never talked about the headlines or world events," he said. "We talked about movies and how hateful people were." She seemed consumed with bitterness, particularly toward Darryl Zanuck and Twentieth Century–Fox. "I never heard that studio get credit for anything," the director claimed. "It was always 'that son of a bitch Zanuck.'" She condemned the whole studio system, resented losing *Captain from Castile* to Jean Peters, and fulminated repeatedly. She complained that directors had neglected her, failed to give her the help she needed, favored other players. "Hell," she fumed, "I get more advice from my hairdresser than I do from these goddamn directors." Joe Mankiewicz was the only director she spoke of kindly, yet she gave no indication she knew him off the set.

"She was a soft, sweet, lovable girl," the director explained. "But she thought she could be tough and rugged when she couldn't. She thought to be mannish was good." She would say, "I could play a part that has balls!" He tried to make a joke, suggesting a more feminine term. "I mean balls!" Linda would storm. They often quarreled, with Linda curling her lip and saying, "Why the hell weren't you there to tell me?" Sometimes her temper would flair, and she once threw a glass at him in an argument. "God, she was an angry woman! She was furious all the time. Eventually that stopped me from seeing her."

The director admitted it was Linda's vulnerability that appealed to him, even though he grew impatient with it. She seemed to leave herself open to hurt, yet at the same time had a devilish streak. Physically she was one of the most voluptuous women he had ever known, but there was always that drink in her hand and her rage, which could burst forth without provocation. The simple fact that he didn't drink gin annoyed her. She belittled his hometown, threw his Ivy League education up to him, coaxed him into drinking more. "Practically everything I did annoyed her," he said. She never slapped him or hit him, but she did shove a great deal, sometimes playfully, sometimes angrily. A gentle, unassuming man, he would file away the things that irritated her and try to avoid them the next time around, rarely with much success. His very eagerness to please seemed to infuriate her, and she spewed out her anger knowing he would let her get away with it. "I must confess that I was afraid of Linda Darnell," he admitted. "There just isn't any other word except fear."

The servants had been dismissed for the evening, and Lola was usually at Pev's. Linda would begin smooching with the director on the sofa, and around eleven o'clock, when she was extremely drunk, she would suggest they go upstairs. "Do you think you can make it?" he would ask. By then he doubted she knew who he was. Linda would grab the open gin bottle, and he'd follow her up the stairs. Sometimes she'd already be undressed. The man found her "inanimate sex," and was certain she hadn't enjoyed it. "I don't even think she knew who was on top of her," he said. "I don't know why she did it." She would pass out, and he would leave quietly.

Linda came to prefer sleeping during the day and staying up most of the night. Often she'd spend the wee hours cooking, usually the spicy foods she adored. She used recipes to give her an idea, but cooked mostly by instinct, adding whatever smelled right. "She was an excellent cook," said Lola. "I think it was something she could do privately that was productive. And Mother hoarded food! I think it came from the days when she was poor growing up." Although Linda would buy her daughter several dresses at a time, she always bought them a size or two too large. "I never had anything that fit," said Lola. "I had to grow into everything. It was just another of Mother's quirks."

At an early age Lola was made aware that she was the daughter of an exceptionally beautiful woman whom everyone treated as somebody special. The girl knew she had no acting ability herself, could neither draw nor paint, and couldn't sculpt. Yet so much emphasis seemed to be placed on creativity. "Mother could do all these wonderful things, and I couldn't do any of them," Lola declared. "I just seemed not to be a creative person. I didn't know that was okay. Not every child is an artist. I used to look at myself in the mirror and think, 'Thank God I'm not ugly, too.'"

At five Lola attended the Sunshine School, a fashionable preschool in Bel Air, where Red Skelton's son was enrolled. The principal discovered the two children in an argument once over whether her mother or his father was the bigger star, although neither really understood what being a star meant. Linda was determined Lola should be equipped to handle any social situation properly, and Pev gave her full support. Table manners were important, as was learning how to shake hands. "Mother didn't grow up with Waterford crystal and sterling, but she insisted that I know about the finer things in life." Friends and family members worried that Linda was too severe with the child, observing how she disciplined her unbendingly, but she refused to change.

Bored and out of sorts, Linda waited impatiently for the start of *Donne proibite* in Italy. By February it was clear that the production would not get underway until at least the end of June. In March she spent a few days at Lake Mead with Philip Liebmann, the head of Rheingold Beer, whom she had met in her own home photographing a commercial for his company. The two had soon been seen on a few dates in Los Angeles. Questioned whether it was true that she and the brewery owner might marry, Linda replied, "I don't want to get married to anybody. I'm having too much fun free."

Late that spring she was rushed into *Second Chance*, again at RKO, and quickly lost a great deal of weight, before flying to Mexico for location work on the picture. *Second Chance* was a thriller about a cable car full of passengers trapped thousands of feet above the ground between two mountain peaks in the Andes. The film was Howard Hughes's effort to capitalize on the current 3-D rage. Hughes produced the picture himself a short time before his final purchase of the RKO studio. He still harbored fond memories of Linda, knew she needed work, and cast her in the role of a former gangster's moll.

When *Second Chance* was released in July, it received favorable notices, with Linda, Robert Mitchum, and Jack Palance all awarded their share of acclaim. Critics agreed that the screenplay was tense and exciting, building to an effective climax. The suspense was brilliantly photographed, and director Rudolph Maté used the cumbersome 3-D process more skillfully than most. There was a spine-tingling fight between Mitchum and Palance on top of the cable car, culminating in Palance's being knocked overboard. Linda departed for Italy confident that she had a commercial hit.

She and Lola flew to Rome in May, several weeks before *Donne proibite* went before the cameras. Giuseppe Amato was at the airport to greet them, obviously treating Linda as more than a lead actress. An affair of sorts had developed between them, although it proved something of a love-hate relationship. They fought constantly. Amato needled Linda, refusing to speak English, knowing her Italian was limited. Their evenings together usually ended in a fight, with Linda getting melodramatic after a few drinks.

She settled into a spacious villa and fell in love with Rome all over again. Lola had no one to play with except the caretaker's daughter, and soon developed health problems. Her mother was convinced that she needed psychiatric help. "I'm shaking with nerves," Linda wrote Pev. "I'm still thin as a rail. You wouldn't recognize my figure, and I'm eating spaghetti like mad. I'll probably feel better when I actually start the picture, but I'm not in a very cheerful mood right now. I have a bad case of opening night jitters on this one."

Filming didn't begin until July 22. Linda was coached on her dialogue by a fine Italian actress, practicing the language with a tape recorder. "I am not worried about my Italian," she said. "It is surprisingly good, and I can always dub the mistakes I make." Amato was directing the picture, so their personal conflicts added tension on the set. The story, Amato's attempt at the new Italian realism, dealt with three women evicted from a bordello, with Linda playing one of the prostitutes.

On June 17, she wrote Pev at wit's end. "Hold onto your hat," she warned. "I am very concerned over Lola. She seems much better physically at the moment, but, darling, she is practically unmanageable. I wish to God I knew what in the world was wrong with her (or with me) and what in the world to do with her." By then Linda's harangues with Amato had grown so stormy they were an embarrassment to everyone present. "My Italian director friend can't handle me," Linda told the press. "He says, 'You American women aren't women. You're men!' I tell him, 'We like it that way.'"

When *Donne proibite* opened at the Rialto in New York in November 1956, critics dismissed it as a feeble Italian drama. "It appears that it was dug, shoveled, and dumped together out of the files of a cheap romance magazine," the *New York Times* said. The dubbed version had limited distribution in the United States, but the consensus was that the picture was a waste of its star's ability.

Driving to and from the studio outside Rome every day, Linda noticed a group of girls, all bedraggled, playing behind a fence. They would run to the gate whenever they saw her limousine pass, and Linda began to watch for them. One morning she had some extra time and stopped to talk to the children. She found out they were orphans who lived in a dilapidated house with a French woman under makeshift circumstances. Linda checked into the situation further and grew determined to raise money for a Girls Town of Italy, to be established along the lines of Father Flanagan's Boys Town in Nebraska. Like Pearl, Linda had her generous side, was involved in all kinds of charity work, but the notion of a Girls Town of Italy became her pet project.

Upon returning to New York, she spent several days with Joe Mankiewicz, who was writing *The Barefoot Contessa*, an original script he planned to produce and direct for United Artists. The story centers on the tragic life of Spanish actress Maria Vargas, who is destroyed by inner conflict. The film was to be made in color, would costar Humphrey Bogart, and from the start had "arty" written all over it. Linda claimed the script was being prepared expressly for her, insisting that Mankiewicz envisioned Maria as the part to carry her to dramatic heights. "It supposedly *was* Linda," an intimate acquaintance said, "because Linda was always barefoot. She hated wearing shoes." Mankiewicz later stated *The Barefoot Contessa* was written mostly in Glen Cove, Long Island, with no thought of Darnell, whereas the actress told friends the script had been written in her bedroom with her help. Linda said Mankiewicz had promised to call her the minute contracts were drawn up on the film. She returned to Los Angeles certain that her greatest role lay just ahead, fashioned specifically to her talents. She soon learned from trade papers that Ava Gardner had been cast in the part.

Linda felt betrayed, sobbing over the loss of the role and what she considered the perfidy of her lover. It was a humiliation from which she never recovered. "That was the bitterest pill she ever had to swallow," Jeanne Curtis said. "She felt exploited. She really did love Joseph Mankiewicz. He was truly the love of her life." *The Barefoot Contessa* spelled the end of their relationship, although friends knew she would have gone running back had he sent for her.

Despondent, Linda remained at home only a few days, then took off for New Mexico. She had no definite film commitments, although she had discussed making a picture in France with director David Miller. When those plans fell through, she was very much at liberty. She spent several weeks at the Hurd ranch drinking heavily and sleeping most of the day, although she did consent to sit several afternoons while Henriette painted her portrait. The two would retire into the artist's studio around two o'clock, with Linda taking a pitcher of martinis along. "That's a difficult time for me to paint portraits," Mrs. Hurd confessed. "I usually work in the morning." She painted just the head and shoulders, with a black scarf tied around Linda's hair. The finished oil captured the star's Madonna quality—her beauty, the pathos, but also her human side. For years the Hurd portrait hung in the hall of Linda's Bel Air home.

Over in a valley close by, Linda found a sheep ranch she wanted to buy. The property consisted of several sections, primarily grazing land, but with a three-room house and a big apple orchard. Linda felt it was an ideal place to retreat from the Hollywood nonsense. At thirty, she realized her time in the limelight was limited, and was fully aware she was no great actress. She thought the ranch, near Picacho, would make a perfect place to relax between assignments. "I'm sick of Hollywood," she told reporters. "I'll be back only long enough to make a film, if I'm offered one. But that's it. I have low blood pressure and need the altitude I've found in New Mexico."

She celebrated the Christmas holidays at home with Lola, and saw a great deal of Philip Liebmann, who had purchased an important brewery on the west coast and was spending extended periods at the Beverly Hills Hotel. The beer baron treated Linda royally, escorting her to all the fashionable clubs and choice restaurants. He obviously worshipped her. "If he'd had his choice," a close observer said, "I think Philip would have wrapped her in cotton to preserve the image he had of her." By late January there was talk that he and Linda would marry. Liebmann had bought her the New Mexico ranch and was urging her to retire from the screen so as to devote herself to a life of luxury as his wife. He promised her travel, time alone, even the freedom to make guest appearances. Finally Linda accepted his proposal. When Alfred Liebmann, Philip's father, inquired about a wedding gift, Linda told him she wanted the money to establish Girls Town of Italy. Between them the elder Liebmann and his son came up with $45,000 for the project. A short time later, in February 1954, Philip and Linda were secretly married.

A Jew converted to Catholicism, Philip was a shy, unattractive man who was first and foremost a businessman. Well educated and knowledgeable about art and music, he was a strange person, sometimes generous, sometimes difficult, given to screaming and yelling at subordinates. Uncertain about his sexuality, he appeared almost a eunuch to some, sexless if not impotent. Superficially pleasant, he somehow seemed lifeless. "There was nothing I could find fault with," Trudi Dieterle remembered, "he was just really gross." A distinguished regular on the *Rheingold Theatre*, a television series sponsored by Liebmann's company, recounted an occasion at Claridge's in London when he watched Philip get out of a bathtub. "I was almost repelled by looking at his blubber," the actor recalled. "He had this big, flabby body. He was tall, but terribly soft, although when dressed, it was well disguised."

A friend of Linda's concurred: "He was a big slob. Liebmann to me was repulsive. Unfortunately he was to Linda, too." But Philip talked endlessly about how perfect and beautiful his wife was, much to Linda's disgust. "He was very fastidious," the star's friend continued. "He used cologne and deodorant and chewed chlorophyll all the time. It was enough to make you sick. He was nice enough, but just a slob."

Gradually Philip's relationship with Linda turned into a business arrangement. "Just be my wife in name only," Philip had told her, "and I'll never expect anything more." Financially he rescued her from serious trouble, and some claimed she married him specifically to get the money for Girls Town. She made it plain his love for her was not reciprocated, and at first he appeared to accept that. But after the wedding it was a different story. Liebmann's family owned a mansion in Rye, New York, which Linda described as an "old mausoleum," although the couple spent most of their time there. It was understood that she and Philip would sleep in separate bedrooms, but her disgust for him was evident from the start. He lavished gifts on her, including an engagement ring insured for $42,000. More than once during cocktail parties at the Hurd ranch she threw that ring across the room. "She hated him," Henriette Wyeth Hurd maintained, "and never should have married him. It was terrible."

During the first months of their marriage the couple saw one another only sporadically. Linda spent most of the spring in Los Angeles, busy making *This Is My Love* for RKO. Stuart Heisler was again directing, and the film had Linda playing the neurotic sister of Howard Hughes's latest discovery, Faith Domergue. When the picture was released in September, neither audiences nor the critics were much impressed with what obviously was a grade B soap opera.

Darnell family members remembered Philip fondly, but felt sorry for him, admitting his marriage to Linda was unhappy from the outset. "He was really a nice, down-to-earth fellow," said Undeen. "You'd never know he was a big executive." They all ate Thanksgiving dinner at Pearl's house that year. Everyone sat on the floor and sang, while Undeen's husband, Harry, played the ukulele. "Philip just had a ball," Undeen recalled. "But he wanted Linda to quit acting and travel around with him to promote his beer, and at that point she wasn't about to give up her career." Monte adored Philip, finding him extremely sensitive. "He and I got along fabulously," she said, "and he worshipped the ground Linda walked on. He would have given her anything she asked for, but for some reason she was just an old witch with him."

Disliking Philip, but hating the hypocrisy of their marriage even more, Linda's frustration turned to anger. Eventually she felt guilty that she couldn't love the husband who obviously idolized her, felt cheapened when he lavished expensive gifts on her, detested him for being blind to her faults, and felt that he exploited her just as Pearl and Darryl Zanuck had done earlier. After a few drinks it all began to fester, and she lashed out at Philip, growing more furious when he allowed her to abuse him. "Anything you want, darling," Liebmann would say. "Anything. You know that."

One afternoon the couple drove over to Encino to swim in

Monte and Danny Wilson's pool. Dick Paxton and his wife were also there. "Linda just cut Philip down every minute," Paxton remembered, "while he was just like a big kid." The six of them decided to eat dinner at a nearby restaurant, where Linda proceeded to pick a fight with Liebmann, causing surrounding parties to stare. She kept at him, getting louder by the minute, until Philip was almost in tears. Embarrassed, Monte whispered, "Linda, let's have a nice dinner." Linda pouted for a few minutes, then started in on her husband again. Monte knew what was coming and began getting angry herself. "Linda," she told her sister, "you don't make love in public, please don't argue in public." Linda's eyes flashed, but she said nothing. A couple of minutes later, she threw her fork down, turned to Philip, and really began letting him have it. Monte suddenly heard her own voice above Linda's. "Tweedles Darnell," she ordered, "shut up! You sound just like Mother!" Linda hated to be called Tweedles in public, and her eyes flashed as if there were about to be a thunderstorm. "You sound just like Mother, Tweedles," Monte repeated softly.

Liebmann arranged a job for Cal at NBC in New York, hoping to lure Linda to Rye permanently. Cal worked for nearly two years in New York, where no one seemed particularly impressed that he was Linda Darnell's brother. Cal welcomed that and felt like his own person for a change. Linda herself avoided the city so far as possible, rushing whenever she could to New Mexico, where she could avoid publicity and booze as freely as she pleased. "Linda hated being married to Philip Liebmann because she was just a bauble on his arm, a stuffed head on some hunter's wall," Cal insisted. "When she lived at Rye, there was a Rolls Royce, mink coats, diamonds, nightclubs, restaurants, café society, and that just wasn't Linda."

Linda took Yvonne Wood to her ranch for three weeks, thinking they would both do some painting. They drove into Roswell and bought all kinds of art supplies. Linda set up an easel and started painting the water tank, then grew discouraged. Yvonne could never lure her back to work, although Linda insisted her friend paint regularly. Since Yvonne was an early riser, she usually went to bed at a decent hour. Linda was a devoted night person, sitting up alone reading, playing an electric organ so softly she could scarcely hear herself, or propped up in bed with a portable typewriter, dashing off letters until four or five in the morning. Once Yvonne asked why she didn't sleep at night and wake up in time to savor the glorious New Mexico sunrises. Linda smiled and replied, "I've seen the sun rise, thank you."

Philip Liebmann flew in and out of Picacho in his private plane, usually staying only a few hours. Linda spent his money freely, buying anything she thought someone needed, plying herself with luxuries, charging everything. She shopped for a wardrobe she thought was appropriate for ranch life and discussed plans for remodeling the ranch house, including tile in the kitchen, extra bedrooms and baths, with a fireplace in every room.

For a while Roy lived at the ranch, taking care of the place when his daughter was away, and fishing and hunting with the owner of the adjoining property. Linda's ranch was next to that of the Flores family, who looked after her grounds and livestock. Their daughter Maria, in her late teens, had been in nurse's training, but had come home following a nervous breakdown. One evening Linda was having guests in and asked Maria if she'd be willing to work for a few hours. Linda liked the girl immediately, asked her back several times, and began to wonder if Maria would be able to work for her permanently. She asked Yvonne Wood whether she thought this young Hispanic woman had skills enough to supervise her household, help pay bills, take care of correspondence and travel arrangements, and all the details Linda hated. Yvonne arranged to spend time with Maria and decided she could handle the job perfectly.

Maria Flores stayed with Linda for nine years, through all kinds of ups and downs. "I was just a little country girl," Maria said later, "who would never have seen the world had it not been for LD. It was a great opportunity for me because of the travel, the chance to see so much, and meet so many interesting people. It definitely changed my life." Linda had Maria's teeth straightened and selected a new wardrobe for her, including a fur wrap. Maria Pia, Linda called her, and the girl went with her everywhere. Sometimes when it was just the two of them, they played canasta or Scrabble. Other times they sat around and gossiped, or Linda talked about "naughty little things," generally something that had happened during the day. "I felt she was a person who should be taken care of," Maria said. "She was the sweetest, nicest, most vulnerable person I've ever met. She needed someone that was strong and protective. She didn't get that in her marriages, unfortunately."

Linda spent Christmas that first year of her marriage to Philip at his father's home on Park Avenue. She looked the part of a Park Avenue matron, driving around the city in Liebmann's Rolls Royce, yet she hated every minute of it. Philip was erratic with money, unpredictable in his moods. He and Linda went into Tiffany's, spent over $7,000 on Steuben crystal for gifts, then he refused to give her $400 to paint her bedroom in the house at Rye. Philip had trouble with the nerves in his feet. He would sit beside Linda in the backseat of his chauffeur-driven car stomping his foot, nauseating her no end. "We just assumed she married him for his money," an actor on *Rheingold Theatre* admitted. "I think he felt that, too. He showered her with gifts, but she didn't treat him well at all. She seemed to be just wallowing in the security he was able to provide."

Linda saw few of Philip's strengths and all of his weaknesses, shuddering whenever he came near her. Occasionally she would sneak off evenings to go dancing with Cal. Otherwise she filled her time with charity work, involving herself in all sorts of causes—aiding blacks, native Americans, Eskimos, the Kidney Foundation, a church in Arizona that happened upon her name and address. "She helped everybody," Maria recalled. "She was constantly sending money to the poor, always doing something for charity. There was not a selfish bone in her body."

Shortly after the New Year, Linda flew to Italy to make her second picture for Giuseppe Amato, this time a comedy with Vittorio DeSica and Rossano Brazzi. Called *Gli ultimi cinque minuti*, or *The Last Five Minutes*, the film was to be shot at Cinecitta Studio and would give her a chance to add final touches on the establishment of Girls Town. She arrived in Rome during February 1955 accompanied by Lola, Maria Flores, and Yvonne Wood. They moved into a villa Amato had arranged, complete with wood-burning stove in case the electricity should fail.

Linda and Yvonne spent most of their time laughing, finding each other hilarious. Since Yvonne was her designer on the picture, they rode to the studio every morning with Yvonne reading aloud portions of letters she had received from her husband. "Linda would just go off into gales of laughter," Yvonne recalled, "and then say, 'Now you've got to let me read your answer.'" Around two-thirty the cast broke for lunch. Amato would have food brought in, and a table would be spread for him on the set. He shared his meal with Linda and DeSica, but offered nothing to the crew, who had been working since five that morning. Linda refused to eat, sending out for enough food for everyone. Amato would scream at her, "You're a fool spending your money." But Linda was not about to eat when others were hungry. "I began to smell a rat," Yvonne said, "that she had paid my wages as designer, not Amato. I think she came home without a penny."

Gli ultimi cinque minuti turned out to be a terrible picture, filmed with each actor speaking his own language. Vittorio DeSica and Rossano Brazzi spoke Italian, Sophia Desmarets spoke French, and Linda spoke English, while Amato yelled at everybody in Italian. Later the parts were dubbed for international distribution. "It was really the damnedest thing to watch," Yvonne Wood remembered. The picture was never released in the United States.

Linda's fights with Amato became so embarrassing that Yvonne tried to avoid going out with them, but Linda always insisted either she or Maria come along. "Talk about overacting," Wood said. "Linda could be very Latin, very melodramatic. When she'd get going, any director would have thrown her off the set." Between the fights and Linda's drinking, Yvonne was ready to leave after six weeks. The picture had another twenty days of shooting left, but with the clothes finished, Yvonne decided to go home early. "I knew Linda was paying the bills," she said, "and I wanted out."

Girls Town had opened at Ottavia, just north of Rome, in quarters donated by Linda and Philip Liebmann. The facilities would accommodate thirty girls, ranging in age from babes-in-arms up to twenty-one. The project, which included a school, was under the supervision of the Catholic Church, with an American nun sent over as head. An appeal was made for clothing and furniture for the home, and Linda stayed in Italy long enough to see her dream realized. "That was really the only time she was happy in all the years I was with her," Maria observed later. "She should have stayed. Italy was where she belonged."

Returning aboard the *Queen Elizabeth* with Lola and Maria, Linda arrived in New York late in June. Philip was on hand to greet them, although Linda's relationship with him moved from bad to worse. "He wanted Mother to be something she couldn't be," said Lola. "Mother was a real person, not a china doll. I think she liked working hard. When she was cut off from her creative processes, everything went downhill, and I think that's what happened when she married Philip." He was good to Lola, although seldom overtly affectionate. "I don't remember his trying to get me to like him," Lola said.

Late in their marriage Philip decided the couple should adopt a child, feeling that a baby of their own would bring them closer together. Despite her love for children, Linda was not enthusiastic, but ultimately agreed, and they adopted a baby girl, which they named Alfreda, after Philip's father. The adoption was never common knowledge, and Linda rarely spoke of the child. "I always thought she was a strange baby," said Lola, "but I was very small and didn't take well to suddenly having a little sister." When they divorced, Philip kept the girl.

More and more the Hollywood princess came to feel like a prisoner and wanted to return to Bel Air, but Philip refused to give her money. "I can't go anyplace," she complained to Cal. Film offers were no longer coming in. She had all the time in the world with nothing to do. So far as American producers were concerned, Linda had simply been out of circulation too long. "After a while," she said, "performing gets into your blood." She wanted work, was even willing to lower her fee. Finally, in August 1955, Linda returned to her old studio. Out of necessity Twentieth Century–Fox had entered the television field, and Linda eagerly consented to make her dramatic debut in the new medium on the "General Electric Theater."

Philip promised to make Linda a producer, which would have allowed her the freedom to select her own scripts and choose the directors, actors, and technicians she wanted, but his price was too high. Their marriage had run its course. Linda appeared in Juarez on December 1, seeking a Mexican divorce. She told reporters she was there for business purposes, "which I prefer not to discuss." Less than two years after she and Liebmann had married, she was granted a divorce on grounds of incompatibility. "There is no bitterness in our divorce," the actress said. "I get no alimony and we each keep our own property." She gave back the $42,000 engagement ring Liebmann had given her and the ranch in New Mexico. "Philip was wonderfully generous to me," Linda said later. "But let's face it, I was pretty unhappy."

Giving up the ranch was the hardest part, although Philip insisted on that before he would consent to a divorce. "He knew that was her dream," Maria Flores contended, "and would only let her go if she gave it up." Five days after their divorce, he married a twenty-six-year-old Los Angeles girl who had been a reservation clerk with an automobile rental firm in Beverly Hills. Their romance began when Philip rented a car from her. He died in 1971.

Immediately following the Mexican hearing, Linda returned to Los Angeles. She settled into her Bel Air house with Lola and later that month made a Screen Gems movie for television, called *All for the Love of a Man*. She was eager to throw herself into work. Liebmann had bought an original script for her called *Constantia*, a romantic drama about a disabled girl, which she hoped to film as an independent production in Portugal, but the picture never materialized. "At thirty-two," she said bravely, "I can see tell-tale marks in the mirror, but the ravages of time no longer terrify me. I am told that when surface beauty is gone, the real woman emerges. My only regret will be that I could not have begun it earlier—that so many years have been ruined because I was considered beautiful." But beauty had been her strength too long; without it, courage was but a veneer of words.

Prince Charming

Herbert Yates, head of Republic Pictures, offered Linda the lead in a low-budget western called *Dakota Incident*, which had the benefit of a solid script by Frederic Louis Fox. Three years before, a major Hollywood actress would have been reluctant to accept an invitation from "Poverty Row," but by 1955 even the biggest stars found work in the studios undependable. Linda was delighted with the offer and pleased to be working with a cast headed by Dale Robertson (whom she knew from Fox), Ward Bond, and John Lund. Lewis Foster, the original author of *Mr. Smith Goes to Washington*, would direct, and Linda accepted the project convinced that the conflict between hardened frontiersmen and Indian reformers lifted the story above Saturday afternoon drivel.

The picture was filmed almost entirely on location. On the evening before the first day's shooting, the players gathered in Linda's motel room to read the script aloud. "That was our first mistake," the actress said later. It was no comedy, but the snickering started with the first page. By the time they reached the part where the stagecoach passengers were supposed to be pinned down in a creekbed by hostile Indians, the session was ripe for hysteria. Then one of the characters accused Ward Bond, playing a politician, of crawling toward Linda with lustful intentions. "I was not!" cried Bond indignantly. "I was just looking for an apple!" At that everything fell apart and wasn't restored that evening. "I can see Linda now," actor John Lund recalled, "rolling on the floor, with tears streaming down that beautiful face. Not a bad way to remember someone."

The company remained congenial, so that *Dakota Incident* proved a generally pleasant assignment. Linda liked the actors she was working with, and they adored her. "In the words of the old song," Lund said, "she was lovely to look at and delightful to know." She was drinking heavily throughout the picture, although it never posed problems during working hours. Every day at noon she'd drink vodka and usually eat something with onions.

"And I'd have to make love to her after lunch!" exclaimed Dale Robertson. "But Linda was a hard worker. She did the best she could."

The film was completed early in January, with the final results less impressive than the original script. Yates insisted on a number of changes, and the song "The Restless Wind," which became a western standard, was eliminated from the opening. The *New York Times* found *Dakota Incident* "an erratic and moralistic western," while Linda was judged attractive and engaging in the role of a dance hall queen, called "ravishingly beautiful" by the *New York World Telegram*.

With the studios cutting back on production, film offers were few and far between. Linda had long intended to attempt the stage, and it now became essential. She planned to test her skills far enough from either coast that none of the major critics would review her. "I have wanted for years to try the stage," she said buoyantly, "where you stand or fall with your acting ability alone." But it took determination to appear with no professional theater background before an audience, not knowing whether she could sustain a live performance or not. She decided to make her debut at the Sombrero Playhouse in Phoenix, Arizona, in Edith Sommer's *A Roomful of Roses*. Linda was aware that having mastered her craft for the screen was slender preparation for the task at hand. She spent six weeks studying her part, staying up nights rehearsing lines with Maria Flores. By mid-February 1956, when she arrived in Phoenix, the wire service had learned of her stage debut and reported it coast to coast, so that critics came flocking into town prepared to be tough. "I've decided to dip my big toe into stage acting," Linda told reporters. "I've hiked my little fanny down to Phoenix to do *A Roomful of Roses*. I thought if I laid an egg nobody'd know about it."

But her notices were remarkably good. "Miss Darnell, making her professional stage debut," the *Arizona Republic* reported, "need have had none of the qualms she voiced before her appearance. She enacted the part of the mother with dignity and poise." Linda discovered she liked theater work enormously. Most of her friends claimed she developed into a better actress on the stage than she had ever been in pictures. "She liked the response of a live audience," Maria recalled. "She was a performer, and she wanted to feel accepted." Cal flew to Phoenix for opening night, giving

Linda the boost she needed. During the intermission she signed a contract with the Coconut Grove Playhouse in Miami to open there early the following month.

For Miami she agreed to play the role of Laura in Robert Anderson's controversial *Tea and Sympathy*, a play in which Deborah Kerr had scored a huge success on Broadway three years before. "I'm scared stiff about *Tea and Sympathy*," Linda told reporters, "but this marvelous magic world of the live theater is one of the high spots of my life." Laura was a difficult part, but quickly became her favorite. Critics again found her performance far better than they had expected. The *Miami Herald* judged the production "a sensitive and absorbing presentation; Miss Darnell gives the role a new dimension."

Linda eagerly agreed to tour with *Tea and Sympathy*, eventually traveling all over the country with it, headlining a number of performances that included young Burt Reynolds. "She was very good in that part," Maria assured, "and did it for a long time. We literally lived out of a suitcase." Those close to Linda agreed that she truly wanted to develop into a fine actress and realized the stage offered her opportunities Hollywood rarely had. The theater gave her a satisfaction her film career seldom provided, and she thrived on the challenge.

Linda's travels were interrupted long enough for her to appear on television programs such as "The Twentieth Century–Fox Hour," "Screen Director's Playhouse," "Ford Theatre," and "Climax!" Live television frightened her, so she appeared on "Playhouse 90" only once, absolutely terrified, although her performance was solid enough. Even though Linda was working steadily, her financial situation remained far from good. She had been informed by the government that she owed a considerable amount in back taxes and there were unpaid taxes on the Bel Air house. Ultimately, to save her home, she was forced to sell some jewelry and expensive gifts she had received through the years, yet consistently refused to accept the generosity of others. "Linda was always proud," her sister Monte said. "Even when she was desperate for money, she would never take help from anyone." Fortunately her friend Jeanne Curtis had a good head for business and helped Linda slowly sort through her finances. Jeanne insisted Linda go on a tight budget until her debts were paid. Sometimes she missed the old days, when she was under contract to Twentieth Century-Fox; other times she felt free. Many of her

30.0 APPLICATION PROGRAMMING INTERFACE (API)

fans remained loyal, eager to see Linda on the stage. Occasionally she felt forgotten. Once in Denver a girl came up to her and enthusiastically remarked, "Gee, you look just like Dorothy Lamour!" Times like that reminded her how transient success can be, how quickly the public forgets.

Linda's language had grown more salty through the years, sometimes offending friends. "The words that came out of that beautiful mouth!" Maria Flores said. Her voice had deepened into what Linda called her whiskey voice. Between engagements, at home in Bel Air, she often was unavailable, sleeping odd hours, withdrawing into her private cocoon. "Maybe only twice did I see her intoxicated," Jeanne Curtis recalled. "However, she did consume vodka, probably a bottle in a day's time. It was a constant thing throughout the day. She would type letters, but would try to avoid the telephone. Her body lacked the proper nutrients from not eating consistently." Maria tried to watch over her, even adding water to the vodka bottles, but Linda caught her and flew into a rage.

More frequently her temper was unleashed on Lola. The more she drank, the more she yelled, at times becoming vicious. On the second floor of the Bel Air house there were stairs in front and back, with a long hall between. Without her glasses Linda had trouble navigating the steps. "If I could run out of her room and make it to the stairs," said Lola, "I was home free. Mother couldn't see very well. I think she probably loved me more than anyone in the world. But when she was drinking, she could be extremely violent. If it weren't for the stairs, I don't know whether I would have made it."

Lola developed an attitude of self-defense, the only weapon she had for protecting herself physically and emotionally. On the one hand she was the spoiled only child, given everything, terribly materialistic; on the other she was packed off to boarding schools or left with governesses. When Linda was home, she saw her daughter only when it was convenient for her and then more for casual pleasantries than any sustained relationship.

The tension between Lola and Maria merely added to the pressure, and intensified as Linda and Maria grew closer. "Lola was not an easy child," Maria remembered. "She could be sweet, but she could also be a Dennis the Menace. She didn't spend much time with Linda and had a grudge against her mother." Having come from humble circumstances, Maria was fiercely possessive of

Linda and the new sophistication she had tasted, eager to protect her protectress. "I think Maria felt threatened by me," Lola said, "by anyone who tried to get close to Mother. I was very nasty to her as a child because I felt threatened, too. She was taking my mother from me."

Linda would sometimes call her daughter into her room for girl talk, usually soon after she'd awakened. She'd still be wearing what she called her "frownies," little pink plastic triangles she wore at the corners of her mouth and between her eyes to keep her face from wrinkling when she slept. As she peeled off the frownies she and Lola would chat. Linda would prop herself up in bed, put on fleshtone glasses, and want to know everything that was going on. For an hour or so they'd giggle and talk, and Lola would suddenly feel close to her mother. Then she was gone—off on another tour, an occasional voice on the telephone.

In July 1956 Linda announced she had signed a contract to make her Broadway debut in a new play entitled *Harbor Lights*. Columbia Pictures had agreed to back the show, hoping eventually to make a motion picture from the script. Since the play was schedule to go into rehearsal in August, Linda and Maria spent a frantic month learning lines, trying to make more of the script than appeared on paper. Cal read the play and told Linda she was making a mistake. "It was all exposition," her brother recalled. "There was nothing happening on stage except a lot of shouting. It was dreadful!" Weak though the script was, Linda was determined to have her fling at Broadway.

Two weeks into rehearsals everyone had grown tense. Linda was having trouble finding her character, and decided to play the role of a young mother realistically, flirting with method acting, then gave up on that approach. She was floundering, and much of the fault lay in the writing, which was full of clichés. The situation looked hopeless, and Linda became a bundle of nerves, wanting Maria in the wings with a script at all times. Liquor remained her constant crutch. Robert Alda, Linda's leading man, recognized the strain she was under. Every day there were new lines as the script was revised. One whole scene was taken out of the first act and put into the third, with no better results. They opened in New Haven in September with the script still in shambles. "The final scene had the players burying a dead duck onstage," *Variety* reported. "Unless there is considerable improvement during the tryout tour, that may prove . . . symbolic."

Then Robert Alda sprained his ankle, making it necessary to postpone the opening in Boston. "This script is a horror," Linda wrote photographer Bill Langley. "We got murdered in New Haven, and justly so." Boston was no better. The company arrived in New York knowing the situation was futile. "I'm fed up with costume characters and cow queens," Linda told the press. "Any actress with serious ambitions must sometime put her abilities to the test, not coast along on face and figure alone. I believe this show offers the range to prove my point." But her efforts were in vain. When *Harbor Lights* opened on October 4, the play was roasted by the critics. Brooks Atkinson claimed Linda Darnell "stood with her arms at her sides, depicting constant fury, and goes through each scene with the same distaste for the characters, the story, the symbolism, and the scenery." The show folded after four performances.

Ann Miller came to Linda's rescue, taking her on a tour of Hilton Hotels in the Caribbean. Soon after returning home Linda met an American Airlines pilot named Merle Roy Robertson, whom she began dating. Everyone called him Robby. A likeable, soft-spoken man, Robby was strikingly different from any of Linda's other off-screen romances. He was handsome, debonair, a giant of a man. "Robby had the body of a Greek Adonis," Dick Curtis assured, "with a very dry way about him. He was the epitome of what a man in the movies should be. He had the women drooling over him." Linda soon became a major conquest. Although she never forgot Joe Mankiewicz, she clearly fell in love with Robby Robertson. "I mean he was a big, grand passion," said Yvonne Wood. "He was a handsome guy and dashing, and she fell for him."

Robby was thirty-nine, six years older than Linda, and lived in an apartment at Redondo Beach. Before meeting her he had had an affair with Jayne Mansfield. Suddenly Linda found herself in a romantic involvement like none she had ever experienced. Robby was affectionate, sexually experienced, suavely aggressive. He called her wherever she went, or sometimes simply showed up in whatever city she happened to be playing. Before long he asked her to marry him. He had never been married and made Linda feel like a desirable woman. He seemed to love *her* rather than her image. They had great times together, and Linda even promised him she'd stop drinking, although she never did.

"Robby was gorgeous," Lola remembered. "I mean I used to

cry over that man with his tan and his silver hair and his beautiful eyes. He was razzle dazzle and fun, and he wore a uniform. Robby was super." He owned a boat and enjoyed taking Lola out in it, the two of them laughing and having a grand time. Undeen met Robby and saw how much her sister cared for him. "He was such a handsome devil!" Undeen insisted.

In February 1957 the couple took out a license, and were married the next month in the chapel of Mission Inn in Riverside. Linda wore a pale pink gown, and Lola, then nine, served as flower girl, giving her new daddy a big kiss after the ceremony. The newlyweds planned to honeymoon in New Orleans and Miami, just as soon as the bride finished a television show, and intended to live permanently in Linda's home in Bel Air.

Robby continued to fly, primarily the Los Angeles–Chicago route, yet immediately became a partner in the Executive Management Corporation, handling tax, insurance, legal, and investment problems for theatrical and professional people. Linda was involved with a new film, *Zero Hour!* for Paramount, her first picture in over a year. Hall Bartlett directed the low-budget melodrama, based on a story by Arthur Hailey, in which Dana Andrews and Sterling Hayden played two airline pilots struggling to get a planeload of passengers safely to the ground.

Zero Hour! would be Linda's last picture for seven years. She had appeared in forty-one films and earned some $6 million. Now in her early thirties, she was virtually a has-been by Hollywood standards. Fortunately she had Robby and for the moment was able to keep her career in perspective. "Things are different," she said philosophically. "The big studios are dying, and of course I'm sad. But after all, I've been very, very lucky."

She looked forward to more television work and making a home for her new husband and Lola. Robby frequently came back from flights exhausted, and Linda enjoyed catering to him. She was grateful that Lola and he got along so splendidly. "They are adorable together," Linda wrote to friends, "and are getting to really love one another." When Linda flew with Robby to Denver to visit Jeanne and Dick Curtis, she admitted how much she already depended on her husband emotionally, and her attitude was more positive.

Linda, Robby, and Lola spent a quiet first Christmas together at home, decorating a white tree. Linda cooked a goose, adding so much seasoning to the vegetables that only she could eat them.

"At first theirs was a fun, happy, good marriage," Richard Curtis observed, "but what happened was that Robby was flying all over the country and Linda was doing her stage work, so that they wound up only seeing each other between performances. Then Linda started to go into a deep depressive shell."

The Robertsons spent time with photographer Bill Langley in New York, during which Langley grew concerned about Linda's drinking. She was always laughing, but Robby indicated she had a problem with alcohol. "I do wish you wouldn't take everything Robby says so seriously," Linda wrote Langley later. "I promise you your fears are groundless. I am experienced enough with this drinking bit to know when I go off the deep end, and so far, everything is still under *my* control. I know how great a thing AA is, and if I ever need it, that's where I'll go right off the bat."

In September 1958 Linda appeared in *The Children's Hour* at the Bucks County Playhouse in Pennsylvania. She still found stage performances exhilarating, less inhibiting than working before a camera. "You underplay everything in the movies," she said. "On the stage you can make sweeping gestures and still not be overacting." During October she was featured in a "Pursuit" episode on CBS television. A month later she was shocked to learn of Tyrone Power's death from a heart attack while filming *Solomon and Sheba* in Spain. "She adored Tyrone," Maria Flores said. "He had been so nice to her. When he died, she was absolutely devastated. She simply adored him."

Around the time of Power's death Linda began sinking into a depression, a mood that deepened over the next seven years. She reached the point where she even disliked Christmas, since the holiday reminded her of her estrangement from her family. She felt guilty for not wanting to see her mother, yet couldn't bring herself to open old wounds. Robby offered support, but eventually she began pulling away even from him. She felt isolated, wanting to reach out, yet incapable of making the effort.

Suddenly she grew nervous about going on stage, even when she had her lines down perfectly. She often felt queasy and even vomited before a performance, and worried about not being able to respond to other actors, afraid she wouldn't pick up on cues. She arrived in Chicago in February 1959 in emotional turmoil. Her personal problems had festered into physical illness. She had been scheduled to perform in *Dial M for Murder* at the Drury Lane Theater, but decided she wasn't up to such a demanding role. The management substituted *Late Love* instead, but she still felt inadequate. In desperation she telephoned a Beverly Hills physician, who suggested hypnosis as a cure for her anxieties. A doctor flew to Chicago, supposedly placed Linda into a deep sleep, then read her lines from the play. She later claimed that was the way she learned her part.

During the Chicago run of *Late Love*, Linda met Rickey Fishburn, a fourteen-year-old boy who was a kidney patient at Billings Memorial Hospital. Rickey had written for an autographed picture, which she promptly sent, and later they talked on the telephone. On Valentine's Day Linda visited Rickey, taking him a box of candy. She fell in love with the child, eventually paying his transportation to Los Angeles so she could show him Disneyland and Marineland. The boy had suffered from kidney disease all his life but didn't know his days were numbered. Linda did everything she could to see that he lived like a normal child and showered him with the attention she sometimes found difficult to show Lola. When Rickey died that summer, Linda was grief stricken. She had kept a bag packed for weeks, expecting a call from Rickey's doctors. When the call came, she flew to Chicago at once, but found the boy unconscious. She was at his bedside when he died.

She immediately threw herself into work for the Kidney Foundation, serving first as chair of the Los Angeles County annual fund drive. Later she led the national campaign, traveling all over the country. "After what I saw that poor child suffer," Linda said, "I am determined to do everything I can to help fight the disease." She buried herself in charity work, finding momentary release from her own anxieties.

In April 1959 Pearl Darnell made news when she was arrested for shoplifting in a Los Angeles department store. She was accused of taking fifteen dollars' worth of costume jewelry, and pleaded guilty to the charge the next day. Pearl, who by then was living in a small house on the back of Undeen and Harry's property, was fined $100 and placed on probation for six months. The judge made it a condition for probation that she not enter a department store unless accompanied by a responsible adult. "Pearl was a klepto," Jeanne Curtis admitted. "Linda told me, but I don't think that particularly disturbed her. She was certainly never the type to be ashamed of her family for anything they did. Maybe because she wasn't that closely involved with them."

That summer Linda starred in *The Royal Family* at the Penthouse Theater in Highland Park, Illinois. The management wanted her for another play the following year, but she turned them down. Robby insisted there was bigger money in nightclub work, and as their financial situation deteriorated, he began talking seriously about a club act. Linda hated the idea, but they already had had to sell her mother's house in Brentwood, and there was barely enough to pay Maria. Eventually Robby sold one of their cars. "Not enough to cover half the bills owing," Linda wrote friends. "Robby is beside himself with worry over money."

He convinced Linda to give up her business manager and let him handle her career. "Honey, you don't have to worry about the bills anymore," he said. "I'm going to take care of everything." Whatever Robby handed her, Linda signed. They hoped for a television series, but when that fell through, a nightclub act seemed the only solution. Linda knew she couldn't sing anymore, couldn't dance, and was terrified of appearing before an intimate crowd without a play for protection. Nightclub work seemed an undignified way of cashing in on her screen reputation, but Robby insisted it was smart business. "I thought it beneath Linda's dignity," her brother Cal said later. "I really felt it was cheap. But Linda did it anyway."

Robby suggested she team up with his friend Thomas Hayward, who had just left the Metropolitan Opera. Hayward, with his strong tenor voice, could carry the musical side of the act, and Linda happened to like Tommy and trusted him. Finally she agreed to go to New York and work with the singer to see what they could put together, yet her instincts warned she was making a mistake. She reached New York to begin preparations for an act absolutely terrified. "I'm trying a new branch of the business," she announced bravely. "Old movie stars never die. Like General MacArthur we just fade away, but I've still got a way to go before the final fadeout."

As an airline pilot, Robby normally had several days off between flights, during which he dabbled in real estate. He bought property from Texas to Long Beach, including two large apartment complexes on the California coast; he had borrowed the money for these properties in Linda's name and soon had become overextended. "There wasn't anything malicious," Jeanne Curtis maintained. "Robby just got into a position of robbing Peter to pay Paul, borrowing a little here and there." He took out a second mortgage on the Bel Air house and eventually two home improvement loans. "We called them the four mortgages," Jeanne remembered. Robby also neglected to pay the property taxes for three years, amounting to around $9,000. He sold Linda's car, then leased a white Lincoln Continental. "This is the way he was operating," said Jeanne, "and he went into debt on this nightclub act, which he cajoled Linda into and which she hated with a passion."

Hayward put up what funds he had for the act, and Robby borrowed the rest. Despite their different backgrounds Linda and Hayward worked well together, although meshing two totally different styles posed problems from the start, She called him Tomasino, while he adored her down-to-earth humor and salty language. "She was marvelous," he remembered. "Everybody loved Linda. She was really a wonderful woman, even though I don't think she was ever the actress she wanted to be."

Work on the act continued at the Haywards' home in New Rochelle throughout the autumn of 1959, and after breaking for the holidays they met in Bel Air early in the new year. For another three weeks Hayward and Linda worked steadily with arranger Bobby Kroll and writer Eli Basse—coming up with ideas, throwing some out, refining others. The team stayed at Linda's house, often working through the night. Frightened and under pressure, Linda occasionally lost her temper. "Please forgive my 'case of nerves' for the past few weeks," she wrote Hayward after his return to New York. "You know damned well that when I *work*, I do *just that*! It's been a rough and tense time for all of us."

In April she returned to New York to rehearse with Hayward, oversee rewrites, and be on hand when the orchestrations of their material were worked out. They decided Hayward would open the act with "Yours Is My Heart Alone" sung in an upbeat tempo, moving into a group of Italian songs. He would then introduce Linda with "Wait Till You See Her." Linda would walk out wearing a low-cut gown, beautiful jewelry, and an albino mink slung over her shoulder that swept the floor in back. "She didn't have to sing," Hayward recalled. "Just to watch her was enough." Linda's voice had become a sultry, low contralto. She did brief scenes from *Forever Amber* and *A Letter to Three Wives*, and Hayward sang a couple of popular arias before they joined for the finale.

Robby booked the act into La Fiesta Hotel in Ciudad Juarez

for the week of April 24–30. Since Hayward had other commitments, singer Bob Newkirk (formerly with Don McNeill's "Breakfast Club" on radio) filled in for him. Linda arrived in El Paso with Robby, nervous and drinking a great deal. Jeanne Curtis flew down to offer encouragement, staying with Linda in El Paso. "Surprisingly enough," said Jeanne, "she had a fair voice. They sat her on a stool and with the proper arrangements to cover up for her not being a singer, she sounded pretty good."

Linda and Hayward spent all of May rehearsing, with the intention of trying out the act on May 26. The first orchestra rehearsals took place at Glen Casino in Williamsville, New York. Maria Flores wrote in her diary on June 20, "First show lousy; second show worse." Her entry the following day read simply, "No comments." After the run-through on June 21, Kroll, Basse, Hayward, and Linda stayed up until five in the morning rewriting, frantically trying to get the material ready to open at the Town House in Pittsburgh three days later.

The Pittsburgh engagement was declared "the best-kept secret in town," since practically no one knew Linda and Hayward were opening. The few reviewers who managed to catch the act turned in generous notices. "Linda Darnell brings to the café field a very welcome addition," *Variety* reported. "The femme film star handles her lines beautifully and is wise enough to let those to whom she paid good money make her big decisions. What they have written she executes perfectly, and it makes for a smart class act that can fit into any of the top rooms in the country."

Off stage Hayward tried to boost Linda's morale. "Linda," he'd tell her, "I'm out there knocking my brains out singing, and I get good applause. All you have to do is walk on stage and the house comes down." But Linda was never convinced. "All those faces right by your ankles looking up at you," she complained. "They're just too damn close. And you're competing with their knives and forks." It made her physically ill, so that her stomach was upset every evening before going on stage.

The act played Washington, D.C. next, then Linda returned to California, spending July in Los Angeles. Lola, then twelve, was home from school, and Linda wanted to be there with her. They fought constantly, especially when Linda was drinking, which was most of the time. "On two occasions Mother tried to kill me," Lola confessed as an adult. "Both times she was drinking, and both times it was with a knife. Fortunately I was able to get away.

I knew if I could make it to the stairs I was safe. Mother was under tremendous pressure, and let's face it, when you're feeling pressured, a kid is handy."

The financial situation had grown worse, making the act's success all the more crucial. Robby had lined up a heavy fall and winter schedule, beginning with Framingham, Massachusetts, near Boston. Linda arrived there on October 16, scheduled to do two shows a night. There was still rewriting going on, but the house was packed the entire week. Next they played Dallas, New Orleans, and Houston.

From Houston Linda and Tommy Hayward left for Miami, where they played the Fontainebleau, followed by an engagement at the Conch Club in San Juan, Puerto Rico. Hayward began to realize just how much Linda was drinking. She would wake up around four in the afternoon, have a piece of toast and a few strips of bacon, and start drinking Bloody Marys one after the other. When they rehearsed, she always had a glass in her hand. "She would finish her afternoon vodka," Hayward recalled, "and by seven o'clock, two hours before we'd go on, she'd start on Scotch. She would finish a whole quart between seven o'clock and when we'd conclude the act and were back in her hotel room talking. By midnight she was ready to start on another one."

Linda was drinking and not eating, and her body was getting weaker. She lost her shapely legs, while her arms shrank to nothing. Hayward saw that she was ill and tried to reason with her. "No, I'm fine," Linda would say. But every night before going on stage she would be soaking wet, terrified she couldn't live up to the image expected. As the deterioration continued, Robby lost patience, growing more demanding with her.

In February 1961 they were playing a month's engagement at the Drake Hotel in Chicago. Linda was really hitting the bottle, and she and Robby were fighting viciously. Neither Maria nor Tom Hayward knew what to do. The last night there Linda struck Robby during a squabble in their hotel room, and he turned her over his knee and spanked her. She jumped up, ran to the window, and threw it open. She started to leap, but Tom Hayward grabbed her and pulled her back. By then Linda was hysterical. The two men put her in the shower, with Linda crying, "I've got to find some way to rest!"

Robby agreed, and engagements in Las Vegas and Hollywood were cancelled. "I want to get away from everybody," Linda insisted. "Yes," Robby agreed, "you need to." They checked her into a hospital for treatment of alcoholism, with Linda promising to stop drinking and pull herself together. All her remaining performances were cancelled. Hayward shortly left for Europe, where he sang in Germany and Italy for nearly a year. It took three months for Linda to dry out and build her strength up. She took protein shots, watched her diet carefully, and worked to slim her stomach. Her doctors forbade her to do anything except rest for the entire summer, arguing that it would be foolish for her to return to work.

Soon Linda grew restless. Her ability to deal with the tedium of motherhood was every bit as tentative as her grasp on marriage. While the ceremonial occasions were exciting, the bad times were horrid; in either case, Lola's life was bursting with drama. The morning Lola turned thirteen, her mother invited the girl into her bedroom to share a split of Mumm's champagne. Linda sat in bed and emptied the bottle into two glasses, handing one to Lola. "Welcome to the adult world," she smiled. Unfortunately, that captured much of Linda's attitude toward parenthood. "We sat in her bed and drank champagne for breakfast," Lola remembered.

During the months she was resting, Linda from time to time received a film or television script to read, and there was talk that she and Robby would set up their own production company. They hoped to launch the company with *The Virgin Heart*, a script Robby described as "a simple, modern European love story" they planned to film in Greece. But their financial crisis made that impossible and necessitated Linda's going back to work before her doctors approved. Early in July she appeared on stage in *Monique* in Indianapolis and later that month revived the act at Walker Air Force Base in Roswell, New Mexico. Since Tom Hayward was busy with opera engagements in Europe, Wayne Tucker became her partner. Robby was determined to go for big money in Las Vegas, but Linda first had to get her timing back and become comfortable working with Tucker.

They played the Cal-Neva Lodge shortly before Lola was due back at school. The girl went along as Linda's assistant, and because she was under age, the management roped off a path through the casino so she could accompany her mother to her dressing room. "We were a great team!" Lola laughed. "Since you had to go through the casino to get to the dining room, I also couldn't eat." The Thunderbird Hotel in Las Vegas was scheduled next, but Linda felt far from ready. As her old insecurities returned, she began drinking again, more every day, attempting to fortify herself for the disaster she sensed was coming.

Linda opened in Las Vegas in mid-September, certain she was not prepared. She earned $10,000 a week, yet the engagement was anything but a success. Critics blasted her, and she drew small crowds, which were often rude. She tried to laugh it off, but agonized over having to face a hostile audience night after night with material she knew was inferior. It was the worst defeat of her career.

In October Linda sailed for Hawaii on the *Lurline* with Maria and Robby, performing the act with Wayne Tucker aboard ship on the way over. They repeated it one last time at Hickam Field in Honolulu, spending three weeks in the islands. They were sailing home when they heard the news that a fire was sweeping through Bel Air. Maria spent most of the trip in the radio room, checking on Linda's house. Fortunately it wasn't in danger.

Linda made a quick trip to Dallas in early December for a fund-raising drive, and returned to find a nervous Maria Flores. While paying bills and going over finances, Maria had discovered that flowers had been charged to Linda's hotel bill in Hawaii. Maria checked farther and found other curious charges. "I really had to dig," Maria said, "before I had proof." What she discovered was that Robby had a girlfriend, twenty-eight-year-old Yugoslavian actress Vera Violetta Gregovic, a former intimate of Marshal Tito. Maria showed Linda the evidence, only to have her turn furious. "Linda wasn't too happy with me after that," Maria admitted. "Maybe she felt she should have been able to find out herself."

"Whether Maria was right in telling Mother I don't know," said Lola. "I used to think she was wrong, then I thought she was right. But what happened in that marriage was not entirely Robby's fault. I'm not defending what he did. But when a man as attractive as Robby comes home to a wife who never gets out of bed, who is in her pajamas, never leaves her room, and is not entirely sober to boot, it's understandable how what happened came about. Mother was drinking a lot."

Linda confronted Robby with Maria's evidence, setting off a series of bitter quarrels. In despair she called acquaintances she had neglected for years. Her dangerous state of mind was clear to everyone, and friends decided somebody should be with her at all times. Yvonne Wood and her husband were living on a ranch in

Oregon at the time. "Linda would get on that phone to me and stay on it for an hour and a half," Wood recalled, "screaming, crying, snarling, just coming unglued over this whole thing with Robertson and Vera Violetta Gregovic." She leaned on anyone who would listen.

Then Linda learned that Gregovic was pregnant with Robby's child. With that the fights became more brutal, physically violent. "I think Mother tried very hard to do the honorable thing," said Lola. "She tried to back out and allow a divorce as soon as possible, so this child would not be born illegitimate." Gregovic later claimed Linda insulted her, called her names, then slapped her face. Linda insisted the buxom Yugoslavian had struck her, knocking her to the floor. Gregovic called Linda a liar, and told the press, "She has twisted stories and even made them up. I couldn't hit anyone so tiny. I was in tears. Miss Darnell had been drinking and was so weak that I could never hit anyone like that."

Linda and Robby legally separated on Valentine's Day 1962. The actress sued her husband for community property and support, complaining that he had humiliated her by acts of cruelty. Money was so short the telephone company threatened to cut off service, and Maria even sold her own car to give Linda funds to pay some bills. With Linda still angry at her and no money coming in, Maria left the house in Bel Air in February, taking a job as a clerk at Bullock's department store, but keeping in close touch.

Shortly after Maria moved out, Linda tried to kill herself by taking an overdose of sleeping tablets. Maria happened by and found her on the floor, woozy from pills, and immediately called Robby. He tried to get Linda downstairs to the kitchen to pour coffee down her, but she had strength enough to cling to a door, screaming until Robby overpowered her.

"I don't think it was that Mother wanted to be dead," said Lola. "I think she simply didn't want to live anymore. She was tired. She was beaten. She drank too much. She was losing her marriage. She wasn't pretty. And when your entire reputation rests on being beautiful and your eyes are puffy and bloodshot, what are you going to do? Mother couldn't get a job at Marshall Field's. Most of us have to get up and go to work. We have to feed the cat. Daddy was still alive, so I could have lived with him. She didn't have anything to get up for in the morning."

After several weeks apart, Linda and Robby made an attempt at reconciliation. "That marriage could have worked with a little more understanding," Jeanne Curtis remained convinced. But in July Linda showed up at Vera Violetta Gregovic's home in Brentwood with a private detective, an attorney, and six witnesses, charging that her husband was inside. The Yugoslavian actress said Robby had been having dinner with her, but had fled out the back door when he heard his wife's voice. Linda created such a scene, according to Gregovic, that she was shown the bedroom to prove Robby wasn't there.

At that point Robby sued for divorce, charging Linda with habitual intemperance and neglecting her duties as a wife. Linda countered, accusing him of "numerous and diverse" acts of adultery with younger women. She also claimed her husband frequently beat her and took advantage of her poor business sense. Robby at first remained silent, even when Linda insisted Gregovic was six months pregnant with his child and listed among their joint holdings half interest in his airline pension. Later he filed a cross complaint denying the allegations. In January Linda obtained a temporary restraining order which prevented Robby from using her credit cards or running up charges in her name. She stated she was unemployed, had no current income, and demanded $1,000 a month alimony.

Jeanne Curtis tried to call in debts that were owing, but friends and hangers-on had suddenly vanished. Jeanne went to work attempting to straighten out Linda's taxes. "I was the go-between," she said. "I would meet Robby and get packets of receipts, so I could work with the accountant. In the meantime everything was spiraling, and the walls were falling down on the financial overextension." Advisors decided Robby should file for bankruptcy. It looked as if Linda would have to file, too, but she was determined to hold out as long as possible. She tried to sell the house in Bel Air, attempting at least to salvage the $50,000 equity she had in the property. Sometimes Maria came over to show the place, but it never sold.

Linda's divorce from Robertson was granted on November 27, 1963. The decree provided that she should receive $350 a month alimony until July 1964, and $250 monthly thereafter through September 1967. Robby was also required to pay the state income taxes owed by Linda. Her financial situation, however, had hit rock bottom the previous May, when the Bel Air house was foreclosed upon.

"That was a confusing time," Lola remembered, "although there were some funny times." When the process servers started coming, Linda nailed sheets to the windows, so no one would know she was home. "We would play hide and seek with these people," Lola laughed. "We could never go to the door, because they would trick us. They would dress up like refrigerator repairmen and postmen. There were some funny moments then. I think Mother and I were closest when all the money was gone."

To avoid the bill collectors Linda made a practice of coming and going through the back door, turning off the headlights before she drove up the hill. "It was real cloak and dagger time," Yvonne Wood recalled. "They were on her like a duck on a June bug." Jeanne kept urging her to file for bankruptcy, but Linda felt that was dishonest. "I owe these bills," she said, "and I'm going to pay them." She slept most of the day and stayed up all night. She rarely opened the draperies, drank continuously, and there was at least one more suicide attempt. "Everything was falling apart," Lola remembered. "Mother was losing everything it had taken her whole life to build. Most of her friends had abandoned her, and there had to have been a tremendous loss of energy, too."

When the Bel Air house went on the auction block, Linda suffered the final blow. "At the time it would have taken very little to save the house," assured Maria, but no one seemed willing to help. Linda's father sent a couple hundred dollars out of his pension check, which touched her deeply. "She didn't ask for it," Jeanne said. "He just felt she needed it."

On a bleak morning in May, while the foreclosure sale was being held at a Beverly Hills bank, Jeanne, Undeen, and Maria helped pack the remaining household items. Considerate person that she was, Linda went around taping keys on doors with notes telling the new owner which key went to which lock. Around four o'clock in the afternoon a car drove up and a man got out. Jeanne answered the doorbell. "I bought the house," the man informed her. "I'd like to meet Miss Darnell." Jeanne refused to let him in. "This is a traumatic time for her," Jeanne said. "She can't see anyone now." The man was still parked in the driveway when Jeanne and Linda went out the back, taping a key to the door as they left. "We drove off," Jeanne remembered, "and that was the last time she saw her home. We moved her in with us for about six weeks."

Later they found a small apartment for Linda on Woodman

Avenue in Sherman Oaks, a few doors from Jeanne and Dick and just down the street from Maria. Pev Marley agreed to pay the rent. "From Bel Air to the Valley in one easy jump," Lola commented. "That apartment was horrendous." Certainly it was modest by Bel Air standards. Jeanne continued working on Linda's finances. Day after day she sat nailed to the typewriter in an effort to straighten the mess out, putting Linda on a rigid budget. The actress's credit had been cut off all over town.

"She felt beaten," Maria Flores declared, "and just crawled into a shell. That's when the Scotch really took over." She no longer seemed to care if it was night or day. Her pride as a woman, as a star, as a person of honor had been destroyed. "That was when Mother first began to realize I was a person, not an infant," Lola maintained. "I got to know her then, and I began to like her. She wasn't so frightening. I think I began to realize Mother was a person, too."

Holding Together

Even before losing her house Linda had been forced to resume stage work. In September 1962 she returned to Chicago's Drury Lane Theater for a production of *The Gioconda Smile*. "What else was she going to do?" an adult Lola asked. "She had to support herself, and there were so many things she couldn't do without ruining her image." Linda would have preferred retiring to Italy, but there was no money for that. Since Hollywood had moved on to new faces, the stock circuit remained the only respectable avenue open. She also appeared in productions of *Critic's Choice* and *Dark at the Top of the Stairs*, which appealed mainly to older audiences. "I miss movies very much," she admitted. "I was in them for years." By the early 1960s there were few long-term contracts, since the big studio system was in its dotage.

During work on a play in Jersey, Linda stayed at the Gorham Hotel, a Manhattan apartment hotel that catered to actors. In the lobby she bumped into Carol Bruce, the Broadway actress she had met years before in Hollywood. Bruce had recently starred in *Pal Joey* in London and by then had become a blonde. Linda invited Carol up to her apartment for dinner one evening. "A lot of time had passed," Bruce recalled. "But I must say I was a little taken aback. Linda had gotten heavy through the middle and looked bloated. That shocked me." Linda's face was still beautiful, yet Bruce sensed her sadness. "I had the impression that life had not been too kind to her," she remembered. "She wasn't the bright shining star anymore."

Shortly before moving from Bel Air, Linda met and began dating Philip Kalavros, a Greek doctor. Kalavros was an attractive man with an accent, dyed hair, and a propensity for white shoes. Linda's friends described him variously as "an emotional Greek," "a charlatan," "a phony," "nutty as a fruitcake," and "a miserable son of a bitch." Monte was fond of him, while Undeen could never stand him. "I was there the night Mother met him," said Lola, "and I thought he was dashing. Never take the opinion of a fifteen-year-old girl on a man. He was strictly show." Kalavros immediately fell in love with Linda. She grew to like him and became dependent on him, although she told Undeen she had no intention of marrying him. Kalavros did his best to keep Linda from drinking and tried to build her stamina. "He picked her up when she was in her mentally depressed low end," Richard Curtis claimed. "She couldn't seem to face the position she was in. He was a means of escape for her. I don't think she had the ability to face the reality that she was no longer a power."

"In spite of everything," said Monte, "Philip Kalavros was good for Tweedles—even though the relationship was stormy at times." Stormy it definitely was. Like Linda, Philip dwelt in a fantasy world. Although he lived simply, he possessed an imagination that easily ran rampant. He constantly called Linda to check on her, spied on her, worried about what she might be doing, and nagged at her. "He was a very volatile person," remembered Lola. "He had temper tantrums regularly."

Linda very likely suffered from cirrhosis, and Kalavros began giving her doses of vitamin B to reverse her liver damage. He also insisted that she was desperately ill with myasthenia gravis, a weakening of the muscles, and probably had no more than a year to live. Jeanne Curtis argued that she must seek another opinion, and took Linda to Cedars of Lebanon Hospital. Dr. Sam Alter, Linda's regular physician, found no signs of myasthenia gravis, yet agreed her health was far from good. Mainly she was run down, in need of rest and a balanced diet. But Linda and Kalavros continued to fight violently over the status of her health. Friends were certain he was playing mind games with her so as to increase her dependency on him.

Linda did have alopecia areata, which as early as 1961 caused her hair to fall out first in a spot over one ear, and then on top of her head. Eventually three or four more patches were quite noticeable. She began treatment with a dermatologist and the hair slowly grew back, yet the alopecia embarrassed her even more than her thick waist.

Jeanne was still sorting through a five-year accumulation of bills, struggling to keep Linda within sensible financial limits. Linda came to look upon Jeanne as a sister, for they became closer than anyone in her own family. "You can choose your friends," she often said, "but you're stuck with your relatives. Only it takes something like this to find out who your real friends are." Philip

Kalavros, however, did his best to tear Linda away from the Curtises, convinced that Jeanne was contributing to her drinking problem. Maria Flores and the Hurds tended to agree, so that the internal friction among the handful of remaining friends became fierce, with Linda caught in between.

When not involved with a play, the actress spent most of her time in the drab apartment on Woodman Avenue, mostly alone. The bulk of her furniture, library, and record albums had been stored. Many evenings she sat at home with Roma, her poodle, watching old movies on television. Lola came home from school for holidays, but Linda seemed to have lost her appetite for celebrations. She showed no interest in buying Christmas presents, even when Dick and Jeanne Curtis tried to shame her into shopping.

After the Christmas of 1963, fifteen-year-old Lola decided to move in permanently with her father. Although the girl had come to understand her mother better, their confrontations had grown severe. "At some point in your life," Lola said later, "I think you have to make a decision to disconnect from something that's not healthy for you. I had done that. I figured that I wasn't ever going back to Mother's place. She was drinking a lot, and her temper was flaring. I felt it was not safe to live there. I couldn't defend myself against her attacks."

By then Pev Marley was filming television commercials and living in an apartment hotel on Hollywood Boulevard. He was engaged to marry Marge Futch, a widow from Palm Springs close to his age, who Lola thought was special. "I would go out on a date and come home, and Marge would be up waiting for me," Lola remembered. "Not to see what time I got home, but to say, 'Have a piece of cake' or 'How was your date?' It felt like family."

Pev and Marge drove up to Ojai to spend the first weekend in February with Lola at school, devoting all day Saturday to shopping for the teenager's first long dress. They ate dinner and returned to their motel, tired. Marge and Lola shared a room, while Pev had the one adjoining. Since *Gunsmoke* was Pev's favorite television program, he and Marge stayed up to watch that after Lola went to bed. The next morning they were planning to go to church. Marge and Lola thought they heard Pev's electric razor, but when he failed to knock for them, they decided he must have fallen asleep. They went in to awaken him and found him dead in bed, having suffered a cerebral hemorrhage.

After notifying the police, Marge took Lola back to Los Angeles, where they checked into the Roosevelt Hotel. "I didn't even want to go home then," said Lola, "which must have killed Mother." Linda was on a train bound for Albuquerque to visit the Hurds. Jeanne and Dick Curtis had just returned home from taking her to the station when they received a phone call about Pev. Linda was handed their telegram during a stop in Phoenix. Within an hour she was on a flight back to California.

Marley's funeral was held on February 5. Over a hundred Hollywood celebrities, including Linda, attended the service. Linda broke into tears afterwards and was comforted by their daughter. "I think it was hard for Mother when Daddy died," Lola said. "I think he was always in the background as a support, emotionally if nothing else. He was so much older than she was, and maybe that made him more tolerant once they weren't living together. They got along very well over the years. But now my alternative was dead, and I had to go back to Mother. After a couple of days, I did."

With Linda not working, her financial situation grew chronically bad, to the point that Jeanne suggested she file for unemployment compensation. Although the thought of going to an unemployment office embarrassed her, she ultimately did file. Linda cautioned Lola that the size of her father's estate would likely be small. "You simply must not get exaggerated ideas about how much money the court will allow you to spend," she wrote in a letter in which she referred to herself as MOM, Mean Old Mother.

A few days later Lola called to tell her mother that she would like to join her on a tour Linda's agent had lined up for the coming summer. "Hooray!" Linda wrote in her date book and became excited about working again. Jeanne and Yvonne Wood helped her shop at bargain stores for dresses that could be remade into appropriate costumes. They stood in a corner and held up fabric so Linda had some privacy while changing. "The three of us got hysterical," Yvonne Wood remembered, "because some of these holes-in-the-wall were totally open across the front. These clothes were cheap, damn cheap—eight dollars for this, twelve for that." Yvonne agreed to redesign them into a wardrobe suitable for Linda's play. Part of her job was to create dresses that would make the actress's middle appear slimmer. Linda still had a mink coat and enough jewelry to spruce up the wardrobe, and it all turned out satisfactorily. "She really looked elegant in those clothes," declared Yvonne.

Since Linda was still not feeling well, Philip Kalavros stopped by the apartment regularly to give her injections, eventually showing Jeanne how it was done. Meanwhile Linda prepared herself for the tour. She flew to San Antonio on June 7, with Lola scheduled to join her the following week, and began rehearsals on *Janus* at the outdoor Peninsula Playhouse in New Braunfels. The money was good—$2,000 a week—but it was far from a prestigious engagement. Still, *Janus* played to a standing-room-only audience every night.

"That's when I got to admire Mother as an artist," said Lola, "and as a person who worked at her craft." Although the play was a fluff piece, it was funny and fast-paced, and Linda enjoyed thoroughly the part Margaret Sullavan had created on Broadway. "I learned a lot about the theater and what goes into being an actress," Lola continued. "It's a lot more than standing around looking beautiful. There are so many technical things that go into acting that I was not aware of. And Mother could do those things! Here was my mother who could do all that and do it well. I was proud of her. And it just so happened we liked each other."

Linda's hair had grown back, but it was not as thick as before. Since her alopecia was a well guarded secret, she could never use the hairdresser the theater provided, so Lola began doing her mother's hair and arranging her wigs. The girl became sensitive to the tensions Linda was under. "It's a tremendous pressure always to have to be perfect," Lola commented later. "Mother couldn't have a broken fingernail or red eyes, which happens to everybody. Some days you just don't feel well, but Mother could never afford that luxury."

Linda talked long distance to Philip Kalavros almost every day and found herself missing him. Sometimes they fought bitterly, and Linda would slam down the receiver. Then they'd be back on the phone, sweeter than ever. Philip met Linda and Lola at the airport when they returned to Los Angeles in late July. The three of them ate dinner in the airport restaurant, where Linda and Philip had an ugly fight. She spent the next week avoiding him.

Linda opened in Houghton Lake, Michigan, to a standing ovation in August 1964. "Mother lit up in front of an audience," said Lola. "It was like turning on a light bulb. She was so beautiful, and her smile was incredible. I saw the show every night that whole summer, and it never failed to amaze me." Much of their time was spent packing and unpacking. After an engagement in Sullivan, Illinois, they flew back to Los Angeles, met this time by Jeanne Curtis. Jeanne was full of talk about a picture deal she had negotiated with producer A. C. Lyles at Paramount. The movie was a low-budget western called *Black Spurs* and Linda's part no more than a cameo appearance, but the prospect of a new film excited her.

The actress reported to Paramount Studios for a wardrobe session on September 2, taking Lola and Jeanne and Patty Curtis with her. She would play a New Orleans madam in the picture, a role almost any veteran could have walked through with ease. Linda received third billing after Rory Calhoun and Terry Moore. Lyles had heard about Linda's drinking problem and asked Jeanne for her personal guarantee that Linda would appear on the set when needed. Jeanne assured him that Linda was a professional and would do her duty. After Labor Day, Linda returned to the studio for makeup and hairstyling, arriving at her dressing room early on September 11 with Jeanne, a hot plate, a garlic press, a cutting board, and all the essentials for fixing lunch. "Everyone was amazed," Yvonne Wood said, "because they had heard she was a drunk and all that."

The cast and crew not only found Linda a consummate worker, but easygoing and fun as well. One morning she borrowed a huge spear from the prop department. She walked onto the set to take her place, planted the prop, and said, "My part's so small I might as well be carrying a spear!" Everyone broke up. Linda cooked lunch for the cast whenever there was time, and her dressing room became a gathering place. The crew teased her about Cafe Lindola, until Jeanne finally hung a sign outside Linda's dressing room.

Black Spurs was Linda's first picture in seven years, and it would be her last. She loved working before a camera again and all the fun and gags that went with it. Linda finished her part in less than two weeks, and had no delusions about the quality of the film, aware it fell into the "oater" category. She described the picture as "a ten-day quickie no one will go to see," but when *Black Spurs* opened the following May, it did reliable business in second-run theaters.

Linda and Philip Kalavros had continued their feuding through the making of the picture, going several days at a stretch without

seeing each other. He ate dinner at Linda's one evening, only to
leave abruptly after slapping her. She ate dinner at her lawyer's a
few evenings later and noticed Kalavros lurking outside. They invited him in, but he left without saying anything to Linda. They
agreed to split up, then dined together at one of her favorite
restaurants.

Richard and Jeanne Curtis called with the disturbing news that
Dick had been transferred to Glenview, Illinois. Linda was sad-
dened, but volunteered to fly to Glenview to help them unpack.
She was in their town house when the movers arrived, telling
workmen where to place various boxes. She spent two weeks
helping Jeanne get settled, before flying to Albuquerque to make
final arrangements on a production of *Janus* at the Little Theater
there. While in Albuquerque she felt tired and nauseated, and
eventually called a doctor to give her a shot. Linda arrived back
in Los Angeles in late November and spent the following week
resting, watching television, and checking on the Curtises in Illinois a couple of times a day. "Alone! Peace!" she wrote in her date
book. She hadn't even unpacked yet from her recent trip, as she
felt tired most of the time. "Everything just seems to be such an
effort for me these days," she wrote the Curtises, "depressing
as hell."

Jeanne was handling Linda's finances long distance, with the
actress mailing her check stubs and deposit slips. Linda stopped
asking Philip Kalavros to mail letters to Jeanne for her, convinced
he was steaming them open. The Curtises had received a number
of envelopes from her that had been sealed with plastic tape.
"Be careful what you send," Jeanne warned. When Lola arrived
home for Christmas vacation, Philip spent most of his time sulk-
ing. Shortly after the holidays, Lola left to visit friends in San
Francisco. In early January Linda grew more despondent, missed
Jeanne, and seemed forever exhausted.

On the evening of January 19, 1965, Linda was booked on a late
flight to Albuquerque, where she was to begin another tour with
Janus. Her sister Monte, recently divorced, had eaten dinner with
an old boyfriend that night, and the two of them stopped by
Linda's apartment afterwards. Since Philip was driving Linda to
the airport, he opened the door for them. Linda was in the bedroom napping. "She's not well," he insisted. "I wish she wouldn't
go, but I can't talk her out of it." Monte and her friend chatted
with Philip for almost an hour before they heard movement from

the bedroom. "It sounds like she's waking up," Monte said. "I'll go in and see."

Monte found her sister still lying on the bed, half asleep. "She just looked so distressed," Monte remembered. "She still had her hair up in loose pin curls, and the expression on her face was just tearful despair, as if she'd been crying." Monte sat down on the bed beside her. "What in the hell are you doing here?" Linda demanded. "Tweedles, it's Monte," her sister replied. "Are you sure you feel well enough to make this trip?" Linda was adamant: "Hell, no, I don't feel well enough. But I've got to get back to work. I don't know how much longer I can stay on my feet, but I'm not going to die in this town."

Linda arrived in Albuquerque and began rehearsals the next day. Audiences the following week responded appreciatively, while critics agreed the show was pleasant entertainment. When the play closed on February 7, Linda immediately packed for Georgia, where she was to repeat *Janus* at the Atlanta Community Playhouse, beginning rehearsals on February 23. She admitted to the local press that she was petrified every time she walked on stage. "I got my start in movies, not on the stage," she reminded reporters, "but I haven't made a decent movie in ten years." Her reviews in Atlanta, however, were excellent.

Few of Linda's colleagues on the road were up to her standards, especially in attitude. She couldn't tolerate lateness and was convinced every audience deserved a polished performance. "I may not be the greatest actress in the world," she frequently told newcomers, "but by God I am a professional! Get behind the sets and work before you're out front. Get back there and learn what the craft is about." During most of her stay in Atlanta it rained, and to add to her depression, she argued repeatedly on the telephone with Philip, banging the receiver down regularly. She felt she must have time to rest and decided to fly to Chicago to spend Easter with the Curtises, arranging for Lola to join her there.

Linda agreed to consult a Chicago physician about her prolonged listlessness, producing another round of stormy telephone conversations with Philip. "Why have you been such a bitch in the past when you could have been soothing, sweet, [and] affectionate?" he wrote her. "Therein lies the vast, brooding mystery that spins my wits." He enclosed articles for her on alopecia, emphysema, and alcoholic heart and encouraged her to remain with the

Curtises until she felt better. "Do not be restless," he cautioned. "There is no doctor in the world, not even the one in Chicago, who can do anything for you!! Deep down in the sacred recesses of your conscience you cannot forever mock and insult and disregard the divine reason and the image of HIM you know. You know what is the truth—what you should do and how to find the strength to do what millions of times I told you, showed you, and proved to you with the profoundest interest. Do not insult your intelligence and do not repeat to me that the doctor in Chicago is going to do something. He will do nothing unless he is a magician from hell."

Linda resolved to free herself from Philip's grasp and with Jeanne's encouragement broke contact with him. In Glenview, Linda and Jeanne spent days cooking and shopping together. While Jeanne was running errands one morning, Linda looked in the telephone directory and found a small grocery that would deliver. She called the store, telling the owner, "My name is Linda Darnell. I'm visiting friends here in Glenview, and I would like some groceries delivered." She sounded so emphatic the owner even agreed to make a couple of stops for her on the way over with the order. Linda had been teasing Jeanne about running out of toilet tissue. "So I've taken care of that," the actress announced when her friend returned home. "I ordered thirty-six rolls!"

Jeanne loved Aunt Penny's white sauce, a shortcut in cooking which was sold in California. She couldn't find it in Illinois, so Linda sent a check to Maria Flores and asked her to buy the sauce and mail it to Jeanne. Maria bought three cartons and sent them air freight. Linda and Jeanne laughed and laughed when the shipment arrived, then spent hours sitting at the kitchen table talking. Linda insisted her friends were lucky to be out of Los Angeles, stressing how much she had come to hate Hollywood. "You know, I never felt accepted in the movie world," the star confessed. "I think that's why I resent my family so. I would never have been an actress if it hadn't been for Mother's insisting. To think I paid a psychiatrist $25,000 trying to work through all that before he finally gave up on me!"

Linda's finances remained deplorable. Jeanne had managed to salvage an insurance policy, and Linda was earning at least $2,000 a week—when she worked. A. C. Lyles was talking about another film assignment, yet it looked as if Linda might still have to de-clare bankruptcy, since her debts far exceeded her assets. Jeanne was working on her 1964 income tax return, trying to gather together all the necessary information.

On April 5 Linda received a letter from Cal in England. He had seen a marquee of a theater in London showing *Black Spurs*. "Here's a letter from Calvino," Linda told Jeanne happily. She tore the envelope open and began shaking her head. "That Cal," she said, "he must have been drinking again. Read this." She handed the letter to her friend. "I had just a terrible nightmare last night," Cal wrote his sister. "I dreamed you were in a burning building, in a shack or someplace. I awakened in a cold sweat. It was just the most horrible dream." Jeanne looked at Linda in amazement. "I'm not afraid to die," the actress said. "I've made my peace with God."

The following Thursday, Jeanne and Linda decided to work on taxes, and spread the papers out in the upstairs sitting room. Dick was in California on business, but Patty was home, eager for Lola's arrival the next week. Jeanne and Linda worked into the night trying to straighten out the disarray of tax receipts. Around midnight they made a telephone call to Linda's lawyer in Los Angeles, asking for information about an alimony payment from Robby. After that they bundled the tax receipts up and got the box ready to mail to California.

Linda had just finished typing a note to her attorney asking about bankruptcy procedures. She left the letter in Jeanne's typewriter and carried the box of tax receipts downstairs to the stereo. As she put the package down, she noticed in *T.V. Guide* that *Star Dust*, her semiautobiographical film, was coming on television at 12:20. She gave a yelp of laughter and, turning to Jeanne and Pat, said, "Let's stay up and watch this. Lola and Patty think they're so sophisticated. Let's show Patty how sophisticated her aunt was at their age. Let's have some laughs."

Fadeout

The cause of the fire was never determined. An ash or a lighted cigarette dropped into the living room sofa may have been the culprit, although Linda was always careful with cigarettes, and Jeanne Curtis recalled carrying ashtrays out to the kitchen after the movie and setting them in the sink. Jeanne also denied that Linda had been drinking heavily that evening. They had sipped coffee while they watched *Star Dust*, something Linda rarely did.

Why Linda went down into the smoke and flames remains a mystery. The press at the time reported she had gone into the fire to rescue Patty, thinking the girl had gone downstairs. Jeanne discarded the possibility, arguing that Linda knew Patty was with them at the bedroom window and had even been the one to suggest that she jump. But the media persisted in turning Linda's tragedy into an heroic rescue effort, leaving Patty with guilt feelings she had to work through later.

Relatives and friends denied categorically that Linda's going into the fire was a subconscious suicide attempt. "She wouldn't have done it that way," Cal maintained. "Linda was always afraid of fire. She was terrified of it, although I think whatever you fear most in life, you probably meet. You have to survive it—unfortunately Linda didn't. But if she were going to kill herself, she would not have done it that way." The Curtises stressed how, during her month in Glenview, Linda had taken a new lease on life. Jeanne and Dick both claimed their friend was simply afraid to jump from the second-story window and felt she could make it out the front door.

A team of doctors at Skokie Valley Community Hospital worked frantically to save Linda's life. She apparently had collapsed from smoke inhalation, while the intense heat fused fragments of her charred pajamas to her flesh. She remained in surgery for nearly two and a half hours as dead tissue was removed from her body. "Her nerve fibers have been pretty well burned out," said Dr. Peter Verges, the first physician to treat her. "There's not much you can do in a case like this but try to relieve the pain and give them plasma." Linda was conscious most of the time, listed in critical condition. A tracheotomy was performed to aid her breathing, and fluids were fed intravenously. Almost the entire surface of her body had been destroyed. Her neck was swollen, and her eyes had closed because of facial swelling. Doctors tried to block the spread of infection and claimed she had come through the operation as well as could be expected. "She responds when someone touches her," a nurse told reporters, but from the outset doctors were not optimistic about her chances for survival.

Dick was still in Los Angeles when the fire occurred, and had eaten dinner the evening before with Gladys Witten. He called Gladys the next morning to say, "I'm on my way home. There's been a fire." He arranged with the headmaster at Ojai Valley School for Lola to fly to Chicago immediately. Lola had had the radio on in her room that morning, but had changed stations when the news came on. She walked into the dining hall to be informed that the headmaster wanted to talk with her after breakfast. After eating she went to see the headmaster, convinced she was in trouble. "I have some news for you," he said. "There has been a fire at the Curtises', and your mother is in the hospital." Lola asked, "Is she dead?" The headmaster said, "I don't think so." Lola suggested they call and find out. She telephoned the Curtises' town house, not knowing the extent of the damage. The phone in the kitchen rang and rang with nobody there to answer it.

Lola was told to pack at once for Chicago. She got out her suitcase, but couldn't think what to take, realizing only that Chicago would be cold. "So I packed my school uniform," she recalled. "I didn't have anything else warm. And I took a white suit. It was all so confused," She left a note for her boyfriend, telling him she would be unable to keep their date that evening, and was driven to Los Angeles, where she found a plane reservation waiting. She was taken in a cart from the ticket counter to the aircraft, which was being held for her. "Everyone knew who I was and was so nice," Lola remembered. "The stewardess was very solicitous and took excellent care of me."

Meanwhile the switchboard at Skokie Valley hospital was jammed with calls from all over the country. Linda rallied enough to express concern over Jeanne and Patty, convinced they had died in the fire. Finally Jeanne had to go in and assure her they were both alive and wanted her to fight for her own life. Doctors agreed Linda should be moved to the new Koch Burn Center of

Cook County Hospital, where advanced treatment was available. Jeanne consulted with her personal physician, who advised making the transfer. Reporters were all over the hospital. The hospital administrator came to Jeanne and said, "I'll set up a conference in the other end of the building to distract newspapermen. We have an ambulance arriving, especially equipped, with the head of the burn center coming to transport her." Linda suffered a sinking spell, so she temporarily couldn't be moved. While the staff was reviving her, Lola and Dick arrived from the airport.

"I was still numb from the death of my father," said Lola. "Everyone at Skokie Hospital was so nice, and I signed some papers giving my permission for Mother to be transferred to the burn center in Chicago." The girl talked to Jeanne, who was bandaged and drugged, and then went to see Patty. "Lola!" her sixteen-year-old friend exclaimed. "You're wearing white shoes before Easter!" Lola was too numb to react. Dick drove her downtown to the burn center, where her mother had been taken. Lola kept saying, "Is she going to make it? Is she going to die?"

When they reached the center, the doctor in charge told Lola her mother had been asking for her. He wanted her to take tranquilizers, but Lola refused. "I wish instead he had tried to prepare me," she said later, "although there is no way to prepare someone to see a person with no skin. It's not a pretty sight. I went in and there was Mother—her hair all burned off, her skin burned off. I understand there was still some skin on the small of her back, but I didn't see that. Something that amazes me about medical science is that they're so careful about a patient's modesty. Mother had sort of a diaper on. There were IVs going in and a lot of stuff that was really pointless. She was so badly burned there was nothing anyone could do. Nothing. She was burned over ninety percent of her body. Nobody comes back from that."

Linda didn't appear to be in pain. "I think when burns are that severe," Lola continued, "there are no nerve endings left. So she couldn't register pain. Mother was reaching for me with her hand, wanting to hold it, which I could not bring myself to do. I just couldn't do it." Linda kept saying, "Who says I'm going to die? I'm not going to!" Because of the tracheotomy, remembered Lola, "she had this horrible voice. She wanted me to put my finger over the tracheotomy so she could talk. I couldn't bring myself to touch her. She didn't know how bad it was. She kept saying she wasn't going to die, which I knew from looking at her wasn't true." Lola fought back the tears, as her mother whispered, "I love you, baby. I love you."

Undeen heard about the fire when a neighbor called around six o'clock that morning and asked, "Is it true about Linda? How bad is she?" Undeen contacted a radio station to check. A newscaster confirmed their report that Linda Darnell had been badly injured. Then Undeen called Monte, who wasn't awake yet. "They said it was second-and third-degree burns over ninety percent of her body," Undeen told her sister. "They don't know if she's going to make it."

The two sisters discussed flying to Chicago at once, but Undeen worried that she and Harry didn't have the money. Both women called the Skokie Valley Hospital, inquiring about Linda's condition. "Please tell her we're on our way," said Monte. "I will get my sister onto a plane as soon as I can. But please tell Linda we'll be there."

Cal was working at the time for a travel agency in London. Alan MacNaughtan, the friend with whom Cal shared a flat, was waiting for him at the airport when Cal returned from a tour of Spain. "Cal," said Alan, "I've got bad news. There's been a fire, and Linda is pretty badly burned." Cal asked, "How bad?" Alan said, "Pretty bad. I've made you a reservation to New York and then on to Chicago. We'll simply have your baggage transferred." Cal sent a telegram to Skokie Hospital: "Please advise patient Darnell brother is on the way."

Meanwhile the switchboards at both Skokie Valley Hospital and the Koch Burn Center were receiving calls faster than operators could handle them. Photographer Bill Langley telephoned from Dallas, inquiring whether he should fly to Linda's side. An attending physician counseled him not to try. "You wouldn't want to see her like this," the doctor advised. But Langley stayed glued to his telephone. Dolly Elder, Linda's high school pal, heard the news from her son when she came home from work. Her children offered to pool their savings so their mother could fly up to be with her friend, but Dolly decided against it.

Telegrams poured in from all over the world. "Dear Linda," wired Anne Baxter, a colleague at Twentieth Century-Fox, "My heart goes out to you." Peter and Henriette Hurd telegraphed: "We are crushed that this had to happen. With our love and our prayers we are thinking of you." Philip Liebmann said: "Thinking of you and hoping you will have a speedy recovery." Ann Miller wired: "Dearest Linda. If there's anything that Mom and I can do, we'll be there to help. In my heart you are my dearest friend in the whole world and always will be. We are saying prayers for your recovery. Love, Annikat and Mommikat."

In the morning mail, rosaries and crosses arrived by the scores and more letters and cards than anybody could count. "Everyone was praying for her," Undeen said later. "It was just really heart-rending." But the ghouls and the souvenir hunters were also out, trying to enter the burned town house. Dick went over to survey the damage, and found a convoy of cars driving by, with people gathered in front to gape. A couple lifted their little girl up through the living room window. Dick shouted for them to get out. The couple replied, "Could we just take some ashes from the fire?" The next day the same thing happened, this time with an eight-year-old boy. Amid the damage were thirty-six rolls of toilet tissue and three cartons of Aunt Penny's white sauce.

Cal spent Saturday morning over the Atlantic, while Monte and Undeen were still arranging a flight out of Los Angeles. Linda was conscious most of the morning, although her kidneys failed and there were additional complications. Dick's cousin, Father John Rankey, was a Jesuit priest and knew Linda through the Curtises. He visited her that morning, knowing how grave her condition was. Although no one could recall Linda's attending church is recent memory, she showed vague leanings toward Catholicism late in her life. Father Rankey went into her room and approached the bed, not sure whether she was lucid or not. "Linda," he said softly, "this is John Rankey. Do you know who I am?" She indicated she did. "Linda, I won't kid you," he continued. "This is serious. Do you know what extreme unction is?" Again she nodded. "Well," Father Rankey asked, "do you want me to administer the last rites of the church?" Linda mustered her strength and in an unmistakable voice said, "You're goddamn right I do!"

Lola and Dick were with her right before the end. They told her there were hundreds of letters and telegrams. "Get the telegrams and read them to me," Linda whispered. Dick and Lola went out into the hall to locate some, but the doctor said, "Don't go back in." She died within minutes, at 2:20 PM on April 10, 1965, thirty-three hours after the fire. Dr. John Boswick, director of the burn center, stated that the primary cause of death was the searing effect on Linda's lungs and breathing passages from the superheated air she had inhaled. "In a sense she suffocated," Boswick said.

Cal arrived at Chicago's O'Hare Field two hours after Linda died. He was met at the airport by two friends who informed him of his sister's death. "When I heard Linda was dead, my mind really went out of gear," Cal said later. "I got the next plane out of there and went back to New York. The curtain just came down, and I knew I couldn't walk into that situation alone. I simply could not go through the formalities." Monte and Undeen finally left Los Angeles around midnight, landing in Chicago early the next morning. The airport was practically deserted. "I'll never forget the two of us walking down that empty corridor," said Monte.

Dick went to the Cook County Morgue to identify Linda's body and helped Lola plan a memorial service. A private service was scheduled for the following Monday afternoon in Glenview Community Church. Linda's remains would be cremated. For years she'd told the Curtises, "If I die, I want you to know one thing. If you hold a funeral for me, I'll come back to haunt you. I want my body to go to science and then a cremation after that. Funerals are for the living." Linda's body was in no shape to serve science, but Lola and Dick planned a simple memorial they thought would be in good taste and would have met with Linda's approval. "Lola showed a great deal of strength," Jeanne recalled. "She helped make the arrangements and took it all very well."

Driving to the service Lola said, "I would like to sit by Mother's casket for a few minutes by myself." Dick told her, "I'm sorry. She's already been cremated." Although Lola understood the Curtises were trying to spare her further hurt, that was her only regret. "It denied me the opportunity to say good-bye to Mother," Lola said later. At the last minute the service was opened to the public, with an estimated ninety people attending, mostly middleaged women. Undeen and Monte were there, and Jeanne Curtis sat in a wheelchair, holding Dick's hand. Burn marks and bandages were visible on her arms. Flowers had arrived all weekend, including a basket with no name; across the banner was simply written a code signature Joe Mankiewicz had used.

Philip Kalavros held a second memorial service on May 8, at a private chapel in Burbank. A picture of Linda was placed in the lobby, and friends were asked to send remembrances to her favorite charity, the home for orphans she had established in Italy. Maria Flores attended the Burbank service, during which a telegram was read from Ann Miller. "To my dear friend Linda," Ann wired, "lover of life and of people, a giver and not a taker. You will always live in our hearts. Farewell Tweedles. Love always, Annie and Mother K."

Lola was aware that Linda had arranged for the Curtises to raise her in the event of her death and knew she would be coming to live with them. "I was numb," Lola said. "I never cried after Mother died. It was about two years later that I really fell apart. I woke up one day before school started, crying hysterically, and I didn't know why." Jeanne and Dick kept her in Glenview for about ten days after her mother's memorial service, then sent her back to Ojai Valley School, from which she graduated in May. Dick later drove her to Northwestern University and filled out an application for fall enrollment. "I'd never even heard of Northwestern University," Lola confessed, "much less wanted to go there. I didn't even know what the Big Ten was." She kept remembering what her nurse Zellie had told her when she had nightmares as a child. "Think about happy things," she heard Zellie say. So after Linda died Lola kept telling herself, "Well, I have a nice place to live. I have food in my stomach. I have clothes. I am in a good school. I'm okay." But she knew she wasn't.

After Cal recovered from the shock of his sister's death, he flew to California to visit his family. Undeen, Monte, and he agreed that Pearl, who had suffered several strokes and by then was confined to a nursing home, should not be told of Linda's death. Cal offered to send her postcards occasionally from his European travels, as if they came from Linda. When he visited his seventy-four-year-old mother in the convalescent home, she barely recognized him. She still kept a picture of Linda on her bedside table and died the following January without knowing of her daughter's tragic end. Roy, however, was soon told of Linda's death.

The Curtises eventually moved back into the rebuilt town house where Linda had died, and although Lola was well cared for by them, she was more traumatized than she realized and did not do well in her studies at Northwestern. Five months after her mother died, she received word that Robby Robertson had been found dead in the Flamingo Hotel in Las Vegas, apparently of a heart attack. Despite her mother's marital troubles, Lola had been fond of Robby and felt more abandoned than ever.

During her freshman year Lola met James Adams, Jr. and started dating him seriously. She never felt she had much in common with the college crowd around her. In her junior year she fell apart emotionally and decided to marry Adams rather than finish school. They married in 1968 and settled in New London, Pennsylvania, a Philadelphia suburb. Linda's granddaughter Valerie was born in 1972; her grandson Jamie followed three years later. "It's a very strange experience," Lola claimed later, "when your own child is the first person you know who is genetically related to you."

Linda had requested that her ashes be taken to New Mexico and scattered over the Hurd ranch, but the Hurds refused permission when the time came. "They wrote us and wanted the most dreadful ritualistic thing of depositing her ashes," Henriette Wyeth Hurd recalled. "We disliked this group so much that we said, 'We're not going to permit it.' If there's any afterlife, Linda knows perfectly well why we couldn't. It was a travesty." So Linda's remains sat in the office of a Chicago cemetery for ten years. Finally, in 1975, after Lola had moved to Pennsylvania and given birth to her children, she asked a local funeral director to send for her mother's ashes and had them buried in the Adams family plot. "It was painful," Lola declared. "It wasn't until Mother's ashes were in the ground that I saw her death was real."

Lola's marriage to Jim Adams lasted until 1979. She devoted the next two years to getting in touch with herself, making peace with her childhood, and coming to terms with the death of her parents. She concluded that her mother wouldn't have wanted to live in a disfigured state. "What would she have looked like?" Lola asked herself. "Not simply from a professional standpoint, but just to get up in the morning and look at herself in the mirror. And what would her health have been?" Slowly Lola worked through her hurt. In 1981 she married Abbott Bunker Leaming and moved to Charleston, South Carolina, where the couple bought a turn-of-the-century house near the Battery. Like Pev Marley, Lola's second husband proved to be a lover of art and music and something of a perfectionist. Occasionally they invite friends in for an informal dinner and watch one of Linda's movies—most of which Lola can't remember having seen before—on television.

As an actress Linda Darnell would be remembered mainly for *Forever Amber*, as Tyrone Power's pretty young wife in *Blood and Sand*, and for the earthy Lora May in *A Letter to Three Wives*. Her final picture, the low-budget western *Black Spurs*, opened on a double bill at the Paramount Theater in New York six weeks after her death. "Poor, departed Linda Darnell," the *New York Times* review began. "The actress did her last turn yesterday—playing the small role of a saloon hostess that almost anyone could have ambled through."

Her fame had come as a "Wampas star," a term used in the 1940s to denote a young screen beauty with little serious training as an actress. Once the first blush of success had faded, Linda came close to being rejected by Hollywood, as many like her were. *Summer Storm* and the vixen roles that followed revitalized her reputation and gave her a new lease on stardom. Gradually she grew into a competent screen actress, although never a great one. Linda Darnell represented the movie star as studio property, a beauty and cinematic personality whom an energetic publicity office and mass advertising could turn into a celebrity. While Linda developed her talents through hard work and strong direction, she emerged as a screen presence of limited dimension. With the collapse of the big studio system, Linda's days as a Hollywood force were cut short, since her reputation and approach were tied to a dying era. Like many of the old silent stars before her, she remained a face fans remembered fondly and respected enough to name children after, yet hated to imagine growing old. Screen beauties in Hollywood's golden age were expected to stay flawlessly young always, a constant the public could return to time and again to reassure themselves that spring in America was indeed eternal.

As a person Linda touched lives and was recalled throughout the film industry as a marvelous human being long after her sudden rise to fame was forgotten. William Holden once said she reminded him of an apple—"beautiful on the outside, delicious on the inside." "She never got bad press in her life," Dallas critic John Rosenfield wrote shortly after Linda's death. "She had one of the most beautiful faces that ever went into a screen career. She never gave a big performance, but she never gave a bad one."

The old neighborhood in Dallas where Linda Darnell grew up is now inhabited mainly by Chicanos pursuing a newer form of the American dream. Most of the old-timers have either died or moved away, but a few remain who still remember the old streetcar line, the hot summers before air-conditioning, and the Bison Theater up on the corner. Louise Lamm, who lived down the street from the Darnells, retired from the same life insurance company that hired her when she graduated from Sunset High School. "I don't move around much," Louise said. Then after a pause she added, "I'm leading the kind of life Monetta would have if people had left her alone."

Chronicle of Performances

Feature Films

1939

Hotel for Women. Twentieth Century–Fox. *Director:* Gregory Ratoff. *Producer:* Darryl F. Zanuck. *Screenplay:* Katherine Scola and Darrell Ware. *Camera:* Peverell Marley. *Cast:* Linda Darnell, James Ellison, Ann Sothern, Elsa Maxwell, John Halliday, Lynn Bari, Katharine Aldrich, Alan Dinehart, Jean Rogers, June Gale, Joyce Compton, Amanda Duff, Sidney Blackmer, Chick Chandler, Gregory Gaye, Evan Lebedoff, Charles Wilson, Herbert Ashley, Barnett Parker, Kay Linaker, Hal K. Dawson, Helen Ericson, Ruth Terry, Virginia Brissac, Edward Earle, Bess Flowers, Allen Wood, Kay Griffith, Dorothy Dearing, Arthur Rankin, Russell Lee, Russell Hicks.

Daytime Wife. Twentieth Century–Fox. *Director:* Gregory Ratoff. *Producer:* Darryl F. Zanuck. *Screenplay:* Art Arthur and Robert Harari. *Camera:* Peverell Marley. *Cast:* Tyrone Power, Linda Darnell, Warren William, Binnie Barnes, Wendy Barrie, Joan Davis, Joan Valerie, Leonid Kinskey, Mildred Gover, Renie Riano, Robert Lowery, Frank Coghlan, Mary Gordon, Marie Blake, Otto Han, Alex Pollard.

1940

Star Dust. Twentieth Century–Fox. *Director:* Walter Lang. *Producer:* Darryl F. Zanuck. *Screenplay:* Robert Ellis and Helen Logan. *Camera:* Peverell Marley. *Cast:* Linda Darnell, John Payne, Ronald Young, Charlotte Greenwood, William Gargan, Mary Beth Hughes, Mary Healy, Donald Meek, Jessie Ralph, Walter Kingsford, George Montgomery, Robert Lowery, Paul Hurst, Irving Bacon, Fern Emmett, Sid Grauman, Lynn Roberts, Elyse Knox, Kay Griffith, Hal K. Dawson, Jody Gilbert, Manton Moreland, Robert Shaw, Joan Leslie, Frank Coghlan, Jr., Philip Morris.

Brigham Young. Twentieth Century–Fox. *Director:* Henry Hathaway. *Producer:* Darryl F. Zanuck. *Screenplay:* Lamar Trotti. *Camera:* Arthur Miller. *Cast:* Tyrone Power, Linda Darnell, Dean Jagger, Brian Donlevy, Jane Darwell, John Carradine, Mary Astor, Vincent Price, Jean Rogers, Ann Todd, Willard Robertson, Moroni Olsen, Marc Lawrence, Stanley Andrews, Frank Thomas, Fuzzy Knight, Dickie Jones, Selmer Jackson, Russell Simpson, Arthur Aylesworth, Chief Big Tree, Claire DuBrey, Tully Marshall, Ralph Dunn, George Melford, Frederick Burton, Charles Halton, Lee Shumway, Frank LaRuse, Imboden Parrish.

The Mark of Zorro. Twentieth Century–Fox. *Director:* Rouben Mamoulian. *Producer:* Darryl F. Zanuck. *Screenplay:* John Tainton Foote. *Camera:* Arthur Miller. *Cast:* Tyrone Power, Linda Darnell, Basil Rathbone, Gale Sondergaard, Eugene Pallette, J. Edward Bromberg, Montagu Love, Janet Beecher, Robert Lowery, Chris-Pin Martin, George Regas, Belle Mitchell, John Bleifer, Frank Puglia, Pedro de Cordoba, Guy D'Ennery, Eugene Borden, Ralph Byrd, Art Dupuis, Hector Sarno, Stanley Andrews, Victor Kilian, Gino Corrado.

Chad Hanna. Twentieth Century–Fox. *Director:* Henry King. *Producer:* Darryl F. Zanuck. *Screenplay:* Nunnally Johnson. *Camera:* Ernest Palmer. *Cast:* Henry Fonda, Dorothy Lamour, Linda Darnell, Guy Kibbee, Jane Darwell, John Carradine, Ted North, Roscoe Ates, Ben Carter, Frank Thomas, Olin Howland, Frank Conlan, Edward Conrad, Edward McWade, George Davis, Paul Burns, Sarah Padden, Elizabeth Abbott, Leonard St. Lee, Tully Marshall, Almira Sessions, Virginia Brissac, Si Jenks, Victor Kilian, Louis Mason, Charles Middleton, Rondo Hatton, Nelson McDowell, Jim Pierce.

1941

Blood and Sand. Twentieth Century–Fox. *Director:* Rouben Mamoulian. *Producer:* Darryl F. Zanuck. *Screenplay:* Jo Swerling. *Camera:* Ernest Palmer. *Cast:* Tyrone Power, Linda Darnell, Rita Hayworth, Nazimova, Anthony Quinn, J. Carroll Naish, John Carradine, Lynn Bari, Laird Cregar, Monty Banks, George Reeves, Vicente Gomez, Pedro de Cordoba, Fortunio Bonanova, Victor Kilian, Adrian Morris, Charles Stevens, Ann Todd, Cora Sue Collins, Russell Hicks, Rex Downing, Maurice Cass, John Wallace, Jacqueline Dalya, Cullen Johnson, Ted Frye, Larry Harris, Schulyer Standish, Paco Moreno, Elena Verdugo, Francis McDonald, Harry Burns.

Rise and Shine. Twentieth Century–Fox. *Director:* Allan Dwan. *Producer:* Mark Hellinger. *Screenplay:* Herman J. Mankiewicz. *Camera:* Edward Cronjager. *Cast:* Jack Oakie, George Murphy, Linda Darnell, Walter Brennan, Milton Berle, Sheldon Leonard, Donald Meek, Ruth Donnelly, Raymond Walburn, Donald MacBride, Emma Dunn, Charles Waldron, Mildred Gover, William Reade, Dick Rich, Francis Pierlot, Paul Harvey, John Hiestand, Claire DuBrey, Edward Arnold, Jr., Robert Shaw, Tim Ryan, Nestor Paiva, Billy Wayne.

1942

The Loves of Edgar Allan Poe. Twentieth Century–Fox. *Director:* Harry Lachman. *Producer:* Bryan Foy. *Screenplay:* Samuel Hoffenstein and Tom Reed. *Camera:* Lucien Andriot. *Cast:* Linda Darnell, Shepperd Strudwick, Virginia Gilmore, Jane Darwell, Mary Howard, Frank Conroy, Henry Morgan, Walter Kingsford, Morris Ankrum, Roy "Skippy" Wanders, Freddie Mercer, Erville Alderson, Peggy McIntyre, William Bakewell, Jr., Frank Melton, Morton Lowry, Gilbert Emery, Ed Stanley, Francis Ford, Harry Denny, Hardie Albright, Jan Clayton, Mae Marsh, Alec Craig, Leon Tyler, Arthur Shields.

1943

City Without Men. Columbia. *Director:* Sidney Salkow. *Producer:* B. P. Schulberg. *Screenplay:* W. L. River, George Skier, and Donald Davis. *Camera:* Philip Tannura. *Cast:* Linda Darnell, Edgar Buchanan, Michael Duane, Sara Allgood, Glenda Farrell, Leslie Brooks, Doris Dudley, Margaret Hamilton, Constance Worth, Rosemary DeCamp, Sheldon Leonard, Joseph Crehan.

The Song of Bernadette. Twentieth Century–Fox. *Director:* Henry King. *Producer:* William Perlberg. *Screenplay:* George Seaton. *Camera:* Arthur Miller. *Cast:* Jennifer Jones, William Eythe, Charles Bickford, Vincent Price, Lee Cobb, Gladys Cooper, Anne Revere, Roman Bohnen, Mary Anderson, Patricia Morison, Aubrey Mather, Charles Dingle, Edith Barrett, Sig Rumann, Blanche Yurka, Ermadean Walters,

Marcel Dalio, Pedro de Cordoba, Jerome Cowan, Charles Waldon, Moroni Olsen, Nana Bryant, Manart Kippen, Merrill Rodin, John Maxwell Hayes, Jean Del Val, Tala Birell, Eula Morgan, Frank Reicher, Charles LaTorre, Linda Darnell, Nestor Paiva, Ian Wolfe.

1944

It Happened Tomorrow. United Artists. *Director:* Rene Clair. *Producer:* Arnold Pressburger. *Screenplay:* Dudley Nichols and Rene Clair. *Camera:* Archie Stout. *Cast:* Dick Powell, Linda Darnell, Jack Oakie, Edgar Kennedy, John Philliber, Ed Brophy, George Cleveland, Sig Rumann, Paul Guilfoyle, George Chandler, Eddie Acuff, Marion Martin, Jack Gardner, Eddie Coke, Robert Homan, Emma Dunn.

Buffalo Bill. Twentieth Century–Fox. *Director:* William A. Wellman. *Producer:* Harry Sherman. *Screenplay:* Aeneas MacKenzie, Clements Ripley, and Cecile Kramer. *Camera:* Leon Shamroy. *Cast:* Joel McCrea, Maureen O'Hara, Linda Darnell, Thomas Mitchell, Edgar Buchanan, Anthony Quinn, Moroni Olsen, Frank Fenton, Matt Briggs, George Lessey, Frank Orth, George Chandler, Chief Many Treaties, Chief Thundercloud, Sidney Blackmer, Evelyn Beresford, Cecil Weston, Vincent Graeff, Fred Graham.

Summer Storm. United Artists. *Director:* Douglas Sirk. *Producer:* Seymour Nebenzel. *Screenplay:* Rowland Lee. *Camera:* Archie M. Stout. *Cast:* George Sanders, Linda Darnell, Anna Lee, Edward Everett Horton, Hugo Haas, Lori Lahner, John Philhber, Sig Rumann, Andre Charlot, Mary Servoss, John Abbott, Robert Greig, Nina Koschetz, Paul Hurst, Charles Trowbridge, Byron Foulger, Charles Wagenheim, Frank Orth, Jimmy Conlin, Sarah Padden.

Sweet and Low-Down. Twentieth Century–Fox. *Director:* Archie Mayo. *Producer:* William LeBaron. *Screenplay:* Richard English. *Camera:* Lucien Ballard. *Cast:* Benny Goodman and His Band, Linda Darnell, Lynn Bari, Jack Oakie, James Cardwell, Allyn Joslyn, Jack Campbell, Roy Benson, Dickie Moore, Buddy Swan, Beverly Hudson, Dorothy Vaughn, George Lessey, Ray Mayer, Billy Dawson, Harry McKim, Robert Emmett Keane, Terry Moore, The Pied Pipers.

1945

Hangover Square. Twentieth Century–Fox. *Director:* John Brahm. *Producer:* Robert Bassler. *Screenplay:* Barre Lyndon. *Camera:* Joseph LaShelle. *Cast:* Laird Cregar, Linda Darnell, George Sanders, Glenn Langan, Faye Marlowe, Alan Napier, Frederick Worlock, J. S. Austin, Leyland Hodgson, Clifford Brooke, John Goldworthy, Michael Dyne, Ann Codee, Francis Ford, Jimmy Aubrey, Lea Sketchley, J. Farrell MacDonald.

The Great John L. United Artists. *Director:* Frank Tuttle. *Producers:* Frank R. Mastroly and James Edward Grant. *Screenplay:* James Edward Grant. *Camera:* James Van Trees. *Cast:* Greg McClure, Linda Darnell, Barbara Britton, Lee Sullivan, Otto Kruger, Wallace Ford, George Mathews, Robert Barrat, J. M. Kerrigan, Simon Semenoff, Joel Friedkin, Harry Crocker, Hope Landin, Rory Calhoun, Fritz Feld, Dick Curtis, Tom Jackson, Edwin Maxwell, Nolan Leary, Dewey Robinson, George Eldredge, Milton Parsons, George Brasno, Ernie S. Adams, George Lloyd, Tom Fadden, Rex Lease.

Fallen Angel. Twentieth Century–Fox. *Director:* Otto Preminger. *Producer:* Otto Preminger. *Screenplay:* Harry Kleiner. *Camera:* Joseph LaShelle. *Cast:* Alice Faye, Dana Andrews, Linda Darnell, Charles Bickford, Anne Revere, Bruce Cabot, John Carradine, Percy Kilbride, Olin Howlin, Hal Taliaferro, Mira McKinney, Jimmy Conlin, Leila McIntyre, Garry Owen, Horace Murphy, Martha Wentworth, Herb Ashley, Stymie Beard, Dorothy Adams, J. Farrell MacDonald, Max Wagner, Dave Morris, Harry Strang, Paul Palmer.

1946

Centennial Summer. Twentieth Century–Fox. *Director:* Otto Preminger. *Producer:* Otto Preminger. *Screenplay:* Michael Kanin. *Camera:* Ernest Palmer. *Cast:* Jeanne Crain, Cornel Wilde, Linda Darnell, William Eythe, Walter Brennan, Constance Bennett, Dorothy Gish, Barbara Whiting, Larry Stevens, Kathleen Howard, Buddy Swan, Charles Dingle, Avon Long, Florida Sanders, Eddie Dunn, Reginald Sheffield, Rodney Bell.

Anna and the King of Siam. Twentieth Century—Fox. *Director:* John Cromwell. *Producer:* Louis D. Lighton. *Screenplay:* Talbot Jennings and Sally Benson. *Camera:* Arthur Miller. *Cast:* Irene Dunne, Rex Harrison, Linda Darnell, Lee J. Cobb, Gale Sondergaard, Mikhail Rasumny, Dennis Hoey, Tito Renaldo, Richard Lyon, William Edmunds, John Abbott, Leonard Strog, Mickey Roth, Connie Leon, Diane von den Ecker, Marjorie Eaton, Addison Richards, Yvonne Rob, Chet Voravan, Helena Grant, Si-Lan Chen, Neyle Morrow, Julian Rivero, Dorothy Chung.

My Darling Clementine. Twentieth Century—Fox. *Director:* John Ford. *Producer:* Samuel G. Engel. *Screenplay:* Samuel G. Engel and Winston Miller. *Camera:* Joseph MacDonald. *Cast:* Henry Fonda, Linda Darnell, Victor Mature, Walter Brennan, Tim Holt, Cathy Downs, Ward Bond, Alan Mowbray, John Ireland, Roy Roberts, Jane Darwell, Grant Withers, J. Farrell MacDonald, Russell Simpson, Don Garner, Francis Ford, Ben Hall, Arthur Walsh, Louis Mercier, Mickey Simpson, Fred Libby, Earle Foxe, Harry Woods, Mae Marsh, Charles Stevens, Frank Conlan.

1947

Forever Amber. Twentieth Century—Fox. *Director:* Otto Preminger. *Producer:* William Perlberg. *Screenplay:* Ring Lardner, Jr. and Philip Dunne. *Camera:* Leon Shamroy. *Cast:* Linda Darnell, Cornel Wilde, Richard Greene, George Sanders, Glenn Langan, Richard Haydn, Jessica Tandy, Anne Revere, John Russell, Jane Ball, Robert Coote, Leo G. Carroll, Natalie Draper, Margaret Wycherly, Alma Kruger, Edmond Breon, Alan Napier, Perry "Bill" Ward, Richard Bailey, Houseley Stevenson, Skelton Knaggs, Peter Shaw, Jimmy Ames, Vernon Downing, Tim Huntley, Ian Keith, Frederick Worlock, Norma Varden, James Craven, Ellen Corby, Tempe Pigott, Cyril Delavanti, Jimmy Lagano, Tom Stevenson, Boyd Irwin, Eric Noonen, Robert Greig, Leonard Carey, Ottola Nasmith, Will Stanton, C. C. "Tex" Gilmore, David Ralston, Victoria Horne.

1948

The Walls of Jericho. Twentieth Century—Fox. *Director:* John M. Stahl. *Producer:* Lamar Trotti. *Screenplay:* Lamar Trotti.

Camera: Arthur Miller. *Cast:* Cornel Wilde, Linda Darnell, Anne Baxter, Kirk Douglas, Ann Dvorak, Marjorie Rambeau, Henry Hull, Colleen Townsend, Barton MacLane, Griff Barnett, William Tracy, Art Baker, Frank Ferguson, Ann Morrison, Hope Landin, Helen Brown, Norman Leavitt, Whitford Kane, J. Farrell MacDonald, Dick Rich, Will Wright, Gene Nelson, James Metcalfe, Milton Parsons, Oliver Blake, Ed Peil, Sr., Ann Doran, Dorothy Granger, Brick Sullivan, Morgan Farley.

Unfaithfully Yours. Twentieth Century–Fox. *Director:* Preston Sturges. *Producer:* Preston Sturges. *Screenplay:* Preston Sturges. *Camera:* Victor Melner. *Cast:* Rex Harrison, Linda Darnell, Barbara Lawrence, Rudy Vallee, Kurt Kreuger, Lionel Stander, Edgar Kennedy, Al Bridge, Julius Tannen, Torben Meyer, Robert Greig, Evelyn Beresford, Georgia Caine, Isabel Jewell, Major Sam Harris, Harry Carter, J. Farrell MacDonald, Frank Moran, Tamara Schee.

1949

A Letter to Three Wives. Twentieth Century–Fox. *Director:* Joseph L. Mankiewicz. *Producer:* Sol C. Siegel. *Screenplay:* Joseph L. Mankiewicz. *Camera:* Arthur Miller. *Cast:* Jeanne Crain, Linda Darnell, Ann Sothern, Kirk Douglas, Paul Douglas, Barbara Lawrence, Jeffrey Lynn, Connie Gilchrist, Florence Bates, Hobart Cavanaugh, Thelma Ritter, Carl Switzer, Stuart Holmes, Patti Brady, Ruth Vivian.

Slattery's Hurricane. Twentieth Century–Fox. *Director:* Andre de Toth. *Producer:* William Perlberg. *Screenplay:* Herman Wouk. *Camera:* Charles G. Clarke. *Cast:* Richard Widmark, Linda Darnell, Veronica Lake, John Russell, Gary Merrill, Walter Kingsford, Raymond Greenleaf, Stanley Waxman, Joseph de Santis, Kenny Williams, Morris Ankrum, Amelita Ward, Dick Wessel, John Davidson, David Wolfe, Harry Lauter, Gene Reynolds, Howard Negley, Grandon Rhodes, Joe Forte.

Everybody Does It. Twentieth Century–Fox. *Director:* Edmund Goulding. *Producer:* Nunnally Johnson. *Screenplay:* Nunnally Johnson. *Camera:* Joseph LaShelle. *Cast:* Paul Douglas, Linda Darnell, Celeste Holm, Charles Coburn, Millard Mitchell, Lucile Watson, John Hoyt, George Tobias, Leon Belasco, Tito Vuclo, Geraldine Wall, Ruth Gillette, Gilbert Russell, John Ford, Phyllis Morris, Robert Emmett Keane, Mae Marsh, Dudley Dickerson, Joe Gilbert, Bruce Kellogg, Fred Libby, Larry Fiedler, George Davis, Sid Marion, John Goldsworthy, Aubrey Mather, Ruth Clifford, John Burton, William Pullem, Billy Graeff, Jr., Ed Max, Joan Douglas.

1950

No Way Out. Twentieth Century–Fox. *Director:* Joseph L. Mankiewicz. *Producer:* Darryl F. Zanuck. *Screenplay:* Joseph L. Mankiewicz. *Camera:* Milton Krasner. *Cast:* Richard Widmark, Linda Darnell, Stephen McNally, Sidney Poitier, Mildred Joanne Smith, Harry Bellavar, Stanley Ridges, Dots Johnson, Amanda Randolph, Ruby Dee, Ossie Davis, George Tyne, Bert Freed, Maude Simmons, Ken Christy, Robert Adler, Frank Richards, Ray Teal, Harry Lauter, Harry Carter, Don Kohler, Ray Hyke, Dick Paxton, Emmett Smith, Ann Tyrrell, Ann Morrison, Eda Reis Merin, Ralph Hodges, Kathryn Sheldon, Will Wright, Jim Toney, Jack Kruschen, Eileen Boyer, Johnnie Jallings, Marie Lampe, Gertrude Tighe, Frank Jaquet, John Whitney, Howard Mitchell, Charles J. Flynn.

Two Flags West. Twentieth Century–Fox. *Director:* Robert Wise. *Producer:* Casey Robinson. *Screenplay:* Casey Robinson. *Camera:* Leon Shamroy. *Cast:* Joseph Cotton, Linda Darnell, Jeff Chandler, Cornel Wilde, Dale Robertson, Jay C. Flippen, Noah Beery, Harry Von Zell, John Sands, Arthur Hunnicutt, Jack Lee, Robert Adler, Harry Carter, Ferris Taylor, Sally Corner, Everett Glass, Marjorie Bennett, Roy Gordon, Lee MacGregor, Aurora Castillo, Stanley Andrews, Don Garner.

1951

The Thirteenth Letter. Twentieth Century–Fox. *Director:* Otto Preminger. *Producer:* Otto Preminger. *Screenplay:* Howard Koch. *Camera:* Joseph LaShelle. *Cast:* Linda Darnell, Charles Boyer, Michael Rennie, Constance Smith, Francoise Rosay, Judith Evelyn, Guy Sorel, June Hedin, Camille Ducharme, Ovila Legare, J. Leo Cagnon, George Alexander, Paul Guevremont, Stanley Mann, Vernon Steele, Jacques Auger.

The Guy Who Came Back. Twentieth Century–Fox. *Director:* Joseph Newman. *Producer:* Julian Blaustein. *Screenplay:* Allan Scott. *Camera:* Joseph LaShelle. *Cast:* Paul Douglas, Joan Bennett, Linda Darnell, Don DeFore, Billy Gray, Zero Mostel, Edmond Ryan, Ruth McDevitt, Walter Burke, Henry Kulky, Dick Ryan, Ted Pearson, John H. Hamilton, Grandon Rhodes, Harry Seymour, Thomas Browne Henry, Emile Meyer, Stanley Pinto, Robert Foulk, John Close.

The Lady Pays Off. Universal. *Director:* Douglas Sirk. *Producer:* Albert J. Cohan. *Screenplay:* Albert J. Cohan and Frank Gill, Jr. *Camera:* William H. Daniels and Russell Schoengarth. *Cast:* Linda Darnell, Stephen McNally, Gigi Perreau, Virginia Field, Ann Codee, Nestor Paiva, James Griffith, Billy Wayne, Katherine Warren, Lynne Hunter, Paul McVey, Tristram Coffin, Judd Holdren, Nolan Leary, John Doucette, Billy Newell, Ric Roman.

1952

Island of Desire. United Artists. *Director:* Stuart Heisler. *Producer:* David E. Rose. *Screenplay:* Stephanie Nordli. *Camera:* Arthur Ibbetson. *Cast:* Linda Darnell, Tab Hunter, Donald Gray, John Laurie, Sheila Chong, Russell Waters, Hilda Fenemore, Brenda Hogan, Diana Decker, Peggy Hassard, Michael Newell.

Night Without Sleep. Twentieth Century–Fox. *Director:* Roy Baker. *Producer:* Robert Bassler. *Screenplay:* Frank Partos and Elick Moll. *Camera:* Lucien Ballard. *Cast:* Linda Darnell, Gary Merrill, Hildegarde Neff, Joyce MacKenzie, June Vincent, Donald Randolph, Hugh Beaumont, Louise Lorimer, William Forrest, Steven Geray, Mae Marsh, Sam Pierce, Sylvia Simms, Beverly Tyler, Charles Tannen, Harry Seymour.

Blackbeard the Pirate. RKO. *Director:* Raoul Walsh. *Producer:* Edmund Grainger. *Screenplay:* Alan LeMay. *Camera:* William E. Snyder. *Cast:* Robert Newton, Linda Darnell, William Bendix, Keith Andes, Torin Thatcher, Irene Ryan, Alan Mowbray, Richard Egan, Skelton Knaggs, Dick Wessel, Anthony Caruso, Jack Lambert, Noel Drayton, Pat Flaherty, Saul Gross, Keith McConnell, Carl Harbaugh, Chuck Roberson, Patrick Whyte, James Craven, Joe Dominguez, Kenneth D. Murray, Salvador Baguez.

1953

Donne proibite (*Angels of Darkness*). Supra. *Director:* Giuseppe Amato. *Producer:* Giuseppe Amato. *Screenplay:* Giuseppe Mangione. *Camera:* Anchise Brizzi. *Cast:* Linda Darnell, Valentina Cortese, Lea Padovani, Giulietta Masina, Lilla Brignone, Anthony Quinn, Roberto Risso, Maria Pia Casilio.

Second Chance. RKO. *Director:* Rudolph Maté. *Producer:* Edmund Grainger. *Screenplay:* Oscar Millard and Sydney Boehm. *Camera:* William Snyder. *Cast:* Robert Mitchum, Linda Darnell, Jack Palance, Sandro Giglio, Rodolfo Hoyos, Jr., Reginald Sheffield, Margaret Brewster, Roy Roberts, Salvador Baguez, Maurice Jara, Judy Walsh, Dan Seymour, Fortunio Bonanova, Milburn Stone, Abel Fernandez, Michael Tolan, Richard Vera, Virginia Linden, Manuel Paris.

1954

This Is My Love. RKO. *Director:* Stuart Heisler. *Producer:* Hugh Brooke. *Screenplay:* Hagar Wilde and Hugh Brooke. *Camera:* Ray June. *Cast:* Linda Darnell, Rick Jason, Dan Duryea, Faith Domergue, Hal Baylor, Connie Russell, Jerry Mathers, Susie Mathers, Mary Young, William Hopper, Stuart Randall, Kam Tong, Judd Holdren.

1955

Gli ultimi cinque minuti (*The Last Five Minutes*). Excelsa Films. *Director:* Giuseppe Amato. *Producer:* Giuseppe Amato. *Screenplay:* Aldo de Benedetti. *Camera:* Carlo Montuori. *Cast:* Linda Darnell, Vittorio De Sica, Peppino de Filippo, Sophie Desmarets, Rossano Brazzi, Pierre Cressoy, Lise Bourdin, Enrico Viarisio, Elsa Merlini.

1956

Dakota Incident. Republic. *Director:* Lewis Foster. *Producer:* Herbert J. Yates. *Screenplay:* Frederic L. Fox. *Camera:* Ernest Haller. *Cast:* Linda Darnell, Dale Robertson, John Lund, Ward Bond, Regis Toomey, Skip Homeier, Irving Bacon,

John Doucette, Whit Bissell, William Fawcett, Malcolm Atterbury, Diane DuBois, Charles Horvath, Eva Novak, Rankin Mansfield, Fred Coby, Eddie Baker, Red Morgan.

1957

Zero Hour! Paramount. *Director:* Hall Bartlett. *Producer:* John C. Champion. *Screenplay:* Arthur Hailey and Hall Bartlett. *Camera:* John F. Warren. *Cast:* Dana Andrews, Linda Darnell, Sterling Hayden, Elroy "Crazylegs" Hirsch, Geoffrey Toone, Jerry Paris, Peggy King, Carole Eden, Charles Quinlivan, Raymond Ferrell, David Thursby, Russell Thorson, Richard Keith, Steve London, Willis Bouchey.

1965

Black Spurs. Paramount. *Director:* R. G. Springsteen. *Producer:* A. C. Lyles. *Screenplay:* Steve Fisher. *Camera:* Ralph Woolsey. *Cast:* Rory Calhoun, Linda Darnell, Scott Brady, Lon Chaney, Richard Arlen, Bruce Cabot, Terry Moore, Patricia Owens, Jerome Courtland, Joseph Hoover, James Best, DeForest Kelley, James Brown, Manuel Padilla, Robert Carricart, Barbara Wilkin, Sally Nichols, Joe Forte, Lorraine Bendix, Patricia King, Jeanne Baird, Guy Wilkerson, Read Morgan, Chuck Roberson, Rusty Allen, Rigis Parton, Howard Joslin, Roy Jenson, Max Power.

Major Television Shows

1953

"All Star Revue." NBC, January 5. *Directors:* Joe Santley and Sid Smith. *Teleplay:* Charlie Isaacs and Jackie Elinson. *Cast:* Jimmy Durante, Linda Darnell, Vic Damone.

1956

"20th Century–Fox Hour." CBS, March 7. *Episode:* "Deception." *Director:* Jules Bricken. *Teleplay:* William Spier. *Cast:* Linda Darnell, Trevor Howard, John Williams, Alan Napier, Gavin Muir, Doris Lloyd, Eleanor Audley, Arthur E. Gould-Porter, Harold Dryemforth, George Doe, Chester Jones.

"Ford Theatre." NBC, March 8. *Episode:* "All for a Man." *Director:* Albert Rogell. *Teleplay:* Karen DeWolf. *Cast:* Linda Darnell, Elisabeth Risdon, Allyn Joslyn, Audrey Conti.

1957

"Schlitz Playhouse of the Stars." CBS, January 18. *Episode:* "Terror in the Streets." *Director:* Robert Florey. *Teleplay:* Maurice Zimm. *Cast:* Linda Darnell, Nestor Paiva, Richard Long, Paul Wexler, K. T. Stevens, Ray Walker, Regina Gleason, Angela Greene, Joe Mell, James Canino, Paul Lambert, Anthony Lawrence.

"Ford Theatre." ABC, March 13. *Episode:* "Fate Travels East." *Director:* Anton M. Leader. *Teleplay:* Jack Harvey and Robert Bassing. *Cast:* Linda Darnell, Craig Stevens, Sheb Wooley, Stacey Graham, Barbara Fuller, Howard Smith, Robert Brubaker.

"Playhouse 90." CBS, May 9. *Episode:* "Homeward Borne." *Director:* Arthur Hiller. *Teleplay:* Halsted Welles. *Cast:* Linda Darnell, Richard Kiley, Keith Andes, Richard Eyer, Rene Korper, Sarah Selby, Pauline Myers, Steve Firstman.

"Climax." CBS, September 5. *Episode:* "Trial by Fire." *Director:* Don Medford. *Teleplay:* Dick Stenger. *Cast:* Linda Darnell, Forrest Tucker, Malcolm Broderick, Byron Foulger, Harry Townes, Ellen Corby.

1958

"Jane Wyman Theatre." NBC, January 2. *Episode:* "The Elevator." *Director:* Allen Miner. *Teleplay:* Michael Fessier and Philip MacDonald. *Cast:* Linda Darnell, John Baragrey, John Hoyt, Dick Wilson.

"Wagon Train." NBC, January 29. *Episode:* "The Dora Gray Story." *Director:* Arnold Laven. *Teleplay:* E. Jack Neuman. *Cast:* Linda Darnell, John Carradine, Michael Connors.

"Wagon Train." NBC, June 25. *Episode:* "The Sacramento Story." *Director:* Richard Bartlett. *Teleplay:* Thomas Thompson. *Cast:* Dan Duryea, Margaret O'Brien, Linda Darnell, Marjorie Main.

"Cimarron City." CBS, November 20. *Episode:* "Kid on a Calico Horse." *Cast:* Linda Darnell, Dean Stockwell.

1964

"Burke's Law." ABC, February 21. *Episode:* "Who Killed His Royal Highness?" *Cast:* Elizabeth Montgomery, Bert Parks, Gale Storm, Telly Savalas, Mickey Rooney, Linda Darnell, Michael Ansara.

Other Appearances: "Your First Impression," "I've Got a Secret," "Verdict is Yours," "Here's Hollywood," "Leave It to the Girls," Cutex commercial.

Stage Plays

1956

A Roomful of Roses
Tea and Sympathy
Harbor Lights (Broadway)

1958

The Children's Hour
The Pleasure of His Company

1959

Late Love
The Royal Family

1960

Monique

1962

The Gioconda Smile
Critic's Choice
Dark at the Top of the Stairs

1964

Janus
Love out of Town

Sources

The bulk of Linda Darnell's story has been drawn from oral history interviews, taped by the author between 1979 and 1989 as director of the Southern Methodist University Oral History Collection on the Performing Arts. Written records have also been consulted whenever possible, and the author is deeply indebted to the Margaret Herrick Library of the Academy of Motion Picture Arts and Sciences, the Billy Rose Theatre Collection of the New York Public Library, the Doheny Library of the University of Southern California, the Louis B. Mayer Library of the American Film Institute, the Fine Arts Department of the Dallas Public Library, and Fondren Library of Southern Methodist University, including its media center.

Most of the data on the early years of Pearl Brown Darnell came from her sister, Cleo Brown Johnson, during sessions taped in Midwest City, Oklahoma (October 27, 1982, and February 26, 1983), supplemented by scrapbooks in Cleo Johnson's possession. Pearl's first marriage was confirmed by the Wayne County Marriage Records, Book 3, Waynesboro, Tennessee; the Geronimo incident is supported by Alexander B. Adams, *Geronimo* (New York: Putnam's, 1971); and the Caddo reservation visit by Muriel H. Wright, *A Guide to the Indian Tribes of Oklahoma* (Norman: University of Oklahoma Press, 1951).

Information on Roy Darnell's family and early years was obtained from a family genealogy prepared by White Darnall, July 1940, now on file in the DeGolyer Library at Southern Methodist University, as well as from interviews in Dallas with Roy's sister-in-law, Virginia Darnell; her daughter, Elaine Darnell Reeves (both April 4, 1980); and Roy's nephew, R. Glenn Darnell (February 5, 1980). A telephone conversation with Roy's sister, Durstine Darnell Heim, in San Antonio (October 8, 1982), confirmed family conflict.

Background material on Dallas and Oak Cliff in the early twentieth century was gleaned from Darwin Payne, *Dallas: An Illustrated History* (Woodland Hills, Calif.: Dallas Historic Preservation League, 1982), John William Rogers, *The Lusty Texans of Dallas* (New York: Dutton, 1951), and Justin Ford Kimball, *Our City—Dallas* (Dallas: Kessler Plan Association, 1927). The Clyde Barrow and Bonnie Parker episode is supported by Walter P. Webb and H. Bailey Carroll, eds., *The Handbook of Texas* (Austin: Texas State Historical Association, 1952) and articles in the *Dallas Morning News*, May 25, 1934.

The major informants on Linda's childhood, as well as much of her adult life, were her older sister, Undeen Darnell Hunter, taped at Lake Elsinore, California (August 19–20, 1980, and July 18, 1982); her younger sister, Monte Darnell, taped in Chiloquin, Oregon (August 2–3, 1982); and her brother, Calvin R. Darnell, Jr., taped in London, England (March 12, 1983). Also helpful were the Darnells' Dallas neighbors: Virginia Crawford Chancey (October 10, 1979), Mrs. Ralph Gilby (November 20, 1979), Mrs. Rojen Soldo (November 23, 1979), Maude Lamm (December 8, 1979), and Rita Crawford Dalton (August 23, 1982), all taped in Dallas. School friends interviewed include Eleanor Kline Solon (October 10, 1979), Louise Lamm (December 8, 1979), Jessie Elder Stone (December 30, 1980), and Charloise Hufstedler Jones (December 30, 1982), also taped in Dallas. Frances Brown Hollis, one of Linda's elocution teachers, was interviewed in Dallas (May 16, 1980). Fellow dance student Pat Nelson McKinnie and her mother, Gertrude Nelson, were interviewed together in Dallas (January 31, 1980). Betty Galbreath Calhoun, who knew Linda and Pearl Darnell from Campfire Girls, was taped in Duncanville, Texas (June 23, 1982).

Linda's high school activities were fleshed out by interviews with classmate Francis Bauman (December 6, 1982) and their principal, W. T. White (September 14, 1982), both in Dallas, as well as a letter from Linda's friend Jeanette Sessions (November 1979), then of Mesa, Arizona. The Sunset High School *Sundial* for 1938 and extensive memorabilia in the possession of Undeen Darnell Hunter provided valuable information. On Linda's adolescent modeling career and early performing efforts, interviews with actress Dale Evans in Fort Worth (April 26, 1982); and photographer Bill Langley (March 16, 1981), Claire Rosenfield (March 5 and April 9, 1982), Inez Teddlie (November 6, 1979), and Pete Teddlie (October 5, 1979), all taped in Dallas, proved vital, along with scattered clippings from the *Dallas Morning News* and the

Dallas Times Herald and miscellaneous correspondence and papers kept by Bill Langley. The Ivan Kahn Collection, now in the Academy of Motion Picture Arts and Sciences, offers a clear record of Linda's discovery by Hollywood, her early screen tests, and her initial contract with Twentieth Century–Fox.

The Darnells' first trip to California was vividly recalled by Dorris Bowdon Johnson in an interview in Los Angeles (August 11, 1981) and by Mary Healy in New Rochelle, New York (October 2, 1982), supplemented by occasional correspondence from Linda to her friend Jessie Elder Stone. In a session taped in Dallas (November 7, 1979), Bill Kline remembered a date he had with Linda after she returned from her introduction to Hollywood. A script of *Sticks and Stones,* in possession of the play's director, Betty Zinn Lewellen, suggests the kind of acting assignments Linda took in Dallas to prepare herself for a motion picture career. Jesse L. Lasky's *I Blow My Own Horn* (Garden City, N.Y.: Doubleday, 1957), written with Don Weldon, details Linda's involvement with the "Gateway to Hollywood" contest, and Gale Storm's *I Ain't Down Yet* (Indianapolis: Bobbs-Merrill, 1981), written in collaboration with Bill Libby, gives a broader view of what that contest was all about. An interview in Los Angeles with Twentieth Century–Fox veteran Joseph Silver includes recollections of Linda Darnell's first months on that lot, and press releases issued by the studio's publicity director, Harry Brand, provide a sanitized version of what teenage stardom was like.

Background information on the atmosphere around the Twentieth Century–Fox studio during Linda's time there was obtained from Norman Zierold, *The Moguls* (New York: Coward-McCann, 1969); Mel Gussow, *Don't Say Yes Until I Finish Talking: A Biography of Darryl F. Zanuck* (Garden City, N.Y.: Doubleday, 1971); Leonard Mosley, *Zanuck: The Rise and Fall of Hollywood's Last Tycoon* (Boston: Little, Brown, 1984); Marlys J. Harris, *The Zanucks of Hollywood* (New York: Crown, 1989); and Dorris Johnson and Ellen Leventhal, eds., *The Letters of Nunnally Johnson* (New York: Knopf, 1981). More immediate accounts came through interviews in Dallas with actors Don Ameche (March 1, 1977) and Cesar Romero (February 26, 1979); and in Los Angeles with actresses Coleen Gray (January 14, 1983), Betty Lynn (July 26, 1984), Terry Moore (August 27, 1986), and Dorothy McGuire (August 29, 1986); actor Gregory Peck (May 27, 1977; August 15, and 21, 1978;

July 28, 1979; and August 22, 1980); dancer Dan Dailey (July 13 and 25, 1974); songwriter Harry Warren (October 24, 1977); makeup artist William Tuttle (August 12, 1976); assistant director Gerd Oswald (July 20, 1979); art director Lyle Wheeler (August 25, 1986); producer Otto Lang (August 7, 1981); film executive Howard W. Koch (August 10, 1981); and film editors Gene Fowler, Jr. (July 20, 1985) and Marjorie Johnson Fowler (August 14, 1986). Biographical sketches of Linda Darnell herself are included in James Robert Parish, *The Fox Girls* (Secaucus, N.J.: Castle Books, 1972) and Patrick Agan, *The Decline and Fall of the Love Goddesses* (Los Angeles: Pinnacle Books, 1979).

A wealth of material on most of Linda Darnell's films was discovered in the memos, story conference reports, and multiple script revisions in the Doheny Library at the University of Southern California. The major reviews consulted on the star's movies appeared in the *New York Times,* and were supplemented by the clipping files in the New York Public Library, the Academy of Motion Picture Arts and Sciences, and the Dallas Public Library. Linda's return home for the premiere of her first motion picture, *Hotel for Women,* was recalled by school friends, family members, and in interviews taped in Dallas and Arlington, Texas, with Bob Coghill (May 29, 1981) and Marge Evans (April 25, 1982).

Interviews with those who worked on Linda's early films include sessions in Los Angeles with actresses Binnie Barnes (August 9, 1983) and Lynn Bari (August 18, 1986); actor George Montgomery (July 26, 1982); choreographer Hermes Pan (January 12, 1983); and directors Rouben Mamoulian (August 19, 1980; and August 15, 1981) and Henry Hathaway (January 6, 1983). Extensive interviews by Thomas R. Stempel with screenwriter Nunnally Johnson in Los Angeles (October 9, 1968–February 5, 1969) in the Oral History Collection of the University of California at Los Angeles proved useful on *Chad Hanna,* as did Dorothy Lamour's *My Side of the Road* (Englewood Cliffs, N.J.: Prentice-Hall, 1980). Mary Astor's *A Life on Film* (New York: Delacorte, 1971) gave interesting insights into the making of *Brigham Young — Frontiersman,* while the movie's premiere in Salt Lake City is well documented in Henry Hathaway's scrapbook deposited in the Mayer Library of the American Film Institute.

Among those who knew Linda Darnell socially during her early days in Hollywood were actresses Carol Bruce (July 16, 1982) and Rosemary DeCamp (July 13, 1982), both interviewed in Los Angeles; and Peggy Moran Koster (July 21, 1982), taped in Cama-rillo, California. Linda's best friend in Hollywood during those years, Ann Miller, tells of their relationship in *Miller's High Life* (Garden City, N.Y.: Doubleday, 1972), while Lana Turner, for whom Linda once served as maid of honor, offers her account in *Lana: The Lady, the Legend, the Truth* (New York: Dutton, 1982).

William Wellman discusses directing *Buffalo Bill* in his autobi-ography, *A Short Time for Insanity* (New York: Hawthorn, 1974) and in an interview with Richard Shickel in his book *The Men Who Made the Movies* (New York: Atheneum, 1975). Interviews with coworkers during Linda's transition to "bad girl" roles in-clude sessions with actresses Anna Lee (August 13, 1981) and Irene Dunne (July 23, 1982), both in Los Angeles; director Otto Prem-inger in New York (January 5, 1982); and an interview with actor Dana Andrews taped in 1958 for the Columbia University Oral History Collection. Otto Preminger, who directed four of Linda's pictures, recounts the making of those films in *Preminger: An Autobiography* (Garden City, N.Y.: Doubleday, 1977).

Incidents within the Darnell family home around the time of Linda's marriage to Peverell Marley were vividly described in in-terviews with family members; Richard Paxton, who stayed a per-sonal friend until the end, recorded in Riverside, California (April 5, 1984); and Trudi Dieterle, who remained close to Cal Darnell until his death in 1984 and was taped in Los Angeles (August 14, 1983) at Cal's suggestion.

Linda's friend Glenn Rose told in a telephone conversation in Los Angeles (January 13, 1983) of the actress's excitement over re-ceiving the title role in *Forever Amber*. The making of that picture was extensively covered by the press and fan magazines of the pe-riod, many of which are available in the Academy of Motion Pic-ture Arts and Sciences. Interviews with fellow workers on *Forever Amber*, in addition to Otto Preminger, include leading man Cor-nel Wilde (August 12, 15, and 20, 1980), screenwriter Philip Dunne (January 8, 1983), composer David Raksin (August 2, 1976, and July 17, 1982), and hairstylist Gladys Witten (January 3, 1983), all taped in Los Angeles; and screenwriter Ring Lardner, Jr., taped in New York (January 11, 1985). An unrecorded luncheon exchange with actor John Russell in August 1983 proved helpful on the mak-ing of *Forever Amber*, as did a telephone conversation in Dallas that same year with studio fashion consultant Della Owens Rice, who helped Linda trim down for the part. Philip Dunne has also written his recollections in *Take Two: A Life in Movies and Politics* (New York: McGraw-Hill, 1980), while Leon Shamroy recalls filming *Forever Amber* in Charles Higham, *Hollywood Cameramen* (Bloomington: Indiana University Press, 1970).

Information on Linda Darnell's private life during her later years at Twentieth Century–Fox was provided by Linda's adopted daughter, Lola Marley Leaming, taped in Charleston, South Carolina (October 28, 1983), where scrapbooks and family memorabilia were also made available. Linda's close friends Jeanne and Richard Curtis gave me free access to the correspondence, telegrams, and boxes of personal effects belonging to Linda that came to them in Glenview, Illinois after the fire, including papers that had belonged to Linda's first husband, Pev Marley, and telegrams from Joseph Mankiewicz. Assistant director Arthur Jacobson, another friend of long standing, offered his observations in an interview recorded in Los Angeles (July 19, 1989). Vivid recollections of Pearl and Roy Darnell's life in Brentwood after their children had left home were provided by Linda's niece, Jan Hunter Nordgren, in a session taped at Lake Elsinore, California (July 18, 1982).

Interviews with directors Robert Wise (July 26, 1979), Joseph Newman (July 23, 1984), and Andre DeToth (July 15, 1987), all recorded in Los Angeles, contain valuable insights into Linda's mature years at Twentieth Century–Fox. In addition Newman (December 21, 1982) and Wise (June 29, 1982) wrote letters telling of their professional experiences with her. Interviews with fellow performers Rudy Vallee in Dallas (October 4, 1975), Joan Bennett in Scarsdale, New York (January 11, 1985), Dale Robertson in Yukon, Oklahoma (April 22, 1983), and Celeste Holm in New York City (March 30, 1988) provided further information. An interview conducted in 1974 for the American Film Institute with screenwriter Howard Koch, who wrote *The 13th Letter,* was consulted in the Mayer Library, as was Koch's book *As Time Goes By* (New York: Harcourt Brace Jovanovich, 1979). Rex Harrison tells of working with Linda on two pictures in *Rex: An Autobiography* (New York: Morrow, 1975), while Veronica Lake mentions *Slattery's Hurricane* briefly in *Veronica* (New York: Citadel, 1971).

Joseph Mankiewicz offers some perceptive views on actresses in general in Gary Carey, *More About* All About Eve: *A Colloquy with Joseph L. Mankiewicz* (New York: Random House, 1972), although the director's biographer, Kenneth Geist, gives only a brief reference to his subject's relationship with Linda Darnell in *Pictures*

Will Talk: The Life and Films of Joseph L. Mankiewicz (New York: Scribner's, 1978). Vera Caspary, one of the early writers on *A Letter to Three Wives,* details in her interesting autobiography, *The Secrets of Grown-Ups* (New York: McGraw-Hill, 1979), the evolution of that script, while Tom Stempel describes the reworking of *Everybody Does It* in his book *Screenwriter: Nunnally Johnson* (San Diego, Calif.: Barnes, 1980). James Curtis's biography of Preston Sturges, *Between Flops* (New York: Harcourt Brace Jovanovich, 1982), contains excellent behind-the-scenes data on the filming of the original version of *Unfaithfully Yours.*

Details of Linda's personal life before, during, and after her marriage to Philip Liebmann were obtained from interviews with designer Yvonne Wood (January 4, 1983) and writer-director Charles Marquis Warren (August 14 and 20, 1980; and July 27, 1982) in Los Angeles; Linda's secretary, Maria Flores in Anaheim, California (August 20, 1983); her friends Jeanne and Richard Curtis in Glenview, Illinois (September 25–26, 1984); artist Henriette Wyeth Hurd in San Patricio, New Mexico (August 27, 1983); and actor Douglas Fairbanks, Jr., taped during an acting engagement in Dallas (October 7, 12, and 14, 1982). A telephone conversation in Los Angeles (January 4, 1983) with Vera Gordon, wife of Linda's frequent date and one-time publicist, also proved significant. Additional glimpses of Linda Darnell during this period were found in Robert Metzger, *My Land Is the Southwest: Peter Hurd Letters and Journals* (College Station: Texas A&M University Press, 1983), while a significant observation about the actress's problematic relationship with Liebmann was made in a letter (October 26, 1982) to the author from Linda's early Hollywood friend Dorris Bowdon Johnson.

Working with Linda Darnell on her last films was recalled by director Hall Bartlett (July 16, 1985) and actor John Lund (August 17, 1988) in interviews taped in Los Angeles. Lund had previously written the author a detailed letter (January 30, 1982), describing his experiences with the actress while making *Dakota Incident.* Linda's professional stage debut was reviewed in the *Arizona Republic* (February 20, 1956), while her Broadway debut was covered in the *New York Times* (October 4–5, 1956). Robert Alda, Linda's leading man in *Harbor Lights,* remembered the troubled play in an interview in Dallas (January 3, 1978), and added to his recollections in a telephone conversation in Los Angeles (July 1982). *Variety* (September 12, 1956) covered the opening of her Broadway-

Sources

bound play in New Haven, and Linda wrote from Boston (September 18, 1956) to photographer Bill Langley of the horrors she was facing with that script.

Insights into Linda's marriage to Merle Robertson and her nightclub act came from interviews in Dallas with tenor Thomas Hayward (April 10, 1982) and entertainment critic Tony Zoppi (September 20, 1982), as well as from a script of the act, correspondence, clippings, reviews, and other memorabilia in Hayward's possession. Maria Flores kept a journal of Linda's nightclub tour, which she read in part to the author during a telephone conversation from California (1984).

Details of Linda Darnell's last months were found in her diary-datebook for 1964, discovered among the personal effects sent to Jeanne and Dick Curtis after her death. A number of letters, several of them written by Philip Kalavros, were included in those boxes. The actress's final tour was covered in correspondence and in the *Albuquerque Tribune* (January 30–31, 1965), the *Atlanta Constitution* (March 1, 1965), and the *Atlanta Journal* (March 3, 1965).

The account of the fire is drawn from a two-day conversation with Jeanne Curtis in Glenview, Ill. (September 25–26, 1982), as well as United Press International reports in the *Los Angeles Times* and the *Dallas Morning News* (April 9–10, 1965, and April 22, 1965).

Index

Index